D1452086

THE TRAUMA OF TIME

A Psychoanalytic Investigation

THE TRAUMA OF TIME

A Psychoanalytic Investigation

IRVINE SCHIFFER

International Universities Press, Inc.
New York

Library of Congress Cataloging in Publication Data

Schiffer, Irvine.
    The trauma of time.

    Bibliography: p.
    Includes index.
    1. Time—Psychological aspects. 2. Personality. 3. Psychology, Pathological. I. Title.
BF468.S3   150'.19'5   77-92182
ISBN 0-8236-6646-8

for Joseph

Contents

Introduction

This is a study about "the killing of time," a theme that invites obvious barbs, but that nonetheless points to a significant aspect of human psychology. Freud elaborated on Oedipus and the fate of the father as a target for murder, a psychological model that he traced to the earliest human group, the primal horde. Rank introduced the trauma of birth, antedating the development of the self and the awareness of one's physical mortality. I offer the abstraction of time as one's earliest target for liquidation, a less incestuous and more narcissistic model than Freud's, and a more structurally based model than Rank's. Man's passion for killing time will be presented as a reflection of his repetitious and compulsive efforts to turn back the clock to that period in his life before he experienced a sense of separation and loss. My thesis explores the illusions man employs to postpone a resignation both to his transience and to biological procreation as the only tangible means of achieving immortality.

To illustrate the efforts of mankind to stem the flow of time, I have drawn upon clinical cases, particularly that of a victim of Hitler's Germany, a girl whose story accentuates the significance of human trust, or more precisely, a dereliction of that trust. It is my hope that examining the effects of the Nazi holocaust on her life will clarify certain aspects of the post-concentration camp neuroses, particularly the elements involved in the distortions of time that are part of the so-called survival syndrome. Although documentations of personal concentration camp experiences, such as Rappaport's (1968), are eyewitness accounts, they are not altogether enlightening on the issue of time. Rappaport tells of invalided women who, out of their compulsion to fill a vacuum and undo a genocide, became addicted to multiple pregnancies and polysurgery. However, in his description of his own postwar reactions and concentration camp flashbacks, neither his curious preoccupation with time nor his compulsive dreams of returning to the scene of the horror are satisfactorily explained; as a motive for his writings, Rappaport offers his desire to bear witness to the tribunal of history. If he were alive today, perhaps he might have yielded to the suggestion that in his recurrent dreams of return, indeed in his very writing about them, he was driven to recapture the macabre, to relive events that had been forced upon him, in the hope that they would become transformed, and thereby allow him a mastery over their traumatic impact.

My story is not of just one person or a few, nor is it only about people traumatized by war; it is a study of ordinary people, of the peaceful society, of the many who sit passively in the cinema or in armchairs in front of television, or who prefer to brave the elements on more active duty as grandstand spectators engaged en masse in the obliteration of time.

I wish to thank Irene Kagan Azarian and Caryl Avery for their editorial excellence, and to acknowledge my indebtedness to those whose writings have given substance to my bibliography. To the patients whose clinical revelations have enriched the content of this volume, I express a special appreciation.

I

The Faces of Time

> Time: That which man is always
> trying to kill, but which ends in
> killing him
> —Herbert Spencer (1820-1903)

Waiting expectantly outside of suburban movie houses or in long queues in front of downtown theaters, millions of people in cities the world over participate in an endless pilgrimage toward the annihilation of time. On the surface, this human phenomenon may be attributed to an escape from the burdens of work or to man's quest for relaxation or entertainment; yet, seated anonymously in darkened cinemas, countless individuals from different walks of life are driven to recapture the imprints of their earliest childhood when their real or imagined invasion of the parental bedroom yielded a first encounter with the enigma of sexuality and their virginal exposure to the maculacy of reproduction.

I begin with the vehicle of film only to dramatize the universality of man's compulsion to manipulate time; except for the detached connoisseur involved in the direction or choreography, the spectator is totally engrossed by the plot, and even the most technically inadequate film becomes legitimized by the overpowering appetite of the masses seeking release from their tensions. Opportunities for

3

exercising a variety of psychic complexes ordinarily dor-
mant become available through the diversity of elements
offered for identification. For nature lovers, domestic
animals or wildlife qualify as transitional bait; for the more
artistic, knickknacks and *objets d'art* are on view; and for
the frivolous or those seeking action vicariously, the desire
for perverse and exotic adventures is fulfilled through the
actions of film hero or anti-hero, transforming us magically
from tightwads into big spenders, from plebeians into
sophisticates, living it up on the French Riviera or sipping
fine wine on a terrace in Caracas, a case of embezzled
treasury notes chained to our wrist.

Orality abounds in the film; not only is there a focus on
food that the ordinary person never gets to eat, but the
gluttony of the audience is heightened by the exaggeration
of delectables captured by the camera. On following the
lead figure from one bistro to another and watching him
offhandedly pick at his food, who among us has not
scavenged, in fantasy, all the succulent delicacies so
casually ignored? Through exploitation of the immobility of
the filmgoer, powerless as he is to translate his psychic
tensions into expressive action, unusual hypnotic effects
induce regression to the lower levels of the time experience.
Objects become shrunken or enlarged at the whim of the
director as the focus zooms in or out, in fast or slow exposure, moving the images forward or backward, catching
them upside down or downside up at the behest of a camera
roving freely in time and space. An opportunity for repetition is provided by endless reviewing of the same movie, a
habit not uncommon in our culture; not only children but
adults frequently stay from noon till dusk, ultimately staggering from their scopophilic debauchery into a twilight of
migraine. The filmmaker's fantasy becomes embellished by
the fantasies of the audience. Although the experience is
only simulation, as in all creative art, for those who hunger

for timeless perfection, it's the real thing. It reminds us of the father who, upon being complimented on the natural beauty of his daughter, boasts "That's nothing, you should see the photographs we have of her!"

Swallowed up by the darkness of your favorite cinema and mesmerized by the lighted expanse of a wide screen, you find yourself a captive participant in the "perfect crime." Sprawled paunchy and balding in an aisle seat, you flinch imperceptibly from the naked bosom and the bared thighs of a screen beauty . . . you suck in your breath like a carp impaled on a fisherman's lure, flustered by the unwavering stare of an unmoved child watching you from close by . . . you hear someone's nervous gasp, an occasional wheeze or titter . . . from behind, a convulsive cough threatens you with virus—and with the odor of rancid peanuts; yet doggedly you sit with eyes transfixed . . . another heave of bosom from the screen . . . furtively you anticipate a baleful glance from your wife . . . out of the corner of your eye, you catch sight of a voyeur across the aisle mouthing popcorn with a ferocity . . . sheepishly you realize that you, too, are one of the many glassy-eyed conspirators in the killing of time!

To support the premise that the abstraction we call time is a primal trauma, its varied faces, which man has created out of his wish both to acknowledge and expunge this uncanny nemesis, can be identified. A historical profile might start with early Greek literature (see Fraser, 1975), which properly characterized time as a tension of oscillating opposites, as in Hesiod's greater and lesser opportunities for agricultural activity or as in Aristotle's rhythmic and cyclic "duration." In a theological framework, the early Hebrews saw time reflected in a tension between Israel and God, and Christianity gave time its biphasic image through the advent of Christ. Kant (1781) proclaimed time a personal sensory experience which became nonexistent once one's intuition was suspended, a concept later embraced by Freud. Where Kant perceived man as creating time, Bergson (1889) saw time as creating man, notwithstanding Bergson's concept of an *élan vital* which transcended the intellect in affording the human soul the afterlife of an eternity. More recently, Fraser (1975) has adopted Kierkegaard's (1849) existential tension in identifying time as the conflicting separateness of certain opposites.

From the dispassionate findings of the mathematical sciences, man's views on objective time became structured around the earth's rotation on its own axis and its rotation around the sun. A more innovative atomic time evolved from Einstein's (1905) conceptualization of space-time as the distance between two events. Historically, the first meaningful dictum on objective time came from Clausius, whose mid-nineteenth century concept of increasing entropy suggests in paraphrase that the world in which we live is running out of time simply because the energy of its inorganic physical processes is being lost at a more rapid rate than it is being replenished (a reflection of the Second Law of Thermodynamics). More recently Prigogine (1955) has offered a reverse theory, geared to living organisms, which proposes that animal life will continue to explore ways and means of discovering inexhaustible supplies of energy. Such theorizing suggests that time may well follow a law of decreasing entropy and increasing organization (infinite timelessness).

The efforts of developmental psychology to gain some rudimentary understanding of how time becomes cognized in early infancy met the natural obstacle posed by the limited access to the ideas and feelings of the preverbal child. Piaget (1927) theorized that the infantile beginnings of cognized time were in the form of a vague awareness of a duration. As the child began to separate out his actions from others' and to connect them with the environmental effects they produced, he achieved an elementary consciousness of a before and an after. With representational thinking, the child apprehended time as a medium like space, in which self and objects were related to each other. The subsequent symbolizations and interiorizations of key people in the early environment imposed a fuller comprehension of the child's sense of cognitive time. Piaget's only significant reference to feelings was a footnoted acknowledgment (see Janet, 1928) that one's sense of duration depended on emotional regulators having to do with the persistence of illusions into adult life.

The significance of these views, whether they are intuitive philosophic speculations, objective scientific facts about our physical world, or findings based on the developmental theory of cognition, can only be enhanced by an elaboration of the instinctual and affective components of mental life that play a part in producing the experience called time. It is only logical to expect from psychoanalysis a contribution that might complement and extend the theme of synthesized opposites, where the subjective and the objective meet on a common ground and where instinct, cognition, and feeling play their respective roles in what we ultimately identify as time.

Birth as the prototype of all periodicities, a view Klein (1923) derived from the infant's rhythmic expulsion into extrauterine life, has become extended by some into a psychoanalytic concept of the origins of the sense of time. Fenichel (1945), for example, offers internal biological rhythms, such as the kinesthetic messages of breathing and pulse, as basic in promoting the child's concept of time. For Erikson (1956), a mounting tension in the infant when its appetite for the mother's breast is frustrated is the original signal for the experience of time. Gifford (1960), too, speaks of the infant's primitive awareness of a periodicity in maternal responsiveness, a rudimentary foundation for the later sense of the outer world's restriction on immediate gratification. Arlow, as reported by Kafka (1972), defines time as a series of successive instants of self-awareness organized by perception into a continuity and connected with memory.

Spitz (1972) attaches feeling to the notion of time as duration, insofar as perception only acquires its existence after feeling has endowed it with biological time. He emphasizes the anticipation evolving out of the infant's conditioned reflexes, something that establishes a bridge between body and mind. Thus, for Spitz, feeling is the main element responsible for the notion of time as duration. Brenner (1974) uses a concept of time to differentiate two feelings, anxiety and depression. He observes that just as the feeling of anxiety is associated with the idea that something bad is going to happen, so the feeling of depression is associated with the idea that something bad has already happened. Implicit here is the concept that time differentiates feelings, as contrasted with the view that feelings give character to time.

Hartocollis (1972), utilizing Piaget's views (1937) on the construction of reality, observes that the possibility of being relieved by the good mother gradually establishes the child's sense of time, first experienced as passive anticipation and later, as active expectation. Hartocollis (1974) demands a formally developed and individuated self in his concept of time, one that has a direct linkage with feelings. Time, for Hartocollis, is determined by the transformation of primitive pleasure and unpleasure into the specific emotions of anxiety and depression, boredom and elation. He (1976) underlines two conceptualizations of time: duration, where the flow of time reflects the strength of one's instinctual drives—time is experienced as moving slowly when wishes are unfulfilled or repressed, and rapidly when they are frustrated by the superego—and perspective, a reflection of the individual's sense of future self-adequacy.

A metapsychology of time can be derived from Freud's so-called stimulus barrier (*Reizschutz*), which he originally described (1895, 1920, 1924) as an outer protective shield, a quasi-organic membrane that defended against traumatic stimuli and served a more important protective function than even the perceptual apparati lodged behind that shield. Freud (1920) suggested that this protective barrier came to be supplied with its own energy (cathexis), enjoying a special capacity for *transforming* such energy in the face of danger from the external world. Although Freud's elaboration on this idea was sparse, he observed that this protective shield was unable to defend against overpowering internal unpleasurable excitations, and that under such conditions, the human organism treated them as if they were coming from the outside by the mechanism of projection. In this way the protective shield was used against internal dangers as well—a last line of defense against the reactions to trauma. This, in turn, was augmented by the alertness and vigilance of one's receptive perceptual apparati, as well as by the narcissistic investment of one's body ego toward a binding of the excitations released during overwhelming trauma. Freud defined feelings (affects) as constitutional endowments determined by the prehistory of the species, whose appearance in mental life he ascribed to the function of instinctual discharge. Interested in the cyclical depressions and elations suffered by those struggling with narcissism, more specifically with problems of self-esteem, Freud (1921) also became preoccupied with the theme of oscillating opposites. Indeed, the oscillating attention and inattention (cathexis and decathexis) of *Reizschutz* and the apparati behind it, a "discontinuous method of functioning," were for Freud at the bottom of the origin of the concept of time (1924). In a subsequent work (1925), he saw the barrier supplied with instinctual feelers, which it sent out and withdrew to test the potential threat from external stimuli. He pondered the idea that there was something about the shield as it operated with time that differed distinctly from its mode of dealing with sensory stimuli.

The concept of oscillation employed by Freud in his efforts toward a cogent psychoanalytic view of time has been largely neglected, except in the writings of Fliess (1961). Fliess accentuated the importance of a self-observing agency (described as an introject). He comes to identify time as the earliest self-observations (on the part of this introject) of one's alternating sucking and biting impulses, transformed and persisting throughout life as a feeling of time. It seems to me that Fliess and Freud have each dealt only in part with the transformatory aspect of the stimulus barrier as it relates to time. Freud accentuated the significance of *projection* (a throwing outward) in dealing with internal excitations; Fliess, on the other hand, emphasized only *introjection* (a taking in) in dealing with the time barrier transformations. Yet the projections of internal excitations triggered by man's first trauma (loss of the breast) are as significantly operative in the stimulus barrier as it deals with time as they are (as Freud noted) with sensory stimuli. In fact, the earliest time sense might well be experienced by the child as a personification or projection of instinctual excitations onto an external time-screen (the images of depriving or frustrating parents). And as Fliess has argued, the introjection of depriving parents as self-observers should also play a role in the transforming of such excitations into a feeling of time. It would seem logical, then, to include in any psychoanalytic definition of the subjective sense of time, the *oscillations of self-regard first experienced affectively, persisting throughout life, and accruing from both the earliest introjections and the earliest projections surrounding the trauma of first loss.* Such an estimable index of time, one of feeling, should naturally reflect not only the immaturities and instabilities of childhood in the form of the child's pendular mood swings, but the later maturities and feelingful nuances of adulthood that narrow the amplitude of these oscillations—a steadying influence promoted in large measure by the harnessing contributions of the genital psychic organization, as well as by the developing conscience (superego), both of which regulate the transformations of one's time sense like a pacemaker.

Certain clinical phenomena give credibility to the idea that the infant's postponement of gratification from its mother's supplies is a trauma, and that residues of infantile reactions to this trauma can be found in the psychology of later years. The Isakower phenomenon (1938) for one offers testimony to such operative reactions in both children and adults. A nocturnal event that commonly transpires prior to sleep, it has components that include an alteration of consciousness (a combination of clouding and alertness), certain amorphous sensory impressions, feelings of floating or sinking, and sometimes giddiness and nausea associated with experiencing vague noises; often there is the sensation of something crumpled or dry in the mouth or on the skin, and almost invariably there is a visual component of a round shadowy object coming nearer and getting larger and then moving further off and becoming smaller. Isakower has explained it as a withdrawal of tension (cathexis) from the external world at the time of falling asleep, by activation of a regressive solution to a conflict between an incestuous fantasy and one's conscience. Basically he postulates a substitution of an early oral gratification in place of a disturbing genital impulse. Lewin (1946) not only supports Isakower's thesis, but in more general terms proposes that the surface onto which all dreams appear to be projected is the flattened representation of the maternal breast (the dream screen). Spitz (1965) links both Isakower's and Lewin's observations to the blend of early sensory imprints of nursing, a blend involving the visual perception of the mother's face (rather than the breast), merged with the infant's touching of the mother's body. I would add the view put forth by Stern (1972), who reads trauma into the Isakower syndrome. To Stern, the syndrome represents a repetition compulsion stemming from excessive traumatic oral frustration, or in my terms, the infant's repetitive hypnogogic efforts to rediscover the lost object (the breast of the unavailable mother).

Kucera (1959) relates the Isakower phenomenon to the eruption of teeth, and one cannot help but perceive this draconic idea as yet another complement to Fliess' definition of time, which involves the transformation of sucking and biting. The associated gastric sensations (nausea) would further support the premise of a primitive cannibalism involving infantile imagery of a "stomach." In addition, I have clinically observed a link between the Isakower phenomenon and migraine (also accompanied by gastric symptoms). Although Greenacre's (1947) series of headache cases involved repressed, traumatic childhood confrontations with the sight of adult genitalia, I am nonetheless led to the speculation that migraine, too, may have its root in that early traumatic period of infancy when maternal sustenance is unavailable, triggering primitive cannibalistic impulses that become projected onto a semi-hallucinatory screen as an externalized infantile gestalt of the unavailable mother (a face-breast image).

The Projected Time-Screen

No portfolio on the various faces of time would be relevant to the reality in which we live without an acknowl-

edgment of the everyday fluctuations that all of us experience in our subjective sense of time. When we look
forward to an upcoming event with relish, time seems to
drag, as it does when we are socially embarrassed or suffering stage fright. As Arlow observes (see Kafka, 1972), our
critical self-observations in such instances become projected
outward and are experienced as a fear of being judged by
others. Generally speaking, time moves slowly for the
young, holding a promise of great things to come. As a
potential healer of the sick, time may hang heavy. For the
imprisoned, it's a stretch to be served, just as for the bored,
it's something to kill. For those maturing into adulthood,
time may be a trustworthy guide, but for those who are
well beyond childhood, it is an enemy to be thwarted, an
unwelcome agent of transience, taking us on all too swift a
journey. Indeed, for those of us over 40, it is enemy number
one—a target for assassination.

From childhood on, we all bend the concept of time to
suit our immediate needs. As Scott (1975) has observed, the
extent to which our omnipotent fantasies are unconsciously
active at any given moment determines how much and in
what way we interfere with time. Among the mechanisms
we mobilize in our tamperings, projection is one of the
leaders, as reflected in the various screens on which we cast
our imagery of personified time. Take our clockmaking (see
Fraser, 1975): the periodicity of nature was long ago
captured in the early shadow clock, in the Tibetan sun
stick, in the Roman hemispherium; man came to employ
these as objectifications of time. His search for objectivity
ultimately led him to nonastronomical devices, to the flow
of water or sand through an orifice, to the rate of burning
matter, to the power from the torque of a water wheel, and
to the pendulum that reflected the beat of his pulse (Gali-
leo). Yet despite his efforts to be mechanically objective in
the service of reality, man's experience of time remains to

this day an unsettling and unpleasurable affair, an intrusive and compromising influence on his intelligence, swaying him in the construction and usage of his chronometers. Even Einstein's successful prediction of curved space-time and faster ticking clocks in gravity-free environments does not completely vouchsafe against the human margin for error when it comes to objectively measuring time; for man's vulnerability rests not in the limitations of his skills or capacities for constructing predictable devices, but in the deeper psychology of his unconscious, wherein lurks, despite his foolproof clocks, his obstinate negation of time.

Because man the clockmaker is also man the subjectively experiencing observer, his mechanics continue to personify time as something less than precise. Indeed, each individual observes and experiences time both objectively and subjectively in his own fashion. Fraser connects his own view of time to the inevitability of the unpredictable event of death, which he feels urges man to increase his mastery of future contingencies through better recall of past events. I have offered the psychoanalytic counterview that time is subjectively experienced in terms of man's separation from the nourishing object, a traumatic event that dictates his defensive projections, whether in the form of his clocks or his timekeepers, or of any other personified scapegoats that he might choose to reflect his endless fumblings with time.

Freud (1925) wrote that all forms of auxiliary apparati invented by man for the improvement of the sensory functions are built on the same model as the human sense organs (spectacles, photographic cameras, ear trumpets). Both Fliess (1961) and Orgel (1965) have observed that though a chronometer cannot be built like one particular sensory sphere (since time is not felt as such), the clock nonetheless stands as a model of the first experience of time; the fact that it possesses a face and hands is not accidental—the face is that of the mother at which the nursling stares, and the hands are those which pluck and snatch at the breast. We fashion the clock in the image of our nursing experience, and though it may approximate an objective measurement of time, it is we who have the mouth to suck and to bite, and the hands to wind the knobs that enslave the clock to our command. Even our televising instrument is constructed in the nursing image. For many it is but another clock, another feeding breast, complete with face and hands; like infants we nuzzle the "boob-tube," twiddling the knobs till overtaken with sleep like the child at the tit, and only the eye of a test pattern (father) discourages our expectations of yet another feeding to come.

The fashioning of our chronometers reflects the ingenuity and creativity of mankind. The flair with which man captures his transitional needs and transformational skills for cushioning the experience of time is amply demonstrated in the colorful variety of timepieces available on the commercial market: there is the clock with the little teddy that runs the numerals with gentle pattering footsteps, offering soft reminders of childhood and timelessness; we laugh at time through the little bird who peeps or chirps the hour, reminding us that time is a little "cuckoo"; when it suits our mood, we pervert time with a wristpiece configurating the physiognomy of an infamous monarch of old Europe or of a corrupt American President. But whether the chronometer chimes the hour from a steeple, or whether the eye of a President winks the quarter, in every instance the message is the same—that we are all still nurslings, hands clutching and mouths drooling in anticipation of the timelessness of the breast.

What about those dedicated to acknowledging time, with their heightened objectivity and their determination to keep our clocks in repair? In our society this is the image of the father, the restrictive "wet blanket" who wakes and who weans, a Father Time who encroaches into the hopes of those who would retrieve their childhood a second time around. And despite the families where mother weans and wakes, it seems paradoxical tó think of a Mother Time, when it is mother who supplies the first cradle. In any event, the image of one parent or the other becomes ultimately projected onto an outside world to configurate our communal custodian of time (or timelessness). These projections color our perceptions of nature and the cosmos, just as they affect our construction and employment of those mechanical proxies that we employ toward the manipulation of our sense of transience—even toward a stoppage in the flow of time.

II

The Repetition Compulsion

The conceptualization of time as a trauma calls for an examination of the repetition compulsion, man's innate response toward the undoing of a trauma. For this I have chosen the clinical history of a patient I treated years ago, whose illness exemplifies the passionate struggle with time. I will refer to her as Lilli, the second of three pivots in this study, the main fulcrum being time.

Although she was 32 years of age when she first consulted me, she was still a wisp of a girl, pale complexioned, with an attractively formed face which gave haven to deep-set hazel eyes, a freckled nose, and casually touched up lips. She had a gaminlike bearing that was curiously aristocratic, and she presented her symptoms in bursts which were halted by tension and a desperately concealed sense of helplessness. She had come on the advice of a consulting psychiatrist who felt she needed intensive treatment. Five months pregnant following a previous miscarriage, she was suffering abdominal pain, a symptom that had begun with an earlier confinement, which resulted in the birth of a daughter. Her symptom of persistent pain at that time had become severe enough to warrant a surgical exploration of her abdomen in her first postpartum; a normal gall bladder was removed. This only reinforced her symptom and further interfered with her relationship to her newborn. Now in her third pregnancy, she harbored a dread that something catastrophic was about to befall her. Her morbid anxiety and pain rendered her incapable of caring for herself, for her new conception, or for her infant daughter. She found it particularly difficult to imagine what her life would be like after coming to term.

As an inmate of Nazi prison camps at Theresienstadt, Auschwitz, Hamburg, and Bergen-Belsen from puberty to late adolescence, Lilli, like so many others, had been abused and degraded. Early on she escaped into fantasy which in large measure succeeded in blurring her sense of time; her dream world took over almost completely during the first few months of her imprisonment. Not that her quest for timelessness during internment or in the years following release proved successful. Even the day of liberation was one of foreboding; festive though it was for the liberators, for Lilli and her fellow inmates who could barely tolerate the smell of food, it meant reemerging into an indifferent world. To some people, however, Lilli was to be singled out as an uncanny object.

Emigration, surgical removal of the concentration camp insignia from her forearm, training and graduation as a nurse, then marriage and a child—none of these accomplished a satisfactory return to the outside world. Helplessness and depression followed her everywhere, as did a compulsive brooding characterized by the hearing of vague sounds of children's screams and the experiencing of nocturnal hypnogogic hallucinations in which there would be a reactivation of the smells of burning human flesh. Haunted by guilt for surviving, as well as by envy of those who had escaped such humiliation through death, and still plagued by nocturnal sweats and flashbacks of her traumata, she finally gave in to treatment.

When Lilli was but a child of six in Vienna, her mother died of cancer. Prior to this, her parents had separated, and she saw her remarried father on only one or two occasions before he fled the country after Hitler's takeover of Austria, just prior to her own imprisonment. She had a childhood memory of him sitting on a bench, watching her play in a park near her home. Difficult as it was for her to recall his physical characteristics, she nonetheless remembered him as a pleasant and affectionate man. She had better recall of two little cousins who were like brothers, with whom she constantly played in those early years. And there were ambivalent memories of a mother, a beautiful but fragile woman whose fatal illness hampered her ability to express a mother's love. Lilli dimly recalled the many trips to the hospital and the mother who died before the mystified child could exhibit a new doll. It was the maternal grandmother who cared for her from then on, right through Auschwitz, until that grandparent's death in a Nazi gas chamber. On liberation, Lilli found a world filled with evasiveness. Friends were unduly solicitous and strangers seemed dispassionate. Even her husband, a professional man, could not sufficiently provide the comfort that marriage frequently offers. Giving birth only complicated Lilli's anxiety, compounding her compulsive need to imprison herself in traumatic memories. One could say that she was living a *present* filled with the horrors of a *past* that had become projected as her *future*.

The first therapeutic task in Lilli's treatment was to take account of her immediate physical needs. Since her repetition compulsion was exhausting her physically and jeopardizing the health of her unborn child as well, it was important that her pregnancy be accommodated towards securing some comfort for both mother and fetus. Only then could there be a proper appraisal of the psychological process that was binding her to her traumatic past. Simply

having a listener helped her, to the degree that her anxiety
had been lessened when she delivered a boy prematurely by
Caesarian section. Shortly thereafter, the analytic work
began.

I offer details of this analysis of someone locked in a
traumatic illness with the cooperation and encouragement
of the patient. Except for the use of the pseudonym Lilli,
the facts have not been compromised by efforts to preserve
the patient's anonymity, since she has outgrown her shame
at having been in a concentration camp. Her candor in this
regard leaves me little excuse in my analytic reporting to
cloak my own reactions and foibles as they appeared within
the therapy; and, in truth, what personally transpired
between Lilli and me played a part, for better or for worse,
in the overall results of the treatment. When she first came
to me, my experience gave me qualms about subjecting a
concentration camp victim to psychoanalysis, though there
were many I had treated supportively in a hospital setting. I
did have some of the defensive cocksureness that commonly
stamps the younger therapist, a brashness that ironically
offers a therapeutic advantage in supporting the struggle of
those patients who are in danger of surrendering to emotional illness.

Not that I wasn't adequately trained for my profession;
I held the routine credentials and was imbued with a
proper enthusiasm for my work. But I had some of the
affectations of the novitiate, including an office appointed
with a suitable aura of Freudianism, including an analytic
couch that was carefully upholstered with fabric reminiscent of the early Freudian circle. I could rightfully be
described as a typical member of the flock. At psychoanalytic conventions I dutifully attended all the colloquia,
while my wife and young children wandered the streets of
New York, window shopping or doing museum tours.
Faithfully I would sit in various convention halls, a willing

respondent to the morning witticisms and the later *Nacht-spiele* of senior colleagues who were busily engaged in upholding the traditions of psychoanalytic intellectuality. Significant in my therapeutic countertransference was the ethnic background I shared with my patient, an automatic identification with those who know what it is to live in a world with sharply drawn boundaries, where the human faults and idiosyncrasies that normally are overlooked have to be justified and defended. Although Lilli may have sensed at the start that her doctor had some personal familiarity with problems of self-esteem, pale as they were alongside hers, perhaps what she didn't know was whether this kinship was going to do her harm or good.

THE SELF

Psychoanalysts in clinical practice usually keep up with the analytic literature in formulating satisfactory diagnoses and in gauging the outlook for treatment. The literature helps today's clinician keep abreast of the current changes in ego psychology that he must consider in differentiating the quality of mental disturbances of our times from that of an earlier era. In the days of Freud's early discoveries, the major emphasis in analytic thinking revolved around the intrapsychic conflicts in man's sexuality. Following a project on which he collaborated with Breuer (1893), wherein neurosis was perceived as a victimization of the patient by his early environment, specifically by disturbed parents, Freud modified his views and acknowledged the significance of the patient's imaginative and fantasying capacities for inventing infantile traumata (1905). None-theless, he rightfully recognized that this very inventiveness was itself a part of the patient's neurosis, the result of a subtle emotional interplay between parent and child. He came to view the causality of these neuroses as distinct from that of conditions resulting from actual trauma, whether elemental or man-inflicted. In describing these other conditions, Freud (1919) introduced "the compulsion to repeat," a demonic force powerful enough to overrule the pleasure principle. He first discerned this compulsion in the play of children and in the dreams of adults suffering from trauma.

Curiously, in relation to group psychology, Freud never changed his mind on causality, as he had with individual psychology; he maintained one point of view on the instigating factor in mass neurosis. He (1913) ascribed the peculiarities of group bondage to an actual historical event, a trauma transacted in the earliest dawn of history by tyrannized and cannibalistic sons, who reacted to their imprisonment in a primal horde by slaying the father who had kept the women for himself. The parricidal deed not only freed the women from the primal harem, it bonded the conspirators psychologically. According to Freud, it was through death that the father became the symbolic leader of the group, now an oedipally stained and guilt-ridden expiative society whose criminal act became the provocation for a mass obsession. And this was supposedly passed down through the generations in shifting forms of totemic ritual and in religious practices that reflected the repetitive neurotic bondage of the group to their original patriarch.

In 1973 I took issue with Freud's theory of actual trauma as the instigating force of mass neurotic bondage. Others have done so as well, including Schimek (1975), who emphasized that just as the past helps shape the present, so our recreations of the present reshape our versions of the past. I realize that humanity, in its creative compulsion to undo a trauma, has a way of altering history and that judicious caution has to be exercised in reappraising historical documentations and assessing new interpretative modifications. A glaring example of a perversion of historical facts is the public defense put forth by modern neo-Nazis who ask us to treat Hitler's death camps as myths concocted by self-serving Jews. Notwithstanding this danger of distorting historical fact, in the case of Freud's explanation for group bondage, I had to question why the slain primal father became a stronger force in death than in life in the minds of the guilt-ridden survivors. I found this point as difficult to reconcile as Freud's unwillingness to offer the counterview that the provocation for mass bondage may have been a concoction rather than an actual murder of a patriarch—a reasoning similar to that which he employed in his understanding of individual neuroses.

With Lilli, I felt I had to keep an open mind as to whether her compulsion to mentally relive her camp experiences related primarily to her real concentration camp trauma, or to seeds already sown in her childhood by imagined family provocations. As to the possible role of time in her traumatic neurosis, I anticipated that the eventual exploration of her earlier years, including her traumatic losses prior to imprisonment, might further explain the psychological enmeshment that brought her to treatment. I felt a need to review in my own mind certain concepts that would be basic to the case, such as repetition compulsion (the phrase that quickly replaced Freud's original expression, "the compulsion to repeat"), the concept of the self, of self-regard, and trauma to self-regard.

A controversy still exists as to when the child has a developed sense of self, an awareness that those in his environment are separate from him. Current views, such as those of Mahler, Pine, and Bergman (1975), emphasize that the earliest phase of infantile autism is characterized by a relative absence of attention to external stimuli. During the symbiotic stage, infant and mother psychologically intertwine, and mother is split into good and bad. During the stage of primary narcissism, the infant experiences the boundless pleasures associated with the omnipotent oceanic feeling of being at one with the universe. From all this, the child at about five months of age appears to emerge with the capacity for psychologically separating his or her own body from that of the mother (separation-individuation). The early symbiotic merging slowly gives way to an unmerging, energized by the elemental thrust toward becoming an individual in his or her own right, a process that affords the individual some measure of continuing conflict, as all people experience residues of this tug of opposites throughout their lives.

Only when the child is walking and has some awareness of her (or his) gender (12 to 18 months) can sense of self and self-regard properly be said to exist. It is at this point that the child's libido comes to rest specifically with the separated self (secondary narcissism). The child acknowledges her existence and movement in the space common to her as well as to others perceived as existing independently of her own personal activity. The world is now objectified and specialized, in contrast to the earlier objectless world of autism and symbiosis. Furthermore, the acknowledgment of a separate self invested with libido carries a particular penalty, in that the child is for the first time aware of a vulnerability to internal and external traumata that have the power to alter her level of self-regard. This contrasts with the earlier infantile period when the child is protected by her inborn unresponsiveness to outside stimuli (primary stimulus barrier).

The traumata to which self-regard is potentially vulnerable accrue from the child's elemental thrust toward emancipation, which provokes fear of losing the care, the protection, and the love of the mother—a conflict which reaches its peak (rapprochement crisis) between 18 months and 3 years of age. Self-regard becomes embattled between the tug toward remerger and the increasing push toward independence; the sense of a lessening of maternal supplies both elevates and lowers self-regard. Coinciding with this, the sexual development of the child heightens the continued splitting of the mother into good and bad, the good images being used by the child in defense against the bad. At about age three, rapprochement optimally resolves by the blending of good and bad internalizations in the transaction of object constancy, as the mother becomes accepted in both aspects. The result is a rudimentary conscience based on values borrowed from such an accepted parent (and from the father later on). The first trauma then to self-regard is one induced by natural developmental forces during the period when the self is most vulnerable to loss of supplies (mother's love). Separation is the major trauma, though diseases, accidents, or unusual catastrophic events serve to compound this trauma.

Piaget's (1937) developmental theory sees repetition as an inherent human function of cognition, a part of general cosmic processes, a form of remembering, which in turn is a form of repeating. Specifically, repetition involves the process of assimilation, of changing the elements of one's environment into a form in which they can be incorporated into the self. This *repetitious assimilation* of external elements or objects *has the reflex quality of instinct*. What is taken in is subsequently either accommodated or not accommodated (like the stomach's assessment of food), and such accommodation serves to stabilize and equilibrate the psychic functions to provide optimal plateaus for new growth and change. Thus, repetition (and assimilation) is the main component of intelligence. The tendency in man to reach out into the environment again and again for objects to incorporate simply stems, according to Piaget, from the fact that man's mind and body were fashioned to incorporate (by divine plan) so that the need to so function cannot be further reduced.

Piaget's developmental model emphasizes the abilities of man to imitate an external event (a repetition compulsion), and to extend the capacities of the assimilative process by altering the elements of his environment through his imagination. Once the realistic deprivations of the feeding mother trigger the capacity of the child for transforming imitation into pretense and make-believe, then this developing imaginative capacity allows the child to internalize symbols (psychic substitutes) of the frustrating or absent feeder in a process known as mental representation. Eventually, representational intelligence allows the psychic apparatus to internally represent an absent event or object, to recall the past, to depict the present, and to anticipate the future in one swift, organized mental act.

Imagination, then, converts assimilation and imitation into internal symbolic imagery. Imagination has been psychoanalytically defined as the capacity to form a mental representation of an absent object, an emotion (affect), a body function, or an instinctual drive (Beres, 1960). Only in man does this capacity for abstract conceptualization and representation exist, and it is *to these representations* that the *energies* of the instinctual drives *are directed* in a process known as *cathexis*. Perhaps the most striking illustration of this imaginative process is the dream and its symbolic images of functions, emotions, drives, and objects. Imagination is crucial in man's ability to test reality, an operation whose aim is to rediscover an object in real perception that corresponds to what is imagined (Beres, 1960). As Freud (1925) observed, man does not simply remain interested in whether something he perceives should be assimilated, but whether some image existing in his ego can be rediscovered in his perceptions of the external world.

Whereas Piaget compares cognitive functions to a

thermostat providing a balance of assimilation and accommodation, with forces of change being counteracted by opposing forces maintaining equilibrium, a concept he borrowed from Mandelbrot (see Apostel, 1957), his observations do not include certain significant features characteristic of the repetition compulsion. He deals neither with the role of feelings derived from the instinctual drives, nor with the element of compulsion, nor with the role of trauma in producing those altered states of self-regard that are so intricately bound up with man's psychological need to reproduce and emotionally relive certain unpleasurable experiences that have remained alien to his ego. It was left to psychoanalysts to first use the term repetition compulsion to designate *a passive reproduction compelled by unconscious instinctual forces which had remained outside the organization of the ego.*

Freud (1920) came to link repetition compulsion with his theory of the death instinct. He proposed in his dualistic theory that in addition to life instincts, there operated in an unobtrusive and subclinical fashion an instinctual drive that was beyond the pleasure principle, that ran counter to the movement of life, a drive which originated in the instinct toward death. In contrast to neurotic disturbances such as phobias, where the disappearance of the danger would bring an end to the unpleasure, Freud observed that in the passive repetition compulsion, the victim continued to function as if the danger had not disappeared at all. This gave the appearance that some demonic force was at work in the patient, and Freud proposed that there was a drive in mankind (a death instinct) to restore an earlier state, in effect, to restore man to his original inorganic substrate. Although he acknowledged that another force appeared to be pushing the human organism toward progress and the production of new psychic structures, he felt such to be deceptive, in that humanity was merely seeking to reach an ancient goal (death) along new paths. Thus, for Freud, the aim of all life was death. He perceived the self-preservative components of instinctual life as assurances that the organism would follow its own path to death, allegedly influenced in this idea by Schopenhauer. He postulated that at the time of its coming to life, living substance was torn apart into small particles which have ever since endeavored to reunite through the sexual instinct. Eros was thus perceived as a life instinct constantly trying to undo the death instinct.

Because Freud's death instinct theory was neither supportable nor refutable, since a psychic representation of death was not clinically demonstrable in the human unconscious, I chose to adopt the pragmatic position that the instinct for life motivated the repetition compulsion, an elemental thrust that at times paradoxically appeared threatening to the very self-regard to be rescued. Not that the theoretical arguments for espousing a death instinct were not tempting, despite the lack of empirical findings in support of such a premise. But in my psychological examination of Lilli, a woman who had been caught in the web of a holocaust and had suffered years of incarceration in death camps, I came to provisionally appraise her compulsion as driven by a wish to restore her self-regard, rather than as inexorably linked with an inchoate attraction to death. Some authors have pinpointed unpreparedness for dying, not problems of self-regard, as the main issue in the repetition compulsion. Lifton (1976), for example, blames impaired death imagery, which leads to a form of psychic numbing when people become subjected to catastrophic physical or mental traumata. This impairment, claims Lifton, attends those who view life as counterfeit because it is not forever; in Rank's terms (1936), it is an affliction of those who refuse the load (life) in order to avoid the payment of the debt (death). Becker (1973) likewise views man as indulging in a denial of death, joining Lifton in embracing a concrete concept of death as something elementally acknowledged even in the unconscious, and therefore a visible enemy with which man can consistently joust in his everyday life.

My own preference now, as when I treated Lilli, is to view anything that is capable of rupturing self-regard and thereby threatening the psychological bond to the mother as a primal trauma. I have suggested that time is such a trauma. Our vulnerabilities in self-regard are consciously reflected in our concern for how we feel about ourselves or look to others when we are overcome with anxiety or helplessness, indeed how we will behave with our loved ones in the face of death. For most people I have examined, the idea of death simply meant another challenge in life, another potential danger to the sense of self, a concern over losing control, of breaking down, or of going berserk. I suspect this kind of preoccupation is encountered in the private imagery of everyone, in the healthy as well as in the sick, in the living as well as in the dying. Even in survivors of death camps like Lilli—faced with physical annihilation every day of their imprisonment—even in these victims, the common ruminative preoccupation was one of losing control or losing face, of being deprived of their option to individuate or reunite on their own terms. Robbed of their sense of freedom and independence by their jailers, they first had the desperate compulsion to restore it, followed ultimately by rumination over a fight never fought or an escape never perpetrated. And like Lilli, they indulged in self-punishment for their own physical salvage at the price of a lowered self-regard, of shame for having survived when loved ones had perished; their repetition compulsion in part reflected their brooding over having been reduced to living as passive, helpless creatures, deprived of the choice of dying with dignity. How many besides Lilli came to the

point of preferring annihilation to helplessness and indig-
nity is a matter of conjecture; but I question whether those
who did were impelled by an instinct to die, or by some
inchoate anticipation of an eventual healing of the rupture
in their regard for self.

As Lilli's therapist, I took the position that two paradoxical elemental forces were operative in her repetition
compulsion. The first was the necessary separation from her
primal objects, her parents. Triggered by the wish to
develop an independent sense of self, such a separation
would logically be experienced as either an active abandonment of, or a more reluctant severing from, the mother; in
either case the developmental thrust was motivated by the
demands for the individuation toward which we all strive,
consciously or unconsciously, in our bid to confirm our
identity. The hovering threat to self-regard associated with
this hazardous transaction for me explained the defensive
quality of the other more concealed ingredient, the counter-
move toward reunification with the mother.

Our day-to-day living clearly demonstrates how much
importance we attach to maintaining our self-esteem,
since the degree of effort we put into bolstering it is of such
staggering proportions. Though we may think of the blows
of fate as major threats to our fragile armor, it is more
commonly the multitude of man-made separations and
human isolations that threaten to overpower our sense of
self and to exaggerate our mental and physical inferiorities,
whether real or imagined. These separations, reinforced by
man's inhumanity to man, become the operative traumata
in the repetition compulsion. To disregard the dereliction of
depriving or unprotecting parents, to underestimate the
child's task of adaptation to the routine competitiveness of
the world, to minimize the humiliations of awkward adolescence or the exclusivities of in-group snobberies—would
be as unenlightened as remaining blind to the compulsive

self-depreciations of the woman who is infertile or the man who is sterile.

The concept of self-esteem, trite and hackneyed as it is, has long been the subject of study by psychologists. Freud's attention to it emphasized the pathological derivatives of one's narcissistic hunger, a focus still being explored by contemporary psychologists who have further refined the significant role of narcissism in the emotional illnesses of our time. Where Kohut (1971) suggests that the narcissistic investment of the self has its own independent development as a nonconflictual process vis-à-vis one's love of others, one must also acknowledge, as does Kernberg (1975), that self-esteem is nonetheless intricately interwoven with the capacity for love of others. Narcissism and object love become so developmentally intermeshed as to reciprocally telescope each other throughout all phases of development—and an impacted herniation of narcissism into object love commonly transpires when undue obstacles stand in the way of an optimal balancing of these investments of libido.

These impactions are particularly common in present times. The floundering self-esteem that they engender is not something that happens only to those traumatized by prejudice and death camps. Nor is it unique to common people. It is a problem of the nobility and the aristocracy, the powerful and the prestigious; it is as agonizing to the scientist trying to make an original discovery as it is to the astronaut back from outer space with no more giant steps to take; it even affects the well-being of our national leaders as they struggle for enshrinement in the pages of history. Self-regard is a mountain without a peak or a pit without a bottom. The more energy used to bolster it, the more energy required to maintain it at its new level; and the level for so many has no bounds. It's like blood pressure; everyone has his own reading; the psyche is obliged to support

self-regard at the individual's particular reading. Although
the level of self-esteem may vary from one individual to
another, the means by which humanity struggles to uplift it
are universal.

INSTINCTS AND THEIR TRANSFORMATION

Many have challenged Freud's death instinct and his
modus operandi of the repetition compulsion, holding to
the Nietzschean view that there can be no such thing as a
return to the inorganic, since humans come to creation not
from inorganic matter, but from a woman's womb. Schur
(1960) draws on the instinctive behavior patterns of animal
life as his basis for explaining the repetition compulsion.
He contends that the origins of traumatic helplessness in the
infant are to be found in an instinctive avoidance and
fright, where the human apparatus is ready neither for
fight nor flight—a view consistent with Rapaport's aphor-
ism (1953) that instinctual drives are the ultimate guar-
antees of autonomy from the environment. In support of a
premise explaining human patterns by comparing them to
patterns in lower animals, Schur cites the writings of
Lorenz (1932) on instinctual animal behavior that in some
degree appears to match the instinctual deportment of
man. Lorenz reserves the term "instinctive behavior
patterns" for those activities originating in inherited path-
ways, rather than in acquired insights resulting from intelligence. For example, in birds he finds little evidence of
intelligent behavior; as far as their social and sexual instincts are concerned, their gregariousness and their ability
to direct their sexual arousal toward humans sufficiently
impresses Lorenz regarding their capacity for tameness.
The ability of newly hatched birds to imprint humans as
libidinous objects leads Lorenz to further conclude that in
most bird species the object of libidinizing patterns is not

innately determined; the freshly hatched gosling looks upon the first living thing it sees with the intent of imprinting the image of that object of instinctual gratification, an irreversible process occurring during a definite period in the bird's physiological development.

The similarities between the sexual deportment of birds and humans is of particular interest to Lorenz. The manner in which human beings fall in love and court their mate is for Lorenz ample evidence that human sexual behavior, too, is marked by a retention of instinctive behavior patterns. Lorenz perceives man, like the bird, responding to innate releasing mechanisms, signals by which his sexual partner is recognized. Indeed, just as the partridge hen apparently falls in love with a human foster parent in a transference to a ruddy colored apron reminiscent of the red thoracic patch of a partridge cock, so the human being seems to respond to the mate who triggers the image of nourishing mother or protective father. The manner in which birds, like humans, are influenced by certain decisive features in their chosen mate—the physiognomy of the head, the timbre of the voice, the unique mode of locomotion—all this substantiates the Lorenzian analogue. And in truth, in the prelude to sexuality, no one can question the startling similarity. The Burmese jungle fowl is by no means a farfetched counterpart of today's modern narcissistic male —the flamboyant colors, the inflatable devices that make up the display (releasers), the conspicuous expenditure of energy so far in excess of what is required to do the job; taking into account the affected preenings and posturings, the stuck-out chest, the strut and swagger, the climactic flight in ever diminishing circles toward a landing by the mate in full wingspread (a jet rendezvous), one has to admit that Lorenz has a strong case to support his theory.

The danger of analogizing between humans and animals is that it all too easily conveys the impression that man is trapped in an instinctive path that forces him to compulsively match the footsteps of the animal. The instinctualist espouses a philosophy that relieves man of the responsibility for being civilized, despite the fact that now more than ever, in a nuclear age when humanity en masse is in danger of passively giving license to the power hungry to decide our fate, there is a cry for the preservation of civilization. Yet the Lorenzian (1950) view sees our society as endangered by domestication, embracing the Darwinian argument that the evolutionary leap from anthropoid ape to *Homo sapiens* has been accomplished by a precarious dismantling of innate behavior. For Lorenz, man's difficulties in the harnessing of weapons of destruction are merely the result of a blockage in their intelligent application. He believes that the invention of weapons only seduces the naive, allowing easy and impersonal killings by the thoughtless tensing of a finger on a trigger. He rationalizes that man's aggressions are due to the flowering of a culture that bottles innate rage, leading to sporadic explosions against human scapegoats made up of anonymous strangers who have encroached on the territorial imperatives of the greedy. For Lorenz, there is survival value in inter-species aggression, one that ensures the distribution of a particular species over an inhabitable area. Far from being seen as diabolical and destructive, aggression is perceived as an essential part of the preservation of the species. Lorenz is convinced that there can be no love without aggression, and rather than seeing society as its ultimate harness, he sees our culture as only serving to aggravate aggression. The thesis that higher psychic structure promotes decompensation and breakdown argues for presenting aggression as necessary for health, implicitly forgivable on the grounds that it's only human. Salvation from superego is not contained in the Lorenzian viewpoint; nor does he count on human creativity for fostering capacities for transforming aggressive tensions. The closest he comes to a formula for taming man's destructiveness is in his vague references to domestication.

Ardrey (1961, 1966), too, espouses a fundamental concept of behavioral evolution based on man's rootedness in the animal past. As far as he is concerned, if one substitutes the notion of the death instinct for the concepts of dominance and territorial defense, then the theoretical differences between his views and Freud's disappear. Hamburg (1968, 1972, 1973) likens the aggressive patterns of chimpanzees, gorillas, and baboons to those found in man, seeing in the human biological primate heritage an anlage of man's genetically transmitted aggressive tendencies that require environmental stimulation for their full development. Hamburg conceptualizes that aggression exists in the service of adaptation to nutrition and reproduction, and involves inherited brain patterns that reflect man's selective learning behavior.

Montagu and Fromm are two of the many who have taken Lorenz and other instinctualists to task in deploring the view that aggression is inherently in the service of life, social rank, and survival of the species. According to Montagu (1952, 1968), the instinctualist offers a myth to divert attention from the debilitating social conditions of mankind. Similarly, Fromm (1973) suggests that aggressions are responses to political and economic circumstances of our own making, rather than biological givens with a spontaneous flow. Fromm's reminder that man is the only mass murderer among the thousands of fighting species (Tinbergen, 1968) is offered in refutation of Lorenz's view that atrocities committed by man only reflect the universality of his animal nature. Not all human beings are murderous, Fromm counters, since everyone is by no means subjected to the same familial and societal forces. He concludes that only when we are willing to carry the

burdens of becoming educated about our insecurity, our
greed, and our narcissism, can we expect our aggressions to
become purged.

Society as provocation for the development of human
aggression is by no means a popularly held thesis among
psychoanalysts. Whereas Freud viewed the instincts as
fused superordinated biological forces with contrary goals,
Anna Freud (1972) emphasized that just as sexual mastery
cannot be achieved without aggression, so aggression cannot be integrated into life without libido. In philosophical
terms, death cannot be attained without the fortunes of love.
Aggression is seen as a prime instinctual force, intermeshed
from the beginning with the various phases of libidinal
development. Although Anna Freud equivocates as to
whether the aggressive drive should be allocated to the ego,
to the id, or to both, she nonetheless views the aim of
aggression as being in the service of libido, and feels that
the mother is the original provocateur of the aggressions of
the child. Unlike libido, she observes, aggression lacks
object constancy; where the good lover demonstrates
fidelity in his love, the good hater is always promiscuous in
his hate. Certainly when one indulges in the theoretical
exercise of screening our Eros from its aggressive companion
in the simple matters of everyday living, the result is a stark
obscenity; our health as well as our social relations demand
the fusion of these two. In beclouding the more muted
aggressive component in the bedfellow relationship, the
clamor of libido helps us project an image of lovingness, an
amiable society bathed in the milk of human kindness. By
agreement of the silent majority, society's murders and
hijackings and rapes gradually disappear from the head-
lines to reappear as anecdotal tid-bits for the inside pages of
our newspapers.

Yet, it is also a fact that instinctual life does have some
capacity to transform and attenuate our aggressions, due

largely to the power of libido to neutralize or buffer these aggressions. Unfortunately it is this same libidinal magic that is responsible for some of the false hopes that people harbor with respect to psychological treatment. So many people see in therapy the promise of a perfect love life, an expectation stemming from the human predisposition to idealize. In truth, idealizations that were initially reserved for one's first object (the primal parent), when displaced or transferred onto other objects, do allow human mating to become a more loving affair. If human beings were not disposed to such transference, there obviously would be no such thing as exogamy, since the reconciliations with reality which ultimately must transpire in our exogamous society are heavily dependent on the earlier expectations of love that were first aroused in relationship to the parent. Even with the help of libido, the glaring imperfections of one's chosen object make it difficult for some to perpetuate object constancy. Yet it is testimony to the power of libido that young lovers, at least, are temporarily able to postpone the breakdown of their idealizations of each other. They become blind to the facts as they gaze at one another in moonstruck rapture, each totally captivated by the other's illusory charms. Indeed we must marvel at the human chemistry that allows the lover to find beauty in a mate who, by all norms of physical appearance, is a definite challenge to plastic surgery! Unfortunately, such illusions do not work for everyone. A patient with an unusual outlook on mating comes to mind. It was part of his fundamentalist rearing that only God could pick him a wife; indeed he married with this premise. His eventual disenchantment with his spouse led to the hypochondriacal conviction that he suffered from a fatal disease—which for this man was preferable to living with the tasteless selection that God made in his case.

Just as the subjective sense of time is the traumatic

trigger for man's aggression, so such aggression calls on the abilities of the libido to neutralize aggressions and to transform one's perceptions of reality. Although it may be circular reasoning, support for this comes in part from our subjective sense of time, since it is the postponement of sexual gratification that gives aim-inhibited thrust to our capacity to idealize our objects. This *readiness of libido to direct itself with the help of the ego to goals esteemed by society is part of the active recreative repetition compulsion* (Loewald's term, 1971). Freud's (1915) original dictum that there is nothing in the id corresponding to the idea of time and that there is no recognition or alteration resulting from time's passage has caused Fraser (1975) to argue that the id cannot possibly remain unaffected by time, or it would survive the body. In an earlier effort to resolve this dilemma, Bonaparte (1940) recalled Freud's (1926) modified concept in which he admitted that repressed psychic content underwent some alteration as impulses became inhibited and deflected from their original aim. Bonaparte suggested that when Freud spoke of a timeless unconscious, he meant either that the unconscious had no knowledge of time, that it was unaffected by time, or that it failed to perceive time. Certainly when it comes to altering our conscious time sense, our instinctual life seems to bend and distort itself in a multitude of ways, as in the dream, where the translation of latent content into manifest content may be carried out by the ego during sleep, but where the distortions, condensations, and displacements are nonetheless processes peculiar to the id (Anna Freud, 1936).

The Ego in the Active Re-creative Repetition Compulsion

Stern (1972) sees human aggression as prompted by the perpetuation of infantile biotraumata in anticipation of the finality of death. His concept of the child's first awareness of death emphasizes the loss of the primal object (the mother). He observes that the fear of the disappearance of both the self and the object is reflected in the ubiquitous experience of *pavor nocturnus* (nightmare). In this common childhood symptom the dreamer feels he is being annihilated, as he unconsciously anticipates the experience of nothingness he thinks his death might bring. Psychologically, Stern observes, it is a conjuring of the early experience of first object loss. I support Stern's view with a personal observation on an episode of *pavor nocturnus* in a two-and-a-half year old (my grandchild), which occurred subsequent to the "disappearance" of her other grandfather (in death). The attack was provoked primarily by fear of the loss of her mother, as reflected in the child's subsequent expression of her first verbal acknowledgment of time, which took the form of an anticipatory observation that with the coming of spring, a mild kitchen burn on her mother's arm would be healed. Eissler (1966) points out that curiously, the analysis of a nightmare is not to be found in Freud's work; he reminds us, however, that for Freud, anxiety dreams in reaction to trauma served the function of reducing that trauma (1900). Similarly, for Ferenczi (1934), every dream was but an attempt to settle the unresolved consequences of a past trauma. Georges Abraham (1976) has even suggested that *pavor nocturnus* might be a reflection of time breaking through into the unconscious.

Eissler's observations on concentration camp victims in some respects do not mirror my own. He gives the traumatic neuroses in general a more favorable prognosis than I would, because he perceives the damage in those cases as more easily undone than in cases where neurosis was brought on by internal forces. According to Eissler, the real trauma acts as a roadblock, inhibiting the further development of the ego, so that removal of the trauma allows the ego to quickly blossom. These findings appear a bit optimistic. In my own experience with concentration camp victims, the traumatic insult was an unusually crushing blow to the ego, superimposed on the internal problems that everyone acquires in childhood. Eissler cites a patient whose traumatic neurosis was brought to an end when he discovered the capacity to be active; though the future still held the potential for danger, the capacity to be active undid the damage of the past trauma. In Eissler's reasoning, just as the mind can anticipate future contingencies, so can it work in reverse; thus, an individual's discovery of activity can have a retroactive healing effect by dissolving the past trauma. I think that what Eissler means to say here is that his patient resolved a major underlying problem that was perpetuating a passive repetition compulsion. The solution allowed the patient to project a more active posture for himself in the future with respect to potential traumata likely to befall him in that future. Unfortunately, Eissler does not tell us how his patient acquired this new capacity for activity. He does go on to say that when old people relinquish their predilection to suffer traumata, they lose their fear of death as well, not a surprising conjunction considering that the acknowledgment of time is almost invariably linked with an acknowledgment of death.

Delving further into the question of activity and passivity, I refer back to Freud (1920), who observes that the pleasure principle dictates that children cannot have their pleasurable experiences repeated often enough, and that they insist that their repetitions be identical. This character trait of childhood, Freud points out, disappears in later life. In my observations, very young children seem to have little desire to exercise repetitious thinking about unpleasurable traumatic experiences. For one thing, the self has to be sufficiently developed for a trauma to be experienced, passively or actively; it follows that only the child who possesses a defined sense of self would be a candidate for experiencing a repetition compulsion in reaction to trauma. Less mature youngsters exposed to stimuli that ordinarily would traumatize an adult—for example, young tots found buried alive in underground pits or extricated from other physically abusive environments—appear to exhibit minimal evidence of any psychological processes approximating the clinical picture of a repetition compulsion.

Lucid explanations for the infant's capacity to convert passivity into activity do not abound in the psychoanalytic literature. Spitz (1957) feels that the infant's eight-month stranger-anxiety and the game of peek-a-boo are related to the conversion of passivity into activity. The infant searches for the mother's face while scanning the face of the stranger, and the sense of estrangement promotes a peeking back at the stranger again and again, the child lifting its face and then hiding it. Spitz describes this as a prelude to negation, wherein an identification with the aggressor allows the shift to activity and to the prerogative for the child to say "no." With the help of the unconscious, observes Spitz, the child takes over the capacity for negation and the ability to use it *against* rather than *with* the adult. Joseph (1959) suggests that an unconscious fear of aggression that might emerge is a causative factor in the failure of some adults to make the shift to activity. She feels that a full sense of self is lacking in such passivity because of a hatred that was never faced; rather than squaring up to certain anxieties, the passive person prefers to unburden his own fate onto the shoulders of others.

Schafer (1968) organizes a differential between active and passive: he designates instinctual aims as active when their gratification depends on the subject acting on an object, and as passive when the gratification depends on the object acting on the subject. In terms of psychic structure, he regards the ego as active when it acts in defense against the instincts, and as passive when it is overwhelmed by them (here he quotes Rapaport, 1953). In terms of object relations, the longing to regress to the nursing situation is offered as an example of passivity, although Schafer acknowledges that such a designation hardly helps distinguish the wish to devour from the wish to be devoured. With regard to subjective experience, Schafer views passivity as reflecting a deficit in the stable internalizations necessary for intentionally doing something to someone, rather than having something done to oneself. Finally, on the subject of experiencing trauma, Schafer cites Anna Freud (1952): it is the unconscious wish of the victim that is decisive in differentiating passivity from activity.

From a practical point of view, I was faced with the task of helping Lilli transform her sense of self as a passive victim into that of a woman with an active stake in her own destiny. I felt that crucial to her acquiring such activity was her *ability to find herself deserving of an active self-defense*, a worthiness that would only come from psychological growth in her sense of self. Her clinical picture confronted me with a crucial question: what was the psychological motive of her compulsive flashbacks? Was the compulsion a kind of revving up, a daily calisthenic that aimed at keeping her in a state of alert, an exercise that prevented psychic atrophy through the regular use of her defensive maneuvers? Or was it designed, as Hartmann suggests (1937), to attenuate the effect that the reappearance of actual trauma would have on her psyche. Or was it, as Schur (1960) proposed, in the service of restoring activity in some way? Bibring (1943) offered as a key component the element of working-off or ventilating; contradicting Freud's "return to an inorganic state," he suggested that it could well represent the repeating of the creation of life. Bibring saw the compulsion as comprised of two opposing forces, one of rupture and the other of reunion; like Schur, he emphasized the aim of restitution through a regaining of activity.

My thinking was further clarified when I reviewed a panel discussion on the subject (as reported by Gifford, 1964). Several of the expressed views struck a chord with my own formulations: Hendrick offered the reminder that unconscious fantasies recovered in adult analytic patients were only the end result of complex developments, and were by no means restatements of primary experiences. Waelder observed that the needs of psychoanalytic patients are contradictory, and that since certain conflicts are insoluble in reality, then a certain creativity is required to find a suitable solution. As for the repetition compulsion in children, Reider suggested that in the imaginative variations of the child's re-enactment in play of a dreaded traumatic experience, there was a tempering of anticipated pain. These views supported Nunberg's (1932) earlier opinion that the repetition compulsion could be deprived of its independence and its driven quality by the synthetic forces of the creative ego.

In line with Freud, Lipin (1963, 1964) formulated the repetition compulsion as a replica-producing activity, a representative of instinctual drives organized by biological processes by-passing the ego and its imagination. He ascribed the cause of the compulsion to a relative lack of essential experiences and to internal and external factors; unfortunately, he was vague in defining these factors. Lipin cited an endogenous re-creation of the distressing experience as the trigger of the process, forcing wave upon wave of repetition, each one coming closer to the original traumatic experience in a *recasting* of distorted functioning toward correctional perception and response.

My own formulations were consistent with Lipin's (and Bibring's) argument that Freud's death instinct could just as

easily be a reflection of a life instinct at work. In my observations of Lilli, I could see her repetition compulsion as a
replica-producing activity in the ultimate service of maturation and restructuring, as Lipin suggested. But as a
model for the process, I preferred the earliest lose-and-find
hallucinations of the infant responding to the trauma of the
absent maternal nipple and its milk, a process in which the
infant first assimilates and accommodates to the loss (and to
the trauma of first postponement) through a primary
creative replication (a retrieving of the traumatizing breast
via hallucination). I felt that later traumata capable of
invoking the same threat (loss of the life-sustaining breast)
would logically be dealt with in the identical way, by a
primary creative replication of the new trauma. In Lilli's
case the repetitive appearance of the camp traumata into
her mental life, like the infant's lost and then hallucinated
breast, was a retrieving of the traumatizing agent, but in
the service of regaining the agent rather than the trauma.
In my view, the purpose here was not to reinstate inor-
ganicity (the death instinct), but the *timeless* union with
one's parents, even if they were only concentration camp
surrogates. Nonetheless, in her passive repetition compulsion, Lilli's trauma lived on as if time had stood still.

Lilli's passive repetition compulsion seemed to me to
have its roots in her infancy, when only a partially internalizing ego (yet one capable of mental representation) anticipated accommodation to a trauma by undoing losses
threatened by that trauma. Contrary to Lipin's view of
recasting as a movement from distortion to actuality, I
found the quality of the recasting in Lilli's compulsion (as
with shellshocked soldiers) to be tinged with a fragmentation and alienation of the mental representation of the
trauma as well as of the self, the aim appearing to be an
alteration toward undoing the loss. I came to view the
whole process as not only a revving up, a refuelling, a ventilating, an attenuating, but as something that *aimed at*

transformation of the trauma by derealization, and transformation of the self by depersonalization, so that both could be *later* recast and resynthesized through certain creative mechanisms that particularly relate to the ego's manipulation of the sense of time (*fausse reconnaissance*). Where Nunberg spoke of ego synthesis subjugating the repetition compulsion, I viewed the compulsion itself (the replication) as the first step toward this resynthesis.

I modeled the actual operation after the manner in which a youngster automatically attempts to revise in his mind an unacceptable outcome of a game, searching in his playback for some means of effecting an alternate outcome for the original event. I felt that this *effort to transform* (to shift cathexis) initially *involved not only instinct, but a largely unconscious ego,* drawing on the capacities of a primary creativity in the service of self-preservation and the maintenance of self-regard. Support for this view comes from the manner in which human memory functions in its prelude to the use of the *déjà* and *jamais* mechanisms of *fausse reconnaissance* on which I elaborate in a later chapter. Freud's (1899) early observations on screen memories clarified that rather than recapturing the images and impressions of a bygone actual event, the human memory reorganizes recollections in accord with the changes undergone by the remembering ego, the latter being no longer identical to the one which initially experienced the event. It was my impression from clinical observations made on soldiers who had just suffered acute battle traumata that such reorganizations of memory, particularly the mechanisms of alienation (depersonalization and derealization), had already been triggered by the time I examined them.

THE THERAPEUTIC PACEMAKER

Early on in Lilli's analysis, I recalled my experiences of several years back, when, as one of the house surgeons assisting in Penfield's (1952) studies, I witnessed electrical stimulation of the temporal lobes during operative procedures to remove scar tissue from the brain. The subjects were afflicted with a form of epilepsy caused by damage to brain tissue. Under local anesthesia these patients dredged up sensory echoes of past experience in the form of recollective hallucinations. The work promoted the speculation that the temporal lobes (as well as the brain stem) were storage systems for memories of past events that could be retrieved through artificial electrical stimulation, albeit without the dynamic repetition of their mode of production. It strongly suggested that the temporal lobe was an integrating station for the past and the present, for inner and outer experience, for projection and introjection. Maclean (1949) referred to it as the visceral brain, an organ of the nervous system that mediates the translation of psychological tensions into somatic experience. Kubie (1953) called it the psychosomatic organ. I thought of it as a pacemaker that regulated the subjective sense of time, comprised of two components—a contribution from the time-bank of the temporal lobes (and brain stem) and a psychological contribution from the mind. This sense of pace is initially experienced as outer protective parents and later as internalized representations of these harnessing figures interacting with the instinctual passions.

I found intriguing the similarity between the memories retrieved under operative conditions in Penfield's study and those I had obtained earlier in a theatre of war from shell-shocked soldiers under hypnotic regression. The past was treated by these traumatized soldiers as though it were the present, as if time had stood still. Often the victims were survivors of dead comrades-in-arms, seeking expiation for an identificatory guilt of survival and hoping to restore a self-esteem left vulnerable by earlier negative environmental forces and further impaired by the latest trauma.

Although the repetition compulsions of shell-shocked survivors had a suicidal quality through identification with their dead comrades, as reflected in their deliria and flashbacks to battle action, discernible in the reliving of their traumata was the effort to transform the actual events through imaginative replay. In the repetition, more initiative could be taken to rescue a comrade, or a belated judicious appraisal of danger might serve to justify the paralytic failure to act on behalf of a fellow soldier.

Lipin's thesis of a passive repetition compulsion motivated by endogenous instinct toward reinstatement of the original traumatic situation could logically be challenged with the argument that the unconscious ego of such a casualty, instead of simply engaging in unpleasurable imitative imagery, was exercising as well a kind of inchoate primitive imagery aimed at not only reinstating the trauma, but at finding a creative restitution therefrom. The price was an acute psychotic state from which there often was a spontaneous and dramatic recovery. The prescription for many of these battle casualties called for sleep therapy, usually a six-day course in which the soldier was sedated to unconsciousness throughout. The aim here was the eventual restoration of more stable rapid eye movement (REM) sleep, which might promote an abreaction through dreaming rather than a hallucinatory psychosis. When sleep therapy was followed by narcohypnosis involving lighter sedation, the patient was able to give vent to underlying conflicts that had been linked with the current assault (such as a "Dear John" letter from home that might have had a devastating effect on the soldier before battle).

In the emotional disorders of civilian life, neurotics often prevent themselves from experiencing their feelings. In fact, Kubie (1953) has expressed the concern that the denatured quality of the memories of patients in psychological treatment, devoid as they are of a true emotional core, poses an insurmountable obstacle to improvement. Kubie thinks the answer to therapy rests in finding a means of penetrating the smoke screen of words in order to circumvent the ego in a cleavage to the gut component. In the instance of the traumatic neuroses, Kubie's concern does not apply; it is the time factor that is important. In Lilli's case, as in the case of shell-shocked soldiers, the past was experienced as the present; the nightmare of the past became the only prospect for a future. It was the annihilation of time that posed the most immediate threat to Lilli's health, a telescoping that had to be stopped if there was any hope of bringing about a rhythm more compatible with the ventilative process. One might say she needed a "transplant," a new pacemaker to replace the one that had broken down—not only from the impact of the death camps, but, as I was to discover, from earlier insults of familial deprivation.

Although I likened the initial steps in the treatment of a traumatic neurosis to the implantation of a pacemaker in someone suffering cardiac irregularities, I could also compare the role of supportive listener to a medicament used to restore natural brain waves in a person experiencing epileptic discharge. Unlike patients with intellectual resistances, where, as Kubie suggests, there may be a call for a psychic scalpel that cuts to the bone, with Lilli the need was for cover. I had the obligation to provide a protective auxiliary to a stimulus barrier that had been severely cracked and left vulnerable to internal explosive forces that were threatening to convert her past into a catastrophe of the present.

My blueprint for engaging Lilli's repetition compulsion was now drafted. I took the position that her compulsive process was motivated by an instinct for life rather than death. Although it was initially triggered by early parental deprivation, it had taken on a morbid quality as a result of imposed concentration camp traumata of genocidal proportions. These traumata had called forth strong restitutive efforts in the victim, including her precipitous agitation to produce new life in the service of achieving timelessness, rather than risk being confronted with the realities of time. I anticipated that in the course of Lilli's analysis, a wide variety of transformatory devices would floridly emerge as passionate expressions of her struggle with the trauma of time. Now it remained for me, as her analyst, to engage the manifest symptoms of her repetition compulsion, specifically the flashbacks and the abdominal pain that still threatened to wreak havoc with her life.

III

The Clinical Investigator

Thus far, the reader has been introduced to Lilli and her adversary, Time. Now the psychoanalyst, as third and last pivot in this narrative, should be acknowledged, so that he can formally take his place behind the analytic couch and bring us clinically closer to the trauma under investigation.

When it comes to understanding the human penchant for killing time, the psychoanalyst has a role similar to that of the sleuth. To compare the two, detective and analyst, we could draw from the literary archives of the popular and classic mystery story. Perhaps just as illustrative as any are the adventures of Sherlock Holmes. It is no coincidence that the great detective invented by Arthur Conan Doyle should be as popular today as when he was conceived. The universal appeal of this fictional investigator attests not only to man's fascination with crime, but also to man's obsession with time. The tendency of contemporary playwrights to link the image of this mythical sleuth with the investigative talents of Sigmund Freud bears witness to the similarity of imagery evoked by these figures, a likeness sufficient to lead one to probe for other features common to the two.

Though it is not possible to analyze the mind of a playwright purely by the products of his craft, nonetheless I feel that Conan Doyle, like other authors of fiction, does reveal himself through his best-known characters—in this instance, Holmes and his companion, Watson. Seen through these characterizations, Conan Doyle indeed seems to bear some psychological resemblance to Sigmund Freud. The comparison might be taken by many as a manifest affront to the memory of the founder of psychoanalysis; some psychologists might disdain even lumping these two figures together. Perhaps the complaints would equal out, since other readers, such as mystery buffs, would probably take offense in the opposite direction. I would take issue with indignation from either side; the tales of Sherlock Holmes faithfully document the imaginative flair of a luminary in the field of mystery, just as the writings of the father of psychoanalysis reflect to this day a unique scientific art.

Both Freud and Conan Doyle were first sons, both mother's boys, offspring of proud and dogmatic matriarchs who exhibited a passion for their son's achievements. Like Freud, Conan Doyle initially found medicine the prime vehicle for his academic interests, and each cultivated teachers who provided inspiration for the alertness of eye and ear that is part of diagnostic intuition. Freud in real life experimented with cocaine; Conan Doyle, through his creation Holmes, did the same. Footprints and fingerprints were to the author of mysteries what dreams and parapraxes were to the psychoanalyst. But what the two men had most in common was their preoccupation with the theme of life and death. In Freud's case, it took the form of an ingenious theory of instincts; for Conan Doyle, it was exercised in literary form in the tradition of the dramatist. The manifest splitting of imagery eloquently reveals the creativeness of both men: Freud, a scientist dedicated to gaining insight into the human psyche, in his personal life allied himself with a significant confidant (Wilhelm Fliess);

Conan Doyle split himself in his writing into the astute Holmes and the satellite Watson.

On the subject of split images, originating as they do with the good and the bad of infancy, and their later protractions into doublings and imaginary friends, I would note that the extension of the process of self-idealization (secondary narcissism) ultimately locates itself in abstract parts of the ego (superego and self-ideal). Logically, however, this abstract idealization (the good) cannot lay claim to standing on its own merit; paradoxically, the negated (originally the bad) aspect of one's narcissistic image remains closely linked with one's ideals in one form or another throughout life. An appropriate term for such negations might be the "subego." In many ways, this subego fragment of one's motivations comes to be treated by the ideal as a defective double or twin, a "poor cousin," so to speak. Indeed, it serves much the same function as the imaginary companion, namely that of auxiliary superego, a vehicle for the unacceptable, scapegoat or buffer, or weapon for expressing defiance. Perhaps most importantly, it assumes the role of the transitional stuffed panda, serving as palliation in the face of loneliness.

It should not be surprising, then, that the hero in the usual mystery story is associated with a side kick, commonly represented in the narrative as an oaflike misfit who, in body and mind, offers sharp counterpoint to the perfections of the hero. As in real-life relationships between friends, a considerable degree of elevated self-esteem attaches to the image of the hero at the price of some denigration of his subaltern. In such a blueprint, the attentions of the reader become subtly shifted from hero to subaltern and back again, depending on the writer's whim and the degree to which he wishes to manipulate the statures of his doubled characters. From the standpoint of the reading public, the insertion of the subordinate figure helps assuage the envies that might be provoked in the reader by the magnificence of the heroic lead; the burden of attaining the hero's ideals and achieving his austerities through instinctual renunciation is softened through an identification with the human excesses of his weaker companion. Often the hero is cast as celibate, demanding of himself a prevailing abstinence, whilst the subaltern to the contrary is permitted an inordinate degree of lechery which offers us a mood of euphoria, a relief from the brooding apathy that we might otherwise be forced to endure. The subego also fosters the illusion of a slowing of time; the introduction of a dawdling dimwit affords us respite from the quick-witted hero. Indeed, the sidekick is often cast as an out-and-out moron, busily engaged in randomly sating his instinctual pleasures without any of the burdens of responsibility.

The origins of this subego image, a created object, can be traced to that early stage of primary narcissism when the mother is being split off, yet still perceived by the child as part of the self. Where there is a failure in one's emancipatory self-idealizations that would lead to a negation of this severed (inferior) aspect of the self, an imaginary companion or a projection onto some outside figure is not an unusual solution; certainly only in rare instances can this lowly aspect be accepted as part of the self deserving equal love. Creative artists, and I include Arthur Conan Doyle in this category, manage to employ means of recycling this unwanted fragment of the self by creating a balance of opposing characters, a countervailing equilibrium between hero and subaltern. A massive dose of subaltern could be lethal; a sprinkling is a spice. Rather than being ejected, dissociated, negated, or projected, he is permitted his symbiotic existence by his close association with the hero. Our self-exaltation comes not simply from an identification with the hero (our self-ideal), but from his juxtaposition to the subaltern (subego) as well. Of course the art form will

conceal from the reader that his idealizations are established through the presence of this sidekick (originally the
split-off mother) modestly showing off his "better half" to
advantage. It is not farfetched to suggest that if either were
psychologically more expendable than the other, it would
be the hero (child) rather than the subaltern (parent).
Conan Doyle may have been intuitively directed by this
truth when, on choosing finally to sever his two creations,
he liquidated Holmes rather than the more primal Watson.

The contemporary mystery takes us one step further in
playing the time-game of oscillating opposites. The synthesis of these two images into one gives us today's version of
the master sleuth. Unlike Holmes or Watson, he is self-
sufficient, stands on his own. A combination of incisive
intellectuality and bumbling stupidity, a blend of realism
and illusion, he both "knows" and "doesn't know." Complete with raincoat and battered hat, half-chewed cigar,
and jalopy ready for the junk heap, today's detective moves
in and out of his adventures with a stupidity that belies his
shrewd deductions. And today's audience anticipates,
indeed demands, this fast-paced sophistication in transitional images, an economic merger of two polarities in one
formula—an instant blend of truth with illusion, of time
with timelessness.

Yet, when one draws a composite of the characteristics
of the consulting detective as profiled by Arthur Conan
Doyle, it is Sherlock Holmes, not our modern shamus, who
captures the essence of the Freudian psychoanalyst (see
Hardwick, 1962, pp. 130-178).

> In height rather over six feet, so excessively lean that he
> seemed considerably taller . . . eyes sharp and piercing,
> in habit of cheerful untidiness . . . cigars kept in the coal
> scuttle and tobacco in the toe end of a Persian slipper
> . . . those strange, exotic visitors constantly appearing

and disappearing from the inner sanctuary of the consulting detective ... with women he had almost
hypnotic power, the laying on of long fingers to an
agitated shoulder ... beyond the violin and the drug-
taking, few hobbies indeed, occasional Turkish baths,
a predilection for whist.

Such a portrait captures the fiber of the investigator, the
master in a variety of disguises, in traditional "Inverness
and deer-stalker" or in more informal houserobe, puttering
about his lodgings on Baker Street, dabbling in cocaine and
heroin, or more restlessly in bouts with morphine. Here is
the intellectual aesthete, the investigative giant who strips
the veils that cloak man's deceits in a baring of naked truth.
   For Conan Doyle, the "truth" was far from acceptable.
Clearly he felt it warranted a buffer of ignorance. So he
introduced the numskull Watson, a middle-sized man
with a square jaw, a thick neck, and a mustache. That's
all, but it's enough! It is not difficult to relate this simple
description to the actual photographic portraits of Conan
Doyle himself (see Haining, 1974). Professional man
though Watson is, a patient listener to the ills of mankind,
with all his medical training, he is nonetheless in a constant
state of bafflement. Surely Watson is as important as the
omniscient Sherlock Holmes in understanding Arthur
Conan Doyle. For every intuitive perception of the brilliant
sleuth, there is an obtuse response from his companion.
Where Holmes is ever cognizant of the guile of the temp-
tress, Watson is contrastingly fair game: "Do you see?"
queries Holmes testily. "I see nothing," mumbles Watson
apologetically.
   Conan Doyle's stories deal with "evil men" apprehended by a master conscience, as represented by the figure
of the great detective. On a surface level, the author may
simply be entertaining us by daydreaming out loud or by

retelling the story of virtue against sin. On a deeper level, one might discover the derivative of an oedipal theme in reinforcement of a communal superego. But examining these adventures in human wickedness further, one can make a case for the author's struggle with primal knowledge and with the preservation of self-regard in the face of separation. Through the split images of hero and subaltern, Conan Doyle may have allowed us a glimpse of his personal perception of the human condition, where man sees what he does not wish to see, and knows what he wishes not to know. Conan Doyle's stories may be of man's rescue of himself through the agency of his own ignorance (Watson), a naiveté that neutralizes the know-it-all, Holmes. Whereas Freud viewed man's negations and illusions largely as drags on the development of an enlightened society (1927), Conan Doyle attacked science (perhaps unwittingly) by demurring at bald facts that, left starkly unclothed, might push man into a hopeless regression.

Arthur Conan Doyle's narrative creatively personifies the danger of factualism in its casting of the arch-criminal Moriarty. It could as easily have been Professor Diptheria with whom Holmes ultimately grapples in his fatal struggle on the cliffs of the Reichenbach Falls (see Hardwick, 1962, pp. 39-40): Moriarty's composite depicts an extremely tall, thin man with shoulders rounded from study and a forehead that domed out in a wide curve, cavernous holes for eyes, and deeply sunk in his head (perhaps the author's self-image whilst cramming for medical exams), an aesthetic-looking face protruding forward and forever *oscillating* from side to side in a curiously reptilian manner (imagery of the pendulum of Time or the snake in the Garden of Eden), a remarkable man who had written a treatise on the Binomial Theorem, on the dynamics of an asteroid, in anticipation of $E = mc^2$. Here, I suggest, we have Conan Doyle's view of science (mathematics, if you prefer) as

Death. The objective measurements of time, space, and causality are represented by Moriarty, and viewed as a threat to mankind—like the tree that baits man's predilection for eating of the forbidden fruit. The author's prescription for the ills of man is the invention of a disease which has no symptom (imagination) and for which man will never invent a cure; it is the production of enigma where there was none before, the fashioning of a detective for a crime never committed, of a sleuth who detects everything but in truth solves nothing. But it is a prescription that brings intrigue where there was tedium, and fascination where there was boredom.

It is not difficult to imagine Conan Doyle's *Weltanschauung* taking shape as a student as he attentively assimilated the polemics of his idol (Joseph Bell) in the clinic amphitheater: "Diptheria, gentlemen, is to be diagnosed before you enter the sick-room—the odor in the hallway is pathognomonic!" How similar to the diagnostics of Holmes: "Watson, what do you mean, you detect nothing," sniffs the great shamus in patronizing forbearance, "surely the irregular footsteps, the labored breathing, the faint odor of stramonium, the regimented metallic knock low-down on the door—they all add up, Watson, we're having a visit from an asthmatic midget, wounded of leg from military service, and with a ring-finger bejeweled by the cursed Star of Ranchipur" (my paraphrase).

Where modern crime stories usually introduce a predictable range of weapons for murder, perhaps a blunt instrument such as a fire iron or a pearl-handled revolver, maybe a touch of cyanide in a teacup, or the ever popular pull-cord from a drawing room drape, Conan Doyle (1901) always goes for the esoteric, introducing "devil's foot-powder" (p. 600) or a "phosphorescent hound" (p. 206) to embellish his narrative. Ritual, talismans, the occult, these abound in Conan Doyle's works (p. 405). On the surface they may reflect the author's passion for mysticism, but "five orange pips" (p. 274) as a presage of death may be indicative of the imprint left on the mind of the physician who had once extracted foreign bodies from children's throats at the clinic. Stark fact was anathema to Conan Doyle, an abrasive trauma to self-regard; mathematics was Time-Death-Moriarty, each square-rooted to infinity. The repetition compulsion of Sherlock Holmes was his relentless effort to track, to trap, and then to destroy the evil Moriarty (Father Time). Some psychologists might diagnose this passion as an exercise in negation, a lifting of repression without acceptance of what is repressed, a successor to expulsion, something belonging to the instinct of destruction rather than to Eros; but in Arthur Conan Doyle's split imagery, I find an affirmation rather than a negation, a repetition in the service of Eros.

Curiously, few psychoanalysts have deigned to offer much in the way of a study of the classic mystery story. Perhaps many consider psychoanalysis too exalted an instrument to apply to a prosaic literary effort such as the mystery story. Rycroft (1957) feels that one reason the detective story so rarely achieves the status of art (and is implicitly disqualified from analytic investigation) is that the identification of the reader with the criminal continues to be denied. According to Rycroft, the writer helps the reader deny his guilt, providing him with a ready-made fantasy in which the compulsive question "who dunnit" is answered by the self-exonerating "not I." To me, this view attributes minimal sophistication to the reader, and I cannot agree with the sentiment that reading detective stories is in diametric opposition to undergoing psychoanalytic treatment. It is a half-truth at best to suggest that where psychoanalysis provides insight, "the mystery" fosters denial or negation. I ally myself with Pederson-Krag 1949), who perceives the detective story addict as attempting to master a traumatic experience by actively reliving what was once endured passively; in my view, the trauma is time and its blow to self-regard.

Like other literary achievements, the detective story creates an illusion of suspended time and merits analytic study. Underlying the themes that authors employ to engage their audience, one can discern their efforts to fulfill their own and their readers' expectations of a creative killing of time. For the young, the manipulation of time may be found in the story of Cinderella, where horse and carriage become transformed at the stroke of midnight into pumpkin and mice. Or there is Frankenstein the monster, the animistic robot of nuts and bolts who staggers his way in and out of the pages of communal myth. The adolescent may prefer a theme of uncanny twins, each experiencing the other's pain in magnificent doubling against mortality. For those in the mid-life crisis, the more sophisticated bedroom comedy may contribute its appeal, where the hero toys with "twenty year itch" in a neurotic escapade of "second time around for everyone." And for the aged, a Shangri-la deep in the Tibetan hills offers respite from hormones and face lifts in the successful slowing of the sands of time.

Eisenbud (1956) observes that the individual's personal experience of time and its relation to the Oedipus complex has been neglected in the psychoanalytic literature. He cites Grimm's *Sleeping Beauty* as a classic that draws not only on the idea of magical control over time, but also on wishful oedipal fulfillment, as exemplified in the story of parents moved backward in time so as to allow their children to catch up with them. Modern playwrights seem particularly disposed toward finding new creative disguises for the Proustian theme of the quest for timelessness. *The Royal Hunt of the Sun* not only reflects the personal identity of Peter Shaffer, its author, one of a set of literary twins (see

Glenn, 1974), but stimulates speculation as to the significance of this fact of the author's birth in providing the
story's undercurrent theme, the "royal" search for timelessness, a saga that seems inspired by the family romance of a
twin.

The theme of timelessness is readily discernible even in
more mundane literary efforts, which might well explain
their survival and popularity. For example, there are the
widely known infamies of the bloodletting Count Dracula,
a semi-cadaver who to this day remains a popular subject
for psychological vivisection. The premise of any episode
with the Count can be established in short order. The
victim is Time, making its appearance in a multitude of
disguises, either beggar or housemaid or perhaps lead
soprano in an opera, and begging for the fangs of Dracula!
Finally the bite and the suck, and the chase is on! Where to
track down Dracula? We can guess—in his coffin, of course,
resting in sanguine tranquility. Retribution calls for a stake
in the heart. But who among us would drive the stake
home? Who has the relish for ridding this world of the
immortal Dracula? On the contrary, "let the poor creature
live," we plead en masse in defense of our anti-hero (all of
us). And so next day, Dracula is up from his coffin (our
nocturnal sleep), ready to bite and to suck (on time) once
more.

Psychoanalysis, too, is one of the great mystery stories of
the century. I would hold suspect the individual who denies
the enigmatic quality that has always been attached to the
psychoanalytic process and to its practitioners. The particular unconscious aspects of human behavior that the
psychotherapist is called upon to deal with are in themselves sufficiently cryptic so as to cast that same aura over
those who would investigate the unconscious. Yet it is not
always out of ignorance that the lay public is prompted to
perceive some practitioners in the category of charlatan or

sorcerer, since there are always those who profess to be therapists by the use of analytic jargon. I am not saying such usage hasn't a place. Not only is it a time-saver, but it is useful as a defense as well. Every profession resorts to its own jargon, whether it be in a psychoanalytic case history, as part of the studied bedside manner of the general medical practitioner or in the polemics of the attorney-at-law. For every fact that humanity discovers about its universe, there is the equally important task of fashioning a convenient cover to attenuate the more dismal aspects of that fact. In medicine, acne is "idiopathic seborrheic dermatitis"; in law (Regina versus Twitt), the case is dismissed on the maxim of "ex turpi causa non oritur actio."

Indeed, it is an astounding fact of our culture that since the days of Mesmer, the public has continued to look askance at those professing capacities in the healing of the human psyche. Yet, although we may be perceived as engaged in hoax or fraud by our critics, we are sought out most frantically by those looking for quick answers to their mental problems. But what about those who are fascinated with the occult, with transcendental meditation, with prophetic foreknowledge, or with extrasensory perception? What about demonology and exorcism, gurus and mysticism, chemicals and mind expansion—indeed visitations from another planet? It seems logical that these cultural passions can only be understood when we familiarize ourselves with the motives behind these psychological props, which are apparently as indispensable today as they were yesterday in caulking the chinks in the armor we wear to ward off our fears. Delving into these motives is indeed the task of the psychoanalyst. Yet to suggest that psychoanalysis itself is not endowed with its own idiosyncratic charade would be a hypocrisy. Take the physical setup itself; it is more than a little bizarre for an individual to lie on a couch, babbling away at a shadow behind him. In any other setting, such a happening would be considered obscene. But intelligent people have come to acknowledge the legitimacy of such a procedure in the unfolding of the patient's conflicts, even though the situation may be reminiscent of the hide-and-seek or blind man's buff of children's play, or perhaps even more deeply rooted in the primal lose-and-find of one's earliest manipulation of the maternal nipple. Such a replay of the infantile is not so absurd an exercise as it seems, when one remembers that the need of many is not to expose the unknown, but to find a way of immersing the dismal facts of their person within the protective foliage of the obscure.

Particularly with respect to the treatment of those suffering the trauma of time does the stereotype of psychoanalysis as a cobweb remover or an "Occam's razor" belie the existence of people such as Lilli who require the protection that comes with hiding rather than exposing. To date, man has not been able to devise a more logical method than Freud's for helping people achieve the creativity necessary to gain that protection. Not only is the psychoanalyst a detective in the best traditions of the profession, but he is an artisan as well. In the transference recapitulation of the patient's life, the analyst learns to understand and temporarily to accept and utilize the role that the patient gives him—whether it be parent, pimp, hairdresser, or god. But Loewald (1975) points out that in analysis, unlike role-playing, the analyst must clarify for the patient the part he assigns to the therapist and the origins of that assignment as well; only in this way can the patient be helped to differentiate parent from others, and past from present. This sorting out of time especially involves the interpretive function of the analyst, with which the patient identifies towards the safeguarding of a future that includes pleasure, even if it is not forever (G. Abraham, 1976).

I suggest that there is more; like Sherlock Holmes, the analyst has to "know" one day, and like Watson, he has to "not know" the next. He must be knowledgeable in the re-creative repetitions in which his patient engages in the transference. A good analyst can also collaborate from time to time in the invention of those necessary mysteries that might enrich his patient's psyche as a protection from the barren void of living with too much truth. To this day there is a controversy between the fact and the fiction of psychic productions. Hacker (1964) has remarked that nothing demonstrates more strikingly the universality of the mythological element in human psychology than the observations of the compulsive urge of the psychoanalytic subject to dig for and unearth myth beneath myth. Rycroft (1962), as well as Loewald (1975), emphasizes that the art of psychoanalysis is to help re-establish connections with the imaginative capacities of the patient toward a change in his way of living.

I concur with the latter authors, as I agree with Hacker on the crucial part that myth-making contributes to healthy self-experience. Yet Hacker rightfully warns against blindly accepting unbroken myth and against failing to discriminate between one myth and another; the extremes, he points out, are pathological, and only in the middle ground does one find the regions of firm character and strong ego. I laud his admission that only by the acknowledgment of therapist as myth-maker can therapy and therapist become stamped with integrity; I take issue with the outrage of those who might view this admission as an attack on psychoanalysis. In keeping with Hacker's thesis, I deem the psychoanalyst the investigator par excellence of the killing of time.

THE SUSPECTS

In the analytic investigation of Lilli, of the traumatic impact of the holocaust on her development, of her efforts to deny time by a flight into the past, the treatment was of course carried on concurrent with my treatment of other patients, who were people from various walks of life. In meeting their daily appointments, some of these patients were invariably punctual and others invariably late. The sessions were often used for acting out a struggle between patient and therapist over the control of time in repetition of the childhood conflict between parent or school authority over the discipline of schedules. For still others, the therapy was less important in terms of actual insight gained than in getting their money's worth in the currency of time.

To understand people bothered by problems of time, we might consider further the theme of narcissism and the struggle for self-esteem. Hartmann's (1950) definition of narcissism as the libidinal investment of the self or the cathexis of the self remains as succinct as any. Kohut (1971) defines the self as a structure within the mind cathected with instinctual energy, having continuity in time, and containing conscious and unconscious contradictory self-representations, as well as object representations experienced as part of the self. Jacobson (1964) observes that normal self-feeling derives from an individual's awareness of an integrated self, while self-esteem depends on the libidinal investment of such an integrated self. Kernberg (1975) adds that neurotic conflicts interfering with the integration of that self bring about disturbed character patterns, which he grades as mild (with conflicts around aggression), moderate (where there is a loving identification with a person that stands for oneself—Freud's narcissistic-object type), and severe (where narcissism replaces object relations so that the afflicted individual is in love with himself).

Any debate aimed at untangling the relationship between self-love (narcissism) and love of another (object love) can only confuse things if there is a failure to differentiate between infantile narcissism antedating phallic oedipal resolution, and those expressions of rescue of self-regard during and following the dissolution of the oedipal conflict. By emphasizing the health-maintaining aspects of narcissism and by acknowledging its role in promoting a climate for increased available object libido, both Kohut and Kernberg have challenged the older view that narcissism can only deplete object libido. The criticism of some (see Hanly and Masson, 1976) that Kohut exalts narcissism in affording it developmental independence in his dualistic concept of libido is in theory valid. It is important to bear in mind, however, that cathexis of the self is necessary for healthy expressions of object relations and object love, since secondary narcissistic cathexes are way-stations toward building adult conscience, allowing a post-oedipal rescue of the parental identifications that are necessary for the genital aspects of object love. The dictum that narcissism can but rob object libido I heartily endorse as a plausible economic concept when applied to pre-oedipal fixations; but in post-oedipal terms, it is clinically no more useful than references to normal and abnormal narcissism, an unfortunate designation of either libido or its cathexes. The clinical issue is more accurately the normality or abnormality of the structural development of the individual, including the distribution of his narcissistic investments. Particularly pertinent is whether such investments are in the service of preparing the individual for discharging his or her responsibilities to others. I comment further on this in my concluding chapter.

For the psychoanalyst, a routine day in the consulting room is by no means comprised of listening to a series of agonizing communications from the desperately ill. I doubt that any therapist would be equal to such a task. Since Lilli could only attend sessions at the end of my working day, the patients who preceded her, far less acutely disturbed than

she, left me with ample reserves for dealing with Lilli's
more critical problems. These other patients, however,
provided me with many examples of the human penchant
for killing time. A survey of some of these individuals might
demonstrate the diverse expressions of their narcissism, as
well as their preoccupations with timing and time. I will
omit any real exploration of these patients and only present
now a range of character types—a dossier colored by the
problems of the therapist, since I, too, as you may have
guessed, am rarely on time for anything. In subsequent
chapters, I will offer a more detailed probing into the
mechanisms that so many of us use in our quest for stopping
the clock.

You're in your consulting room ... there's a knock on
the door (a suspiciously gentle tap) ... your beady eyes
rivet on your first subject as he austerely navigates toward
the analytic couch. But let's stop for a moment. Here you
have your first clues—the gait, the stiff, haughty deportment, the imperceptible bracing of the shoulders, the deliberate regimented hallmark of a gentleman's gentleman.
Blend these with the mock obsequiousness, the solicitous
"how are you, doctor" (meaning I trust you're sick), add the
flaring of a nostril detecting a smelly cigar, the telltale
posture of expectant waiting (for a miracle)—and you have
the profile of "the butler."

This individual would probably be described in the
psychoanalytic literature as one of the milder narcissistic
types, one of the more common personalities in our society,
whose hypertrophied character tendencies derive primarily
from mechanisms aimed at bolstering self-regard. Generally, the conflicts of such a person relate to early childhood disappointments in parents. The hunger for idealizations (and disenchantments)—an appetite which in those
less neurotic ordinarily becomes attenuated—persists as an
excessive preoccupation (often unconscious) with borrow-

ing or inheriting the assets of others who appear stronger and better endowed. Such hunger is reflected in the apparent manipulative quality of object relations. Envy is exaggerated and often repressed, flawing more positive feelings. Masked by a dutiful concern for others or by a cloak of disarming servility, this envy often takes the form of sniffing for evidence that the envied person is in deep trouble. One such patient was quite comfortable in his unconsciously fantasied ʾexpectation that each year of therapy would add an inch to his penis, while subtracting the equivalent length from his therapist's. Curiously, these feelings of inferiority are often found in reasonably motivated individuals. As I have indicated, the social deportment of such mildly narcissistic people is in itself a giveaway; the undue solicitude with respect to the health of others, understructured by an inordinate alertness to people's catastrophies or misfortunes, financial or physical, provides the justification for extending the euphemistic "butler" image to that of "the undertaker."

A pre-oedipal avarice in exacting supplies permeates the character profiles of other narcissistically disposed individuals in my dossier. For example, there's the "garburetor." Lest the reader presume that I am maligning trusting patients (not beyond an unconscious possibility), I should point out that the characteristics I am describing apply to just about everyone (perhaps little assurance to the reader). It seems that we all strengthen ourselves at someone else's expense, albeit in varied amounts; so, in truth, all of us contribute to the colorful spectrum of human narcissism that makes up our society.

The "garburetor's" hunger for collecting the strengths of others is of a particularly gluttonous and indiscriminate quality. A garrulousness that passes for independence helps promote an aura of courageous dissenter. The compulsion is not only to collect other people's views, but to jealously claim them as one's own. At the same time there is usually a subtle put-down of the people from whom one so avidly borrows. The doctor-patient interaction is pathognomonic:

Therapist: "Then your elated mood was triggered by the telephone call?"

Garburetor: "In other words, you see a connection between the mood and the call?"

Therapist: "Well, I was simply . . ."

Garburetor: "In my terms, I would consider the telephone call as a provocation for the elation."

Therapist: "Well, that's what I . . ."

Garburetor: "Doctor, perhaps what you mean to say . . ."

The siphoning of other people's ideas is often effected in a largely automatic and unconscious manner, like a well-oiled sump pump that drains off the contributions of others so that they flow from the garburetor as original. Analysis will uncover the deeper springs of this mechanism, that of short-cutting the time and effort involved in figuring things out for oneself. The success at tapping the tolerance of those unwittingly sucked in by this time-saving machine is most striking, as evidenced by my own gullibility in early practice, when I was unenlightened as to my own collusion in such exercises. One has to wonder, of course, how many of us in the field of psychology, in our own interpretations and embellishments of our patient's verbalizations, unwittingly sump their ideas through our own analytic "garburetors."

Contrast such acquisitive traits with expressions of mid- and post-oedipal narcissism, as seen in individuals with some especially esoteric hobby, a circumscribed and parochial vocation that instantly demarcates them from others. I call them "bird-watchers." Back in medical school days, certain students became so obsessed with particularly rare physical conditions ("birds"), such as some tropical diseases, that they earned the label of "bird-watchers" or "birders." These personalities are to be discovered not only in the medical field, but in other professions as well. Those in the field of psychology are by no means exempt from this category. Some have ambitions that can only be satisfied by their acquiring some special or unique recognition in the field. Perhaps their bolstering of self-regard may have received an impetus through an identification with parents' expectations or in the satisfying of unfulfilled parental ambitions.

The inordinate rivalries among "birders" frequently pushes them to fly in ever higher circles for the fulfillment of their particular goals. Their compulsive academic zeal should be quite familiar to many, applying as it does to practically any academic vocation. I remember having two especially colorful "birders" in analysis simultaneously, colleagues in psychology known to each other. The pace was typical: before their analyses, one had chosen a medical school in his home town, the other had promptly enrolled in a school in Switzerland. The first had graduated with honors, the second had won a prize in psychology. One embarked on a traditional residency in psychiatry, the other had opted for ethology at a prestigious European center; his return from abroad had been an epiphany—the advent of the psychobiologist! The last I heard of the two, subsequent to their analyses, one was writing a paper on the Eskimo; the other, I believe, was churning out a *magnum opus* on the salamander (it may have been the whooping crane). Ironically, it is from such "bird-watching" that we often get major discoveries in science!

There are phallic narcissistic adults whose sexual symptoms reflect a heavy burden of *timing*. These include the self-styled *bon vivant* and the *femme fatale*, whose sex lives are pretentious exercises of the ego rather than manifestations of instinct. Where phallic narcissism has long afflicted

the male, sexual license has likewise become a common trait
in today's female, freed as she is to join the male in taking
pride in the number of "affairs" they each can transact.
They often suffer exquisite mortification at that period in
their lives when the biological drive starts to wane; the
encroachment of time wreaks havoc on their sexual behavior. One menopausal nymphomaniac was so avid in her
craving for having her genital (a lower mouth) stuffed with
male organ for endless periods that one of her exhausted
partners practically ended up *in extremis*, recouping his
vitality at a local spa. A male counterpart at his climacteric,
fearful that his sexual virility was coming to an end,
bemoaned at some length how his "timing was off." In his
own baseball metaphor, where he had always prided
himself on hitting home runs, now in his twilight he was
ready to settle for a bunt. Variations in timing problems are
also found among younger people. I particularly remember
one chap who suffered what he considered to be the repetitive intrusions of fate into his abortive attempts at sexual
consummation. Despite Herculean efforts, something
always seemed to go wrong; just listening to the narration
of his frenzied fumbling about for misplaced contraceptives
at crucial moments would leave me in a cold sweat.

A chaotic disturbance of a wild young man who sought
consultation for an unusually disorganized problem involving his excretory and sexual functions comes to mind.
Ferenczi (1923) might have labelled this patient a casualty
of amphimixis. (I am still uncertain as to the actual psychological mechanisms that this term embraces.) Where Freud
clinically differentiated the erogenous zones and the levels
of libidinal development, and where Anna Freud drew
attention to the developmental telescoping of these sequen-
tial stages, Abraham blueprinted the construction of one
stage upon the dissolution of an earlier one. It was Ferenczi
who employed the term amphimixis to describe the blend-

ing of the contributions from each of these zones by the ego toward the "thresholding" of the primacy of orgasm. It is awesome to contemplate how the cathexes from these various sources meet like the spokes of a wheel at a central hub, but it is even more impressive when one appreciates the intricacies by which they all become coordinated (or uncoordinated) to permit the component instinctual drives to defer to each other in a juggling of thresholds.

Perhaps further light will be shed on the concept of amphimixis by exploring the symptoms of amphimixis gone awry. In mechanistic terms, one might describe my patient as suffering from a poor connection in his time-circuits. Physiological responses normally held in abeyance in those free of such emotional disturbance became unhappily triggered at the most inappropriate times in the case of this young man. On experiencing sexual excitations, he had the urge either to urinate or to defecate; conversely, peristalsis following breakfast stimulated him to defer either to urination or to sexual emission. Going to the toilet was a blind gamble for this patient, his "wires being so badly crossed" that he never knew in advance just what he was going to accomplish there. More embarrassingly, he had the same uncertainty in his few heterosexual attempts, since for this miserable chap, women in a sense were merely toilet bowls.

His timing problem was sufficiently catastrophic so as to cause me to have him checked out for possible brain damage or spinal cord injury, although he had ostensibly been troubled by his symptoms from puberty. He was found to be organically sound. Psychologically, his disturbance first appeared to be related to an erotization of his physiological functions. He volunteered the suspicion that a prolonged tendency to postponements, whether of eating, urination, or defecation, represented a cover for a build-up of sexual tensions. He diagnosed himself as someone constantly engaged in a sly form of masturbation, one that involved a deferment of the call to physiology in favor of a build-up toward explosive sexual discharge. On another level, I discovered that even before puberty, his functions had become compromised through an unconscious exercise in ascetic self-frustration; calculated tolerance tests in waiting had contributed to what was basically a repetition compulsion involving excretions and secretions in order of their developmental appearance. The syndrome proved to be in the service of overcoming early, passively experienced traumata whereby the patient had been victimized by indulgent as well as depriving parents. The symptoms reflected a struggle to master these traumata.

Moving on to Dracula, I have thus far drawn mostly on symptoms illustrating the narcissistic component of every-day neurotics. There are, however, other reflections of narcissistic development involving the psychological complex known as the family romance, which engages the fantasies of children as they relinquish their infantile over-valuation of parents. The child's disenchantment with his or her parents is commonly triggered when he or she perceives for the first time that father and mother are sexual people, blemished, as it were, and no longer deserving of pure childhood respect. This recoil from the facts of life and the tarnishing of the parental mystique becomes softened by a displaced fascination for more aristocratic and immaculate adoptive figures in society. Because of the closer relationship of the child to the mother, the fantasy of having been brought into the world in some clandestine fashion by people of nobility usually involves finding a substitute for the father, although a truly disappointing maternal figure can provoke a quest for a better mother as well.

The rather benign expressions of the family romance that unfold in the psychology of the average child are less aggressive than in children with easily traumatizable narcissism, where a pernicious mutation of the family romance invades object relations and persists right on through to adulthood. In this aggressive type, the people chosen for idealization are psychologically disposable, unlike the benign version where positive feelings toward family figures (or their substitutes) prevail. In the pernicious type, undercurrents of old sibling rivalries extend themselves into the adopted milieu; such a "romanticist" harbors the archaic anticipation that his rivals will kill each other off in a triumph of attrition (claim to the family prize, the adopted mother). Occasionally, there is a fantasy in which the predator simply bleeds his "donor" like a parasite.

This is Dracula, someone out for blood, indeed ready to ravage his victim! It can be the intellect of another person that is plundered, his know-how, his life-style; in some instances it can even be a more desirable genetic lineage that is usurped. Biblical narrative recounts the struggle for birthright, and though I am not a student of biblical writings, I believe that this dynamism is clinically relevant to what I describe. It is a theme that the novelist, the poet, and the dramatist often utilize in their creative art. Television commonly offers it as entertainment. The hero starts out as an orphaned vagabond struggling in a heartless world, but he is adopted by ailing nobility, grieving over a lost child, and there is a fairy-tale ending. In another version, the lowly hero, while wandering abroad, suffers a blow to the head which leaves him with amnesia, and he awakens in an aristocratic four-poster. Again, there is the fortuitous transformation from the dregs to the top. These sagas bring hope to the underprivileged, as well as provide harmless entertainment. Emerging in a psychoanalytic setting, however, the theme of birthright merits closer scrutiny.

I have implied that Dracula is stunted, since the incorporation of other people becomes his way of life. Because oedipal conflict is unresolved and conscience left wanting, the capacity for internalization is deficient. Although he and other Draculas may appear to enjoy a family romance, there is something deformed about their adoptions. In the usual romance, there is a positive tone to the objects of idealization, since positive relationships were earlier established with parental figures and carried over to extra-familial objects. With Dracula, there are few affectionate ties to family; in fact, there is strenuous ambivalence and only partial object-relatedness. When Dracula looks to the outside world for heroes, it is to *replace* them rather than to *idealize* them. The victim is usually someone whose position (rather than whose person) is prized. The aim is to incorporate the victim totally, so that no trace of him is left.

One of Dracula's main traits is envy, coupled with the associated need to be envied. Rather than emulating or identifying with those whom he envies, Dracula wishes to replace, to end up wearing the other person's shoes. His alertness for potential victims is like that of a trained blood-hound sniffing for prey. The infantile self-perceptions emerging in treatment are pathognomonic, such as images of climbing into a new skin, or crawling up the bowels of the victim like a tapeworm, or entering the blood stream like a parasite invading its host.

Talented and skilled as such marauders often are (curiously), their capacity to evoke the envy of others is not that astonishing. Some are experts in exuding good news, aware of the havoc they can mobilize in their vulnerable victims by their well-timed bragging. I had a few "good-news killers" from time to time on my couch. One in particular was quite remarkable; he could convert the most stable of individuals into a shambles of envy. His tour de force had been provoking a heart attack in one of his more envious competitors. "Good news," he'd complacently announce to me, "I just made a killing in the market." A few sessions later: "Good news, meet your new boss, I've just been promoted as your senior at the university!" Naturally the well-trained analyst can handle himself in these situations, relying as he does on his detached analytic neutrality. With this type of patient, I find it helpful to keep checking my pulse or to munch an antacid or two.

You began your day with a fresh and incisive mind, eager to discover how people seek out a timelessness in recoiling from the trauma of time. Now you sit muddled and dejected by the futility of the day's work. So far, most of the patients you have examined have merely demonstrated an unusually heightened orality in search of the obliteration of time. Mechanically you nod to your next patient—and then you realize you're trapped. Even before this patient opens his mouth, you know you're in trouble; you are caged in with the classic bore.

Boredom is a disturbance of mood. Jacobson (1957) differentiates moods from feelings, defining moods as temporary fixations of feelings induced by significant experiences, and whose patterns of discharge give a specific characterological stamp to the individual. Their most dramatic characteristic is their pervasiveness; repetitive emotional discharge protects the ego from the dangers of sporadic eruptive explosions. According to Jacobson, moods lack an object other than the self. Consequently, they are vehicles for taming feelings that particularly revolve around narcissism. In pathological moods, suggests Jacobson, the precipitating event has either been repressed or denied. With a mood spectrum that stretches from elation to depression, apathy, and boredom, an examination of the less colorful polarities, such as boredom, offers an opportunity for understanding the relationship between feelings and time, since in clinical work, boredom is a common complaint. As a universally experienced mood suffered by individuals more than ready to unburden themselves, it is readily accessible to examination.

Both Grotjahn (1942) and Fliess (1961) perceive boredom as a state in which time hangs heavy. Grotjahn describes it as an ego starvation, a state of imprisonment or bondage. Fliess likewise identifies a claustrophobic element, and both authors agree that the victim fears an unseemly discharge of libido as a result of the panic that often goes with boredom. Greenson (1953) perceives a basically oral state characterized by feelings of emptiness and a demand for being filled, along with an agonizing sense of a slow passage of time which Greenson relates to a delay of impulse discharge. He describes the bored person as in a state of tense emptiness, where the superego's repression of instinct produces hunger; and because the individual does not know what he hungers for, he turns to the external world for satiation. Greenson finds that people with strong oral fixations are particularly predisposed to boredom. Similarly, Eisnitz (1974) views a fantasy of oral attachment to the mother as the key. Schilder's (1936) interest in boredom centers on the problems of the psychotic's handling of time. He describes the bored depressive for whom time moves too fast (rather than too slow), attributing this subjective experience to the mobilization of the patient's fear of his own aggression.

Some states of boredom involve a poorly defined self-ideal. Here the victim does not blame the outside world for his boredom, but rather blames himself; that is, he feels bored with himself. One might say that he is unable to supply the necessary nutriment for raising his own self-regard. Despite a well-functioning ego, he often experiences an excessive loss of energy without the satisfactions of a superego exaltation (failure in self-idealization). Such a bored (and often boring) individual commonly experiences an associated sense of frustrating envy, seeing others (but not himself) as busy accomplishing things. With this tendency toward comparative self-depreciation, his time sense is paradoxical—the passage of time seems alarmingly accelerated (as applied to his own sense of transience) and subjectively slowed (as applied to his sluggishness in locating goals deemed worthy of his interest). The result is a despairing sense of paralytic immobility, as if he were standing still while others were passing him by.

People afflicted with this kind of boredom often have considerable insight, recognizing that their own difficulty in choosing values and goals makes them a captive audience for bores and leaves them amply qualified to bore others. In terms of energy cathexis, boredom involves an emphasis on the ego, usually at the price of an impoverished superego (or self-ideal). Although narcissistic cathexes of the ego often enhance performance (which may further increase the state of boredom), often producing achievements of superior quality, the yield in a subjective sense of success is minimal. Reactionary measures are often undertaken to offset boredom; mysticism, drugs, and other time-blurring devices are fruitlessly employed as medicants to the ego, while the superego remains languishing.

Weinberger and Muller (1974) explain this type of boredom as a problem in phallic narcissism rather than in orality, an affliction of the youthful society. Like Icarus, they see our present generation of young high-flyers ignoring all caution in their soaring so high as to melt their wings in the sun (boredom)! They support Bibring's (1953) conviction that in boredom, the repression of goals interferes with the ability to reach these unconscious goals, and since substitute goals become rejected as inadequate or prohibitive, the resulting directionless state yields the feeling of emptiness and boredom. They perceive those afflicted as victims of the failure of inadequate fathers to attenuate the incestuous bondage of children to their mothers, leaving unrealistic and unrealizable incestuous goals intact. The authors blame a society that supports youth in boundless phallic flight, youth doomed from the start by the inappropriate psychology that was nourished by parents.

Whether one views oral or phallic problems as predisposing to boredom, any explanation has to include failure in goal attainment and an identification of the goal left unattained. In general terms we can identify the unattained goal as an exaltation of self-regard. The failure to achieve this elevation becomes reflected in the experience of time as paradoxical; on the one hand there is a quickening of one's sense of personal transience, and on the other, a slowing of the passage of time.

Everyone experiences boredom at one time or another. It may come on when one feels trapped in a situation such as an after-dinner speech or an academic presentation, from which one cannot easily extricate oneself without social embarrassment (a time claustrophobia). In these circumstances, a person might feel a panic over stifled sexual impulses long ago deemed inappropriate to such situations; while listening to a boring after-dinner speech, a sense of emptiness, or time lag might be experienced, or even a fantasy of hurling food leftovers at the podium. Most psychoanalysts have at least someone in their case load who possesses that special talent for provoking the painfully distressing mood of boredom. Not that an analyst disposed to being bored by his patients doesn't reflect his own unresolved problems; nonetheless, boredom has to be considered a hazard of the profession. McLaughlin (1975) attributes its high incidence in analysis, particularly in those who treat passive, obsessional, or narcissistic patients, to the shift that he claims therapists undergo from paternal to maternal role. I suspect that the boredom of the analyst relates more to his own personality than to his role-playing function or to his type of patient.

I have discovered that those patients who made the "honor role" as all-time bores are indelibly etched in my memory. I can almost relive the boredom just thinking about some of their analytic sessions . . . the feeling of going under, the prodromal claustrophobia . . . the tug from consciousness . . . the apprehension of the patient's catching me snoring . . . the painful muscles and the gurglings of the stomach . . . then the panic . . . strange thoughts of my doing something unprofessional, like crying out in torment, or simply turning resignedly (and secretively) to the *Daily News* (respected analysts have admitted to acting on the latter fantasy)!

The last session of the day with Lilli had a way of jolting me out of any residues of boredom that might have lingered from the hour preceding. Although her analysis had begun with thoughts about her pregnancies and her pain, it did not take long for memories of camp horrors to erupt. Almost imperceptibly, her analytic narration became a stream of random flashbacks, of grisly obscenities delivered in half whispers, sufficiently chilling in their macabre content to unsettle me considerably, of her grandmother being led to her death, but not before blessing her grandchild with the recitation of the Shema (Hear, O Israel), recollections of the deprivation of food that had diminished Lilli's will to live, the ravage of fear and disease, typhoid, dysentery, hepatitis, babies in Auschwitz screaming for their mothers amidst the odor of burning flesh, criminals and political prisoners performing musical entertainment for inmates awaiting the crematoria, Lilli in the lineup for "Russian roulette," a game the guards played, in which the rules called for any inmate who moved to be shot.

Although Lilli's associations seemed fragmented, it was

not difficult to discern that they all reflected the theme of
loss. As she lay on the analytic couch, touching her abdomen in recall of the abdominal pain of her pregnancies and
the terror first experienced on feeling the movement of life
within her, she drifted toward old feelings of depersonalization. She described the strong sense of unreality attached
to her pregnancies, the feeling of having something foreign
inside her which had led her to drugs in the hope of obliter-
ating not only the gnawing pain, but the memory of the loss
of her grandmother to the gas chambers. Her mind drifted
to the gallbladder she had lost through surgery, the
menarche she had lost on imprisonment in Theresienstadt;
thoughts of a father who left home and who then fled the
Nazis, memories of mother who had died of cancer. With a
sense of foreboding, she recalled a recurrent nightmare that
she had first reported to her referring psychiatrist. It was
always the same dream of fleeing for her life with a baby in
her arms in a desperate escape from a public official. Lilli
wondered out loud whether there was any truth to her
childhood notion that her conception and birth had aggra-
vated and hastened the death of her mother. The theme of
birth led to the memory of her only childhood doll, a doll
that her mother never got to see before her death.

IV

The Transitional Ladder

I have described the repetition compulsion as a lifelong phenomenon having its inception in childhood, long before an understanding of death is acquired, and dedicated to dealing with separation and loss. In its earliest semi-delusionary stages, even before the ego and the superego institute their re-creative efforts to actively engage traumata, the compulsion to transform has a passive, instinctual reflex quality. Flashbacks of my patient Lilli were a symptomatic reflection of this particular quality of the compulsion. Her seemingly illogical tendency to let her mind drift to the past, filled as it was with horror, stemmed from her inability to anticipate a future that held promise for an adequate sense of self-regard. Her hopes of finding a tangible means of redeeming her losses and giving her life a sense of continuity through biological reproduction were all too heavily infiltrated by the premonition that these hopes would only end in abortion. In effect, a primary insult to her narcissism in childhood had been seriously compounded by the holocaust, causing her psychological development to be suspended.

Many psychiatrists can confirm from their own dealing with their patients that a direct or indirect threat to the capacities of such patients for biological reproduction (such as from certain physical conditions involving the reproductive organs) often heightens their sense of urgency to procreate. This is particularly true of women, geared as their sexuality is to fulfilling a biological fecundity, in contrast to the male's emphasis on pleasurable ejaculation. It is also a common clinical fact that such compensatory urgency to procreate is unconscious and ego-alien, and of a driven quality so typical of the repetition compulsion. This was so in Lilli's case.

Consciously unwanted pregnancies result from just such a state of affairs operating in the minds of many women; contraceptive devices fail in many instances because of the unconscious wish for a pregnancy to occur. It is important for the physician to be on the alert for such a dynamism existing in women seeking abortion or sterilization; if the physician fails to look beyond the physical, theological, and ethical issues, he may improperly evaluate the unconscious emotional effects of a therapeutic abortion, even when such is indicated on medical grounds. A woman may consciously accept and even desire abortion: unconsciously, her state of pregnancy may in fact have been the result of a repetition compulsion toward procreation.

To understand the regressive psychological process that accounted for Lilli's flashbacks, and more specifically for the abdominal symptoms that persisted after she became pregnant, I found it helpful to bear in mind *the transitional series of illusions* that universally surround the theme of self-replication—a spectrum of human re-creative efforts that are energized first by primary and then by secondary narcissistic cathexes, most of them mental substitutes developmentally antedating the realization of one's actual biological capacities for reproduction. In adult traumatic neuroses, a regressive return to such transitional mental states reflects the degree of conflict experienced by the victim and the quality of the past development of the traumatized individual.

In order of its developmental progression, which is bonded by the common factor of illusion (or sometimes delusion), the transitional series begins with the infant's hallucinatory creation of the maternal nipple (or the face-breast gestalt of the mother). From there it progresses to the creation of the transitional object (the soft cloth or the doll). In some instances it may proceed to certain physical symptoms, known as conversion phenomena, or to an illusory reduplication of body parts, or to the development of imaginary companions; in the gifted, it may elaborate itself into higher creative devices, such as art or humor. The series peaks in certain expressions of scientific, religious, philosophic, or charismatic devotions, some of which are often accomplished through reinforcement from the group. As a result of Lilli's developmental obstacles, including her camp traumata, I found her position on the transitional ladder to be frozen well down on a rung commensurate with her lack of opportunities for creativity. Compared with those more gifted in the sophisticated and loftier expressions of the transitional series, Lilli was not in an optimal position to attain one of the higher perches of the ladder. She never, however, developed psychotic hallucinatory phenomena, which I had witnessed in several camp survivors. I suspected that a combination of body ego defenses (conversion), augmented by the use of drugs, had acted as a safety net in breaking her fall. Schur (1960) felt there was an ominous clinical prognosis when somatization pervaded the clinical picture of the repetition compulsion. I would emphasize a more positive aspect of somatization, where the body ego, in acute distress, acts as a bastion against more serious disturbance, sacrificing a part in order to protect the whole.

With her stimulus barrier in need of propping, it was

not surprising that Lilli's reservoirs of object libido had been depleted in proportion to that required for the reinforcement of her sense of self. Early on she showed an undue accentuation of the need to manipulate people (such as her husband). The surreptitious way she went about using drugs demonstrated a subtly disguised corruption of her superego. And, of course, there was the obvious disturbance in her subjective sense of time. It was also a fact that her camp incarceration had posed a serious obstacle to her biological development, provoking an insatiable and precocious thrust to conceive and bring new life into her world. To use the analogy of driving a car in winter without snowtires, her attempt to negotiate the icy incline of sexual procreation was met with the danger of falling off a cliff (abortion); terrified of slipping backward (regression), her shift into overdrive (repetition compulsion) only led to the futile spinning of wheels (her exhausting flashbacks).

The Transitional Process

A Freudian maxim in psychoanalytic work is that when the patient dwells on the present, she may be avoiding establishing connections with her past, and when she dwells predominantly on the past, she may be avoiding confrontation with her present. Ordinarily the therapist would deal promptly with this in treatment; in Lilli's case I chose not to do so. I let her drift without confrontation in her own quest for an explanation of her illness; I also felt that she desperately required this escape, to postpone dealing with the anxiety associated with the incredible traumata to which she had been exposed. In truth, her slipping back to childhood memories offered analytic benefits, lifting into view all the intermediary way stations of her self-replicating series, which were stamped with the illusory elements that make up the fabric of the transitional process.

In health, the illusions that ordinarily permeate our object relations become gradually subjugated, particularly because of phallic development, by a maturing psychic structure that facilitates the adequate adaptation of our biological reality to the society in which we live. Even in healthy states, however, meaningful vestiges of illusion characteristic of the transitional process linger on. In certain neurotic disorders, particularly in the traumatic neuroses, the struggle to escape into timelessness promotes a hypertrophy of the transitional elements, sometimes to the point of delusion and hallucination. Lilli's flight never went that far; it did, however, run a wide gamut of transitional pathology. Her loss of menses, for example, was an almost immediate reaction to her initial incarceration in Theresienstadt; she had unconsciously chosen to turn off her main (and most ingeniously constructed) timepiece—her biological clock. For an adolescent girl with a biological cycle only tenuously established, camp imprisonment was hardly the milieu for furthering her pubertal development. She remained without her periods throughout her concentration camp imprisonment, her cycle returning only following liberation five years later, and then linked with her compulsion to reproduce. It was to the transitional elements of this compulsion that her treatment had to address itself if her illness was to be properly understood.

The transitional process, which begins in infancy, belongs to the advance armamentaria deployed toward the maintenance of merger between infant and mother when this first clashes with the elemental process of individuation. "Transitional" implies a bridge between one phase of development and another. Crediting Fairbairn (1952) with coining the term, Winnicott (1953) conceptualized transitional as any thought or idea experienced in what he called an intermediary area, which, in adults, included a broad spectrum of cultural elements such as art, religion, and scientific work. Later, Winnicott (1960) spoke of infants so impinged upon by traumata from early environment as to be forced to withdraw the rudiments of their individuality into the formation of a secret self which existed by not being found, a self whose inner core never communicated with the world of perceived objects. Traumatic experiences, Winnicott (1965) observed, continued to pose a menace to this isolated core, either threatening to alter it or to bring about some communication with it.

Winnicott's thesis demands our full attention, particularly because of its relationship to the subject of illusion, a theme of the utmost significance with respect to the subjective sense of time. Not that I conceptualize trauma as something that *threatens* to alter a secret self; rather, I see it as *promoting* an alteration in the self. It is precisely this altering or transforming ability (a secret *of* the self, if you will) that is destined to play a meaningful part in the subsequent evolution of the transitional process. Indeed, it is this transforming quality that should command our full interest if we are to understand man's fascination with "twilight zones," with parapsychology or the occult, with demonology, exorcism, or ghosts from the beyond. It is illusion, which is energized by wish and not necessarily a contradiction of reality (as is its more infantile predecessor, delusion), that fashions our transition into the broad realm of cultural passions which we develop to maintain our self-regard.

To Winnicott, the term transitional denotes a process that begins in the first few months of life, somewhere between the time the infant first introduces its thumb into its mouth in erotic stimulation and its later attachment to an object. Winnicott locates this developmental event between 4 and 12 months, when the infant, still only partially capable of recognizing and accepting reality, chooses its first "not-me" possession—commonly a soft cloth or a teddy, and later a doll or a toy—which Winnicott terms a transitional object. He points out that although the significance of such an object to the child may become reactivated in the face of some major deprivation, ordinarily the first object becomes gradually relegated to limbo, being neither internalized nor repressed, neither forgotten nor mourned. It loses its meaning as the transitional process diffuses over a vast intermediary territory between inner psychic reality and the external world, a diffusion that comes to expression in such things as art and religion. According to Winnicott, although the transitional object is symbolic of the mother's breast, it is its actuality rather than its symbolic value that is important to the infant. Standing as it does between the subjective and the objective, the whole process is especially important to Winnicott in giving root to the symbolism of time.

The transitional object depends for its viability on the child's perceptions of the mother. It is the good-enough mother who provides the lifeline for the infant's illusion that an external reality exists corresponding to the infant's capacity to create. The transitional element affords a neutral and unchallengeable area of experience to the infant. The mother nourishes both the representation of herself as internalized in the child's psyche and the child's interest in the transitional object. Her failure as a good mother brings about devaluation of both. The object is neither under the child's magical control (as is the internal representation of the mother) nor completely outside the child's control (as is the external mother). But the child nonetheless has a manipulative stake in the fate of the object. For Winnicott, the transitional process is the foundation of illusion, a process that belongs only to human beings, who may come to understand the process but are unable to surmount it. Constituting the greater part of the infant's experience, it becomes a lifelong investment in imaginative adult living.

Greenacre (1969) was the first to draw a clear differential between the transitional object and the fetish. She emphasizes that though both resemble each other in certain aspects (both being inanimate and adapted for the maintenance of a psycho-physical balance under conditions of stress), they nonetheless differ strikingly in their origins and roles. Where the transitional object ordinarily belongs to infancy, the fetish, standing as it does in Greenacre's view (as it did in Freud's) for the female phallus, becomes adopted in much later development, especially in males, as a common prop for securing adequate sexual performance. In fetishism, emphasis on the visual sense contrasts with the importance of texture and odor attached to the transitional object. In addition, the nonviolent implications of the latter contrast with the aggression and the castration panic associated with the fetish. Expressing a narcissistic rather than an object need and reflecting a flaw in body image of the genital area, the fetish, to Greenacre, differs from the average child's transitional play in self-mastery, which is a normal creative act that arises at a period of development before aggression has become an object-directed hostility. Greenacre sees fetishism, unlike the transitional object, developing against a background of neurotic parents who promote sexual confusion and expose their offspring to physically traumatic acts.

A significantly different version of fetish was offered earlier by Wulff (1946), who drew no distinction between the transitional object and the fetish, perceiving both as reflecting object choice in early childhood. Wulff perceived an initial substitution of the entirety of the mother's body by the fetish or the transitional object. This early oral experience became translated during the anal phase into a matter of possession, and still later, in the phallic and genital stages, into a valued penis threatened with castration. Milner (1952) agreed that the transitional object served the need in some children to discover a pliable medium for creativity. She felt that it was important for parents to foster in children a partial feeling of maternal fusion; prematurely forcing a child to break with the illusion of oneness in order to develop an awareness of separate identity could lead to severe anxiety which might disrupt the creativity derived from the illusion. Milner felt that therapy should support the illusion that object and self are still merged, allowing the child to tolerate a goodness that is not its own. By contrast, Sperling (1963) pointed out that in pathological fetishism, mothers, out of their own pathology, prompted a child's attachment to an inanimate object. Clashing with Winnicott's acceptance of the normalcy of transitional objects, Sperling claimed that these mothers fostered such objects out of their own inadequacies. And unlike Winnicott's and Milner's more optimistic view that in the healthy child the transitional object was gradually decathected, it was Sperling's opinion that such objects could easily return in the form of a fetish.

In an opposing vein, Coppolillo (1967) feels that a parental or environmental intrusiveness could have deleterious effects on the child's transitional development. Kahne (1967) properly raises the question of how a transitional object, so crucially significant to psychic development, can undergo a decathexis without mourning. Fintzy (1971) expresses the feeling that in some people, the transitional object may never disappear, but may simply go unnoticed. In certain borderline patients, Fintzy feels that the object becomes disguised by a shift to substitute objects chosen not for themselves, but for properties with which the patient's imagination endowed them. Roiphe and Galenson (1975) have more recently observed that when there is an emergence of serious castration anxiety in the

face of unusual stress, the transitional object, no longer
serving its ordinary function, becomes replaced by a fetish
that is more focally involved with aggressive trends, as well
as with concerns about genital intactness.

I believe that the first transitional object follows a
developmental blueprint which begins with the infant's
innate tendency to assimilate and imitate. In the infantile
phase of merger, replication originally takes the form of
projective hallucinations and delusions with respect to the
absent nourishment of the breast; with the beginnings of
individuation and maturation of the perceptual apparatus,
the attending mother's presence is no longer satisfactorily
secured in such a fashion, and the child is induced to more
tangibly replicate itself *outside its own body* in a form that
imitates a primal physiological model. With the child not
yet capable of meaningful internalization beyond imitation, I see the mother's milk and the child's excrement, both
physiological extrusions from the body, as the earliest
models for the infant to draw upon as a rudimentary proxy
or imitation of its self. Rather than the mother's breast or
body, the infant's earliest transitional objects are more
accurately a blend of the substances of the nutritional
process, namely the mother's milk and the child's waste.
Both the texture and the smell of the soft cloth specifically
relate to these two materials, and the manner in which the
infant manipulates its cloth (as it does milk and feces) is in
keeping with the importance that Spitz (1965) and later
Pacella (1975) attach to the mother's face. The nuzzling of
cloth (milk-feces baby) to nose and face indeed imitates the
mother-infant nuzzlings; the mother has *her* baby (the
infant) and the infant likewise has hers (the cloth impregnated with milk-feces odors). In truth, the child comes to
treat its baby (the cloth or doll) much the same way as it is
treated by the mother; there may be a cuddle one moment
and casual neglect the next, one minute a kiss, the next
minute a frown.

The Abdominal Conversion

Somatic symptoms involving a narcissistic cathexis of the body in a compromise of physiology represent a later stage in the transitional process. Although these do not deserve the stamp of an active re-creative repetition compulsion, they nonetheless frequently find their way into adult living, particularly under certain conditions of stress when reactivation of the conversion process transpires, particularly in people genetically endowed with a tendency to somatize emotions. It is because this tendency appears to have a familial cast that some consider it a constitutional endowment.

Although both observation of infants and retrospective verbal communications from adults can only lead to a deductive reconstruction of infantile development, they nonetheless strongly suggest that the infant's earliest rudimentary self is composed of its own bodily sensations, intermingled with sensory impressions (touch, taste, sound, smell, and sight) emanating from meaningful outside persons (parents and siblings). Such a blend could logically be described as a rudimentary body ego, a network of body symbolizations that identify a rudimentary self as well as objectify those outside persons giving representation to that self. This body ego is the first structure to reflect physical signals of the infantile organism's separation from its symbiotic host (the mother). As mentioned earlier, where Freud and others, including Lewin, emphasized the tactile quality of the maternal breast in part-object symbolizations, Spitz and Pacella viewed as equally significant the infant's visual impressions of the mother's face, which they regarded as a more practical model for object constancy than the maternal nipple that is periodically withheld.

Just as the need for replication gives thrust to the transitional "stillbirth" of milk and excrement, so does it continue to operate in the ensuing body ego defenses which, like the more sophisticated mental constructions that develop later, aim at altering one's sense of time. Felix Deutsch (1959a) elaborates on a *conversion process* that is mobilized by the child in its earliest months to safeguard its body unity (merger of mother and child). He describes it as a body language, a psycho-physiological phenomenon manifesting itself in the form of bodily symptoms activated by the trauma of loss. Reporting on a patient plagued by physical complaints, I (1962) described a woman burdened with losses whose body parts became veritable warehouses for the symbolic representations of family members. A threatened loss of one of her children, whether real or imagined, would be signalled by a flare-up of symptoms in the corresponding body part, like an alarm system warning of impending danger. This symbolization and incorporation of family figures into her body scheme at times led to an actual impairment of the physical function of the particular body part.

My clinical evaluation of Lilli's pain (abdominal conversion) was naturally influenced by the ideas, feelings, and memories she expressed in direct association to her symptom. Unlike the artist whose instinctual life becomes invested in a creative process that symbolically unites him with his primal objects, Lilli's capacity to mourn was limited by her neurosis, as reflected in an underlying, unresolved ambivalence toward her mother, as well as in the way she had bound herself to early objects by encapsulating them into a body conversion symptom (her particular compromise position in the transitional series). Because her libido was not free to move toward more mature investments of newer objects, there was always the danger of its regressive release from bodily bondage (a likelihood that would have probably resulted in the actual abortion of her pregnancies). I was particularly on the alert for any premature abandonment by Lilli of her conversion symptom, which not only served to bind her aggressions, but functioned as a face-saver as well. Psychiatrists are familiar with the role of conversion symptoms as face-savers in their everyday practice, particularly when an over-zealous interpretation aimed at providing a patient with quick relief brings premature abandonment of physical symptoms at the price of acute depression.

That Lilli's abdominal pain was intricately bound up with her thoughts about pregnancy was clear; the development of her symptom coincided with her first conception. Other associations to her abdominal pain, from the most recent to the most remote, included sundry diseases incurred during her camp incarceration; a bout of infectious hepatitis which had become linked in her mind with having eaten something bad and which, in turn, began an associative chain that led back to thoughts of her mother; her mother's fatal illness and the pain her mother had endured in giving birth to her only daughter; the feelings of responsibility for her mother's cancer which had spread from breast to abdomen while she carried Lilli. All these seemed to be a screen for certain deeper hostilities. Although there was no history of a familial predisposition to the expression of emotional conflict in the form of bodily symptoms, Lilli admitted that the development of her abdominal pain had originally served the function of saving face. Reluctantly she even confessed that the failure of exploratory surgery to find an organic problem left her feeling robbed of a crutch; she felt that everyone thenceforth would perceive her as either seeking attention or faking for other reasons.

THE FLIGHT TO THE TIMELESSNESS OF DRUGS

Compounding the mystery that enshrouded her abdominal symptom was Lilli's heavy use of drugs during her pregnancy. Drugs not only provided relief from pain, but allowed her an escape from the terrifying premonition that something catastrophic was going to befall her. I was aware that many people who used drugs suffered anxiety about the passage of time. Early on, Rado (1926, 1933) observed that by diminishing or removing the sensation of pain, drugs supplied a shield against stimulation from within (he did not specify that it was the sense of transience that was involved). Acting as a second line of defense in paralyzing nerve substance, the drug shield acted centrally at the sensory approaches to the mental apparatus. Rado, in fact, described a pharmacogenic orgasm, where a spreading sense of well-being from the diffuse reactions to drugs offered an erotic satisfaction that rivaled sex. Once drug intoxication became a sexual aim, Rado observed, addiction was sure to follow, a process that deepened with each failure to achieve genital orgasm. Drug users, he pointed out, also commonly experienced an alimentary orgasm, a diffuse feeling in the stomach similar to the oral gratifications of the sucking infant; the addict played a trick on biology so to speak, copying the function of nutrition in developing an alimentary mode of orgastic experience. All three types of orgasm—the alimentary, the genital, and the pharmacogenic—had a common goal, the amelioration of erotic tension.

Addiction, Rado claimed, was an illness psychologically triggered by tense depression. By his emphasis on the initial increase in self-regard produced by drugs (especially by mood elevators), Rado pointed to the problem with time. In the relief gained, there was a temporary restoration of omnipotence and self-love (and a subjective sense of timelessness), a narcissistic fulfillment that compelled the user to repeat the cure until the torment and self-reproach for helplessness and drug dependency disposed the victim to addiction. Eventually becoming inadequate in sexual performance, the addict would wreak vengeance on what he or she held responsible for the tension, the disappointment in genital sex. Drug users often try to shake off their difficulties by a flight into masochism or into homosexual activity, or by clinging to heterosexuality with the aid of a fetish to rescue imperiled gender-defined sexuality. Indeed, such a rescue is particularly apparent in those who seek in alcohol the royal road to sexual arousal (especially in males, where the drinking to another man's health even today expresses hope for a lengthy sexual life). In fact, a man's capacity to hold his liquor still earns the same respect as his prowess in sex; the teetotaller, by contrast, gets the label of weakling. Of course, this does not apply to women, who, even in our liberated culture, continue to be censured if they succumb to inebriation.

Szasz (1958) was particularly impressed by the addict's need to repeatedly expose herself or himself to the dangerous effects of drugs in order to master the fear of passivity and helplessness and to develop resistance against surrender (via repetition compulsion). Savitt (1963) compares the addict to the infant who requires a specific substance of nutrition, but from an undifferentiated source. Savitt acknowledges the issue of time by observing the hard drug addict's intolerance of delay, a desperation that forces abandonment of the oral route in favor of the more primitive intravenous channel. Dora Hartmann's (1969) research stresses the sociological significance of drugs; the advertising of the satisfaction becomes an important part in the infectious process, and the jargon, the ritual, the being in fashion with the cult all become crucial face- savers on the road to addiction. Her investigation of parents of addicts uncovers significant pathology, more so in the mothers than in the fathers. Hartmann also makes the clinically verifiable point that drug users have a need to seduce others to the habit. This need was significant in

Lilli's case, and her husband became the prime target for a *folie à deux* of this order. (This behavior can be compared with the guilt-reducing tactics of overeating mothers with respect to the feeding of their offspring.) In Hartmann's subjects there was almost always the need to replace a loss, whether the loss of a parent or of some other meaningful figure. It was also found that, as in Lilli's case, an encounter with severe illness during the early years, particularly the illness of another family member, formed part of the profile of the addict's childhood.

Observing that drugs are not selected indiscriminately, Wieder and Kaplan (1969) draw attention to the addict's choice of chemical. These authors attach symbolic importance not only to the agent chosen, but to its portal of entry into the body, as well as to the associated physiological sensations. LSD has been found to alter body image, producing fantasies of merger and fusion, the "trip" representing a cracking of the stimulus barrier as the addict tries to regress beyond the early autistic stage. Opium intoxication, or being "on the nod," produces a lethargic state of blissful omnipotence, whereas amphetamines and cocaine increase the sense of impulse strength and diminish awareness of fatigue, both at the price of decreased judgment and accuracy. Alcohol and marijuana are noted for promoting an alteration in the subjective sense of time. Overall, I concluded that as with all drug users, the signal motive for Lilli's use of drugs (codeine, barbiturates, and amphetamines) was to rid herself of the feelings of lowered self-regard and unbearable tension that had originated with her early experiences of loss (and of time).

MENTAL SELF-REPLICATION

Individuals with traumatic neuroses have a wide range for expressing their passion for replicating themselves psychologically in reaction to trauma. The spectrum includes twinning fantasies, multiplication of body parts, creation of imaginary companions, and more sophisticated defenses, such as *fausse reconnaissance* and the so-called *alienations*. Changes in body imagery are a very common response to both separation and castration anxiety. One patient, a man who was quite dependent on his mother, described regular childhood beatings by his mother, an irritable, phallic woman, often armed with an umbrella, who would belt him about his arms and legs while they walked in the street. The abuse caused him to develop an unusual childhood body image that persisted into adult life—the image of a centipede with a thousand eyes lodged in each extremity. The patient's fear of castration (displaced from his genitals to his extremities) had its origin in the oedipal voyeurism that was prompted by the sexually seductive mother, who had a predilection for exhibiting herself nude to her son during his formative years. His limb-replicating imagery disguised a heavily repressed oedipal complex which was primarily reflected in the disturbed body imagery rather than in overt sexual conflict. Amputees frequently experience an illusory (though startlingly real) restitution of the missing part, the so-called "phantom limb" syndrome. Although often attributed to nerve-ending sensations linked with mechanisms of the temporal lobe (see Ostow, 1958), from a psychological standpoint these illusory reduplications reflect the defensive work of the ego engaged in the reduplicating mechanism. Ostow (1960) also speaks of autoscopy, a primary narcissistic mechanism of almost reflex quality, which involves visual self-replicative images and is modelled after the infant's hallucinatory response to the absent maternal breast.

In his exploration of the uncanny, the novelist finds reduplication a favorite subject, and perhaps while he is conceiving his product, he is himself doubling in such a "pregnant" state of mind (union of mother and self). Kupper and Rollman-Branch (1959) are among those who draw attention to Freud's designation of the playwright Schnitzler as his *Doppelgänger,* an implicitly uncanny second representation of Freud. They speculate that in Schnitzler, Freud encountered his spectral double (an insurance against destruction), whose life Freud could have realized but chose not to live. Folk superstition holds that seeing one's double may be a presage of death. In many ways, the development of the superego might even be considered an example of the doubling process.

The *imaginary companion* is another manifestation of the replicative process, appearing considerably later than the transitional object, somewhere between two-and-a-half and three years, and commonly reactivated between nine-and-a-half and ten years. Burlingham (1952) feels that the fantasy of possessing a companion or twin is often triggered by disappointment resulting from unfulfilled oedipal wishes; she believes that the fantasy serves not only as a replication of body parts in the face of oedipal castration anxiety, but as a compensation for either losing or not acquiring a loving and ever-present companion in real life. According to Arlow (1960), a person's mirror image is identified as his (or her) twin before he realizes it to be a reflection of himself. Arlow observes that there is a vast difference between the fantasy of having a twin and the reality of being one; the ambivalent relationship between twins in terms of their accentuated rivalries, projections, denials, and corruptions of superego, make for a clinical syndrome in its own right. Nagera (1969) finds that the imaginary companion serves as an auxiliary not only for the ego but for the superego as well. He observes that better endowed children produce more vivid imaginary companions, which, like imaginary twins, serve as vehicles for

the discharge of impulses unacceptable to the ego, as scapegoats or buffers for mitigating difficult situations, or for
prolonging omnipotence in a defiance of parental authority. Beyond impersonating primitive ideals outside the
child's reach, perhaps they act most of all as buffers against
loneliness, neglect, and rejection. Nagera contends that the
imaginary companion is not as jealously guarded as wish-
fulfilling daydreams or the fantasies of latency, that it promotes less withdrawal and strengthens rather than weakens
the ego's capacities to test reality. I cannot entirely agree
with this, having seen instances in which imaginary companions were extended into adolescence, where they served
to distort rather than strengthen reality testing, allowing
illusions to permeate the perception of self and objects. It
seems to me that any excessive need to secure comfort by
narcissistic replication of the self must go hand in hand with
some perversion of the reality sense, especially when it
comes to phallic development, where illusion can even blur
one's sexual expressions of love.

Benson and Pryor (1973) describe children who abruptly
abandoned their imaginary companions as a direct result of
parental intrusions, the companions under such circumstances being no longer qualified to serve in their capacity
as narcissistic guardians. One thinks of the manner in which
transitional illusions of infancy become similarly undermined when they receive an unempathic response from the
mother. A rather instructive corollary involves the intrusion
of offspring into a parent's private illusion, illustrating how
an imaginary companion persisted into the twilight years of
an aging man. I cite the case of my father, who in his last
years, following the death of my mother, maintained an
illusory companion with whom he could be heard com-
municating right to the end of his days. My first assumption
was that he was simply talking to the mate whom he
imagined to be still by his side. It became apparent, how-

ever, that he was conversing with an earlier derived "soul mate," and his animated conversations with this transitional companion were unchallengeable, put aside only temporarily by the occasional queries of snooping members of the family. Clearly, from a body ravaged by aging, a spirit or soul had become split off as an indestructible aspect of the sense of self. It is of some interest that my father never came to know his mother, since she had died giving birth to him. I suspect that his soul companion was originally this ethereal figure (later blended with the image of his wife). I speculate that his mother had always been an imaginary companion, as unmovable a spirit as an infant's first not-me possession. Perhaps this is an instance of a transitional companion never being relegated to limbo, but remaining throughout life as an "immortal soul."

The phenomena of *fausse reconnaissance* and the *alienations* are more intricate mechanisms by which the human psyche deals with the subjective sense of time. Freud (1899) first described them as *transformatory reactions* to situations disagreeable to the ego, introducing his ideas on the subject when he identified certain early memories as screens for later events, and certain later memories as screens for earlier events. For Freud, the value of a screen memory was to be found in its relation between its own content and that of some other repressed memory. He observed that when a screen memory introduced the presence of the subject himself as an object among other objects, this could be taken as evidence that the original impression had been transformed, and that it had become translated into a plastic visual form on the date of its arousal as a memory. This kind of Freudian thinking implies that our childhood memories are in considerable measure only distortions, wherein the locale of an event can become shifted or the scenes and people merged or substituted one for the other. For Freud this reshuffling served the purpose of repressing disagreeable impressions, so that rather than having memories *from* our childhood, we really retain memories *relating to* our childhood.

Freud's (1900a) interest in *fausse reconnaissance* took further shape when he described dreams of landscapes or other localities which emphasized the dreamer's conviction of having been there before. For Freud, this type of *déjà vu* invariably referred to the mother's genitals, since there was no other place about which one could assert with such conviction that one had been there before. Freud's attention to the phenomenon reappeared in 1914 in his description of analytic patients who expressed a conviction of having already related to the analyst something that in fact they had not (*déjà raconté*). He ascribed to *déjà raconté* an attempt at screening a repressed recollection related specifically to the castration complex, which served the purpose of correcting an unwelcome perception. Freud included all *déjà* phenomena under the heading of *fausse reconnaissance*.

Fliess (1956) viewed *déjà raconté* as a transference delusion occurring in nonpsychotic people. He went along with Freud in classifying it with *déjà vu* so far as content was concerned. According to Fliess, the patient experiencing a *déjà raconté* feels as though he has told his castration experience before (although he knows that he has not), laying claim in so feeling to the maternal breast as something belonging to his ego. The mechanism of the patient's *déjà raconté*, as reported within the transference to the analyst, works as follows: "*I am in danger of re-experiencing castration. . . . To protect myself, I have regressed to an early stage where owning the breast is what matters and, having transferred upon you the early mother, have incorporated yours . . . you must now let yourself become the victim of a* folie à deux *and join me in my delusion*" (Fliess,

1956, p. 226). Why is it, Fliess asks, that the patient tells his castration experience for what to him is the second time? What compels him to negate that he is telling it for the first time? The answer for Fliess lies in Freud's view of *mastery via transformation into activity*. In Fliess's view, traumatic experiences are surrounded with fragments of infantile ego, so that when these experiences return from the repressed, the patient becomes totally seized by the wave of infantile reactivation, the shock of castration having been initially experienced passively and as something annihilative to the infantile ego. According to Fliess, experiencing an initial recounting as if it were a second recounting, a *déjà raconté*, aims at mastery through activity and reconstruction (a repetition compulsion).

Although I support the thesis of remerger with the mother, I see no reason to single out castration anxiety as the precipitating factor in the *déjà raconté*, convinced as I am that the trauma of separation is an equally valid provocation. Rather than postulating a return to an incorporation of the mother's breast, I view the reactivation of the transitional process of self-replication as the more likely point of return, particularly since the storyteller in the *déjà raconté* is searching for the listener's empathy (the mother's approval). The story-telling performance itself is like the soft cloth or the doll, or like show-and-tell at school, all of which are derived from the self-replicative activity of the transitional period. Thus, in my terms, *déjà* experiences are illusory rather than delusionary. Kohut (1971), too, perceives the telescoped screening of memories as not necessarily related to castration anxiety; rather, it can be due to separation anxiety undergoing transformation by an ego seeking to convert passivity into activity.

Déjà raconté is not only a transference phenomenon of analytic treatment, but an event that can occur in everyday social intercourse as well. It is also a common feature of the analyst's countertransference; indeed, it can occur long after treatment has been terminated. On two separate occasions, both of which involved some socializing with former patients, I found myself experiencing a *déjà raconté;* both times, it was I who was now the storyteller. On examination, I discovered that the operative factor in each instance was my wish to change a situation that was once passively endured by me (listening to those two patients during their analyses) into a more active situation, where I had the opportunity of turning the tables and doing the talking. In both instances, the analyses had not been what I would describe as classic. Both patients suffered narcissistic disorders that called for dealing with mirror transferences, and which unquestionably provoked narcissistic responses of my own. Indeed, I am sure that this had everything to do with my own willingness to engage in the socializations that subsequently took place well after these analyses had been terminated. One might even say that undercurrents of separation anxiety operated on each side of the dyad—in the physician as well as in the patients. The *déjà raconté* could be perceived as a way of extending the analytic relationships, as a means of turning back the clock to the time when these two individuals were patients, albeit with reversals and transformations that unquestionably were in the service of manipulating my sense of the passage of time.

Marcovitz (1952) perceived the *déjà vu* as primarily expressing the wish for a second chance. Arlow (1959) regarded the mechanism as a compromise formation, a transitory, circumscribed disturbance of a specific ego function in which there is an unpleasant feelingful component with a quality of the uncanny; as far as Arlow was concerned, the second chance element was purely a secondary gain, rather than a signal of repression of unachieved instinctual gratification. Arlow diagnosed *déjà vu* as a disturbance of reality testing, rather than a disturbance in the sense of reality. Silbermann (1963) reports on the *jamais raconté* (here the patient, who has in fact previously given an accounting of a past event or memory, repeats the account with the belief that he is offering it for the first time). Silbermann observes that the *jamais raconté* can range from a simple and easily reversible idea to a firmly fixed conviction and, like the *déjà*, appears under normal as well as pathological conditions. Silbermann postulates that the dynamic factor is a fragmentation energized by the aggressive drive, a specialized form of denial in contrast to the synthesis of the *déjà* experience that is nurtured by the sexual drive. I am not entirely in agreement with Silbermann on this, although I can only cite one case in dispute of his point of view. A man in treatment twice related a traumatic incident of latency, an episode in which he had been passively molested. His *jamais raconté* served as a screen for the memory of a much later and more traumatic event, in which he had been defiantly active and had felt threatened with castration at the hands of his father. I am led to speculate that what Silbermann describes as a fragmentation motivated by aggression may be rather the energetic and aggressively defensive efforts of the ego to both hide and soften (to secretly transform) one aspect of his sense of self that, if acknowledged, would invoke his fear of castration. In his *jamais raconté*, my patient introduced a more passive surrendering self, and one less prone to castration (and more prone to perversion). This example would suggest that the *jamais* too should be included as a synthesizing rather than a fragmenting mechanism of the ego. I further suggest that the double recounting of the *jamais* in my example is itself a duplicative screen defense, unconsciously set up to support the ego's efforts to transform the self, a self endangered on one level by castration, and on a deeper level by separation.

Boesky (1973) emulates Arlow's (1959) comparison of

the *déjà vu* to the dream by affording the same treatment to the *déjà raconté*, perceiving the *raconté* aspect as capable of being decoded, analyzed, and shown to be a familiar product of condensation, displacement, and symbolization analogous to the secondary revision of the dream process. Boesky views the *déjà* element as a screen memory equivalent, a defensive, dynamic resynthesis on the part of the ego, rather than an accurate reproduction. Instead of remembering something painful, there is a remembering of something less painful; instead of recognizing the similarity between the present situation and an earlier threatening fantasy, there is a displacement of the feelings of familiarity onto some neutral, pleasant, and reassuring screen aspect of the present situation. Boesky also sees both the *déjà* and *jamais* phenomena as efforts to reintegrate early experiences; both are failures in memory in the service of defense, yet both are rich in adaptive implications.

In relation to time, Boesky sees the *déjà* as a coalescence of past and present. Reminding us of Kohut's (1971) observations on the tendency of the psyche to telescope generically analogous experiences, Boesky views the *déjà* as a manifestation of the synthesizing capacity of the mind to express early trauma through the medium of analogous psychic contents that are closer to secondary process and verbal communication. Boesky feels that the screen is designed not only to conceal painful feelings, but to convert them into pleasurable experiences, and that the defensive reversal of passive into active is particularly visible in the *jamais* experience. In effect, he sees both the *déjà* and the *jamais* as related to the repetition compulsion; both are for Boesky, efforts on the part of the ego to actively remember and recreate the past through a parapraxis, which, when interpreted in analysis, fosters a new creative resolution of conflict (this is in line with Loewald's thinking, 1971).

Neu (1973) recalls Freud's dictum that even hysterics suffer from reminiscences, that they, too, are victims of their past. Neu warns that simply helping an hysteric to reintegrate incompatible ideas into consciousness in order to facilitate insight is not enough for a cure or for a resolution of conflict; what is needed is a reattachment of feeling to idea. The conditions that kept the feelings from being discharged in the original situation should not be duplicated in the treatment, since these feelings (strangulated affects) cannot be simply discharged in just any fashion. Since the unconscious fantasies inherent in hysterical symptoms are real in so far as they are mental aspects of an impulse, then for Neu, the hysteric, too, engages in a repetition compulsion, in an unconscious attempt to alter the past by embellishing or informing current impulses with unconscious memories or fantasies.

Rather than explaining *déjà vu* as a revival of feelings of familiarity with the mother's genitals, as Freud did, Pacella (1975) sees the phenomenon as ultimately derived from the face-breast gestalt of the mother. He draws on the work of Spitz (1965), who first described this gestalt as one of the early crucial organizers of the psyche, wherein a shift from tactile to visual perception during the first few months of life takes on paramount significance in the infant's later development. For Spitz, in contrast to the need-gratifying perception of the maternal breast which is repeatedly lost and regained (the lose and find of infancy), the perception of the mother's face remains relatively constant. Spitz suggests that breast and face become partially fused as a total experience and that visual perception, because of its greater constancy and reliability, becomes the leading perceptive modality in man, serving as the anchor element of the mother's psychological essence.

For Pacella, the sense of the familiar in the *déjà vu* represents the earliest awareness of the child's sense of identity as a component of the nonsymbiotic dyad with the mother. Pacella sees it as a derivative of the infant's lose-and-find or peek-a-boo re-creations of fusion with the mother. According to Pacella, the *déjà vu* is a controlled regression, a search by the adult ego for the visually imprinted core of the omnipotent mother established in infancy as a basic memory. This maternal image, dressed in the cloak of the familiar (*déjà vu*), is superimposed on a real perception, such as a landscape. *Déjà vu* serves to recapture the primal love object, avoiding castration anxiety through an encapsulation with that object, yet, ensuring the distancing necessary to avoid too much regressive merger with the object. As to why there should be in *déjà* such regressive movement back to the visual signal of the mother, rather than merely back to the oedipal object, Pacella simply emphasizes the power of return to the imprinted core that persists throughout life as a basic memory. Mahler (1975a) supports this view, observing that when the ego is threatened by unusual danger, security measures more basic than oedipal mechanisms become reactivated. In times of the greatest danger from without or from within, this blissful symbiosis becomes the ultimate reservoir, as in the *déjà vu* of soldiers before battle.

As a counterpart to *fausse reconnaissance,* whereby one seeks to accept memories of events as belonging to the self, Freud (1936) described the so-called *alienations,* which included *depersonalization* (wherein the subject feels that the sense of his own self has become estranged) and *derealization* (wherein the subject feels that a piece of external reality has become estranged). Freud felt that these alienation mechanisms were efforts to shut out unpleasant memories from belonging to the self. Fliess (1956) drew a differential by emphasizing that cognitive judgment was not impaired in the alienations, as it was in *fausse reconnais-*

sance. In Lilli's case, there was little evidence in the early phases of her analysis of the use of either the *déjà* or *jamais* mechanisms; from the beginning, however, she did suffer from episodes of derealization and from frequent bouts of depersonalization. Jacobson (1959), in her observations on a group of political prisoners of Nazi Germany, found depersonalization to be a very common response to trauma. She described victims whose body parts, including the genitals, were experienced as dead, estranged, or changed in size; even the sexual act became an estranged experience for some, who assumed the role of spectator observing someone else's performance. Jacobson properly emphasized that such depersonalizations were to be observed in normal individuals, in neurotics as well as in psychotics, and particularly in individuals with a narcissistic personality structure.

There are differing opinions as to the elements involved in depersonalization. There is general agreement that there is a split in the ego and that feelings of estrangement result from sudden shifts of libido from the object to the ego. Schilder (1935) stresses a sadomasochistic element. Bergler (1950) views depersonalization as a defense against anal exhibitionism transformed into voyeurism, which, in turn, becomes accepted by the ego as self-observation. Oberndorf (1950) compares depersonalization to the simulative behavior of animals who play dead when confronted with danger. For Blank (1954), the phenomenon is called into play when other defenses fail to keep dangerous feelings repressed. Jacobson favors Fenichel's (1945) view that depersonalization is a special type of defense against feelings that have become intensified as a result of an increase in the narcissistic cathexis of the self, and is experienced primarily in the hypercathected organs.

Jacobson describes depersonalization in victims who anticipated a battle of wits with the Gestapo; the feelings of familiarity which were ordinarily enjoyed before incarceration gave way during imprisonment to the detachment of depersonalization. For some, the ensuing traumata propelled them toward brainwashing, an acceptance of the criminal role ascribed to them by the enemy. Some even identified with the aggressor, becoming "Nazis" themselves under the pressure of active archaic identifications which were promoted by the seductive and sadistic prison officials. To successfully withstand such a fate often required an overinvestment of the thought processes at the expense of feelings. The struggle between contradictory self-representations in which efforts become mobilized to deny or negate unacceptable and archaic criminal identifications becomes particularly expressed in symptoms of depersonalization that involve the upper body parts. According to Jacobson, these parts become most commonly depersonalized because of the role they usually play in people's fantasies of attacking and being attacked. Unlike Fenichel, Jacobson thought repressed aggression was also involved in depersonalization.

Most authors, Jacobson included, perceive depersonalization as the pathological result of a narcissistic conflict of identifications within the ego, although Oberndorf views the process as linked with unacceptable superego identifications, particularly with the parental figure of the opposite sex. Sarlin (1962) emphasizes a pathological identification of the self and the object, which results in an impairment of the sense of identity (an impairment of the differentiation between the self and the non-self). Hunter (1966) views depersonalization as a splitting of the ego which represents a perverted form of seeing oneself as others do. Arlow (1966) to some extent allies depersonalization with the *déjà vu*, perceiving the former as generically related to dreaming (where a split into observing and participating self-representations permits a sense of estrangement from bodily organs), to the transitional phase of development (where self and non-self are not clearly demarcated and where the child still perceives his own extended feces as connected to the self), and thirdly to a phase of self-discovery in the image before the mirror (where the self-image is treated as an external object). This kind of linkage I found helpful in giving the spectrum of mental self-replications a sense of continuity, wherein one could view the trauma of time as the trigger for both the transitional process as well as the dream. All of the self-replicative compulsions, ranging from passive to active re-creative, are aimed at transforming the trauma through the workings of the ego.

My own clinical findings suggest that both of the so-called alienations are further examples of the workings of the repetition compulsion in reaction to trauma. Involved is a shifting of cathexes within the secondary stimulus barrier, the flow being from self to object representations in the case of depersonalization (where the danger is projected as external) and in the reverse direction in the case of derealization (where the threat is perceived as coming from internal excitations, including from one's subjective sense of time). In self-replicative terms, as with transitional objects, mirrors, twinships, or imaginary companions, the predilection of some to "step outside themselves" for periods of self-observation not only reflects a splitting of the ego, but a defensive doubling in the face of danger. Patients who have survived an approximation to clinical death have described serene states of depersonalization in which the soul was separated out from the body. I have had patients who have used the alienations to avoid the reactivation of primal scene images. One narcissistic patient, a sculptress suffering recurrent bouts of depersonalization, perceived her upper body as an "all-observing head and neck" divorced from the reprehensible "animal" aspects of her lower parts. The perception of herself as "sculptor's bust" reflected her

almost catatonic vigilance toward sexual stimuli. Her face
and shoulders had a curious immobility that gave her upper
torso a sort of "Mount Rushmore" look. Other patients have
described an intellectual guardedness in their depersonalizations, like being armored in a time capsule. Such defensive maneuvers appear to be attempts to retrieve the kind of
fortification associated with the primary stimulus barrier
that once offered immunity in infancy. Hunter (1966) has
particularly noted the strong desire for sleep in one of his
patients, a symptom that subsided as the patient's need for
depersonalizing diminished.

A clinical detachment similar to the isolation of obsessional neurotics is often the feeling state of individuals
predisposed to the alienations. One patient in particular
comes to mind, a schizoid man whose fear of aging was so
strong that he was averse to excitement, "which would age
him." He came to treatment complaining of emotional
impoverishment and lack of spontaneity in all his relationships. The flavor of this man's personality is typified in the
way he handled his aggressions. Where others would give
vent to outright anger, this man would only become
"vexed." He gave the impression that he was above even
perspiring, let alone being burdened with any of the basic
human responses. In truth, I assumed that his symptoms
were merely obsessional until I became aware of his recurrent bouts of derealization. Some of these episodes bordered
on the absurd, particularly one which occurred in a session
early in his analysis, when a berserk patient of one of my
colleagues across the hall began smashing the furniture in
the foyer just outside my office door. I had been in the
midst of urging my patient "to say everything that came
into his mind," an admonition that was customarily met
with a grimace and the deliberate mastication of a few
carefully chosen words. It was at this moment that the
bedlam in the hall caused me to run out to see what was

going on. When I returned to my patient, who was still "laid out" on the couch, he simply resumed talking precisely where he had left off.

"Hold it!" I stammered, "What about the orgy in the hall?"

"No sweat," came his hollow reply, "I'm at my best in a crisis." In truth, in his derealized state, he had hardly noticed the commotion.

Returning to the *déjà* and the *jamais*, they, like the alienations, are by no means peculiar only to the transference situations of psychoanalytic treatment. *Fausse reconnaissance* experiences are common in ordinary social life, especially in the raconteur who specializes in telling droll stories. Ostensibly aiming to exhibit or disarm, such a storyteller often demonstrates the underlying expressions of his repetition compulsion. Unlike the good mother with the child's first not-me possession, or the appreciative audience of the creative artist, the dyadic listener in the *déjà raconté* is often disinclined to offer an empathic response. Indeed in *déjà raconté*, the storyteller has ample cause to fear that he is boring someone with his "second time around"; even when informed that it is a "first," he still feels rebuffed, for hidden in the *déjà raconté* is the lowered self-esteem attached to an earlier repressed trauma suffered at the hands of an unresponsive mother during the transitional period of illusory infantile offerings.

Mental self-replications are not always successful as re-creative repetition compulsions, but the screen elements justify their use as adult defenses. The veiling of one memory by another allows something that was experienced passively to be transformed into something more active; it allows a re-creative reversal, as well as a telescoping transformation of painful memories. Something in the more immediate past is screened by something in the more remote past, or vice versa. Indeed, it is through such mechanisms that the oedipal son later becomes the oedipal father, just as in some families (or cultures) the oedipal father, aged and debilitated, once again becomes the oedipal son.

THE DOLL

Well into the first year of Lilli's treatment, I could more clearly formulate the crucial aspects of her transitional illness, as well as some of the underlying narcissistic pathology that had been the *anlage* for the traumatic reaction that came later. With respect to her position on the transitional ladder, it was obvious that trauma had heightened self-replicative phenomena causing her to make a precocious attempt at giving birth to new life. Unfortunately her developmental position lagged behind her biological ambition. Her abdominal conversion symptom was one expression of her narcissistic fixation.

I was able at this juncture to identify at least some of the characteristics of Lilli's narcissistic character structure—the disdain for others, the subtle grandiosity which existed side by side with shyness and a feeling of inferiority, and all within an ego that had remained relatively intact until the concentration camp trauma. Even then, her ego had not fragmented, as it was rooted predominantly in an underlying grandiose self (see Kohut, 1971; Kernberg, 1974), a specialness that from childhood had defended her against feeling overpowering rage toward disappointing and depriving parents. It was not surprising that in the transference, her idealizations were feeble and shortlived, interrupted by shifts toward devaluation or even veiled contempt. Although these shifts prompted fear that the therapist would retaliate, they at least served the purpose of allaying an underlying depressive current that related to repressed rage against a mother who was seen as cold and ungiving and a father who was perceived as selfish and betraying.

It was important that I allow the fullest possible emotional reenactment of Lilli's struggles with her parents (transference neurosis) and that I avoid making premature interpretations that would stop the flow of material. It was at times easy for me, however, to succumb to the more positive and pleading aspects of my patient's seductions, unconscious ploys aimed at bringing me into the kind of alliance that she had enjoyed with her husband. It was in fact only later that I found out about the *folie à deux* in drugs in which her husband had eventually colluded. This is not to say that I didn't suspect an undercurrent of mutual destructiveness in this symbiotic dyad. Temporarily at least, I managed to withstand the role of rescuer, an obvious pitfall in countertransference that would have caused me to lose the opportunity to deal with the more negative components of her transference. I knew that if there were any hope of eventually helping Lilli renounce some of her narcissism in favor of more meaningful relationships with husband and children, it depended in some degree on my capacity to withstand being drawn into her sadomasochistic replay of concentration camp horrors which, on one level, offered her special status and secondary gain.

To reconcile my understanding of Lilli's transitional pathology with respect to her "doll pregnancy," I found it helpful to refer to Freud's (1919) paper on the uncanny, in which he made reference to "ingeniously constructed dolls" having the capacity to excite the impression of a mechanical automaticity working behind the ordinary appearance of mental activity. Recognizing that the idea of a living doll produced little fear in children, Freud went on to state that the source of the uncanny effect it produced in adults was derived from the infantile wish for a child. In listing characteristics of uncanny experiences, Freud drew attention to the unfamiliar, foreign, and demonic qualities of such experiences, as well as to the aura of secrecy and automaticity they engendered. He recognized that uncanny experiences were often invaded with the theme of *lex talionis*, particularly in neurotics predisposed to castration anxiety. The uncanny effacement between the real and the imaginary allowed occult ideas of ghosts and hauntedness to become reactivated. Freud concluded that as soon as something actually happens in our lives that seems to confirm our old discarded beliefs, we get a feeling of the uncanny—not from being shaken in our beliefs, but because of the return of the repressed.

In theory, a neurosis-free world would imply a surmounting of all the primary elements of the transitional process of infancy, abetted by the adult sublimations of religious, creative, intellectual, or scientific pursuits. Yet infantile transitional fears, for example, fear of silence, fear of solitude, fear of darkness, are by no means completely eradicated in the average adult. Perhaps it is fair to suggest that it is in situations where for one reason or another our efforts at transforming the fact of our transience into illusion break down, that the trauma of time is experienced as uncanny. Lilli's threatened abortions were largely related to her unconscious efforts at transforming the biological fact of conception into a transitional twilight of childhood. Psychologically speaking, during pregnancy her fetus became a doll. Just as on imprisonment she had aborted her menarche, so on liberation she tried to convert conception into something nonbiological. She came to treatment feeling that a demon, rather than a fetus, was inside her, which was pushing her with an automaticity to a fate contrary to her biological drive to procreate. In her illness, it was a "thing" inside her, an inanimate doll. Yet it moved! Something that was supposed to be inanimate inside her was alive—and frighteningly so! What was to confirm a regression to the familiar past was in fact propelling her forward to a new future, thereby threatening to separate her from, rather than unite her with, that infantile past. As far as Lilli was concerned, she had something inside that was not ready for an outside world. One might say that she felt that time was being thrust upon her before she had outgrown timelessness, a thrust that had received impetus from a holocaust that had threatened (and promised) to abort her of her biological potential. On a deeper level, Lilli's drive to procreate was conflicted by childhood imprints of "death from procreation," conditioned by the connection she had made as a child between her own birth and her mother's fatal cancer.

Despite all the degradation she had experienced in the concentration camps, Lilli had found in that very horror a haven from intrapsychic conflict and the trauma of time. Bizarre as that camp setting had been, it had nonetheless allowed her a regression to a twilight existence. Some of her companions had even submerged themselves in a world of delusion and hallucination. On liberation, with biological procreative functions unconsciously reactivated, and with new objects demanding her investment, Lilli nonetheless felt trapped, with one foot still in the past and the other only tenuously in the present. With a child in her belly, not only did she feel threatened by new life, but by the demands for love that such life would make on her; she could not anticipate protecting and defending a child against future dangers. Pregnancy for Lilli was an invalid affair on all levels. Sociologically it was illegitimate, something to be hidden from the world (cf. the dream of running with her baby in the darkness from a public official; the "public" was the Nazi position on Jewish procreation, something punishable by genocide). Psychologically, in order of its regressive stages in the transitional series, pregnancy meant harboring a fetus that countermanded the incest taboo;

deeper still, pregnancy was a penis; and on a still deeper level it was an animated doll or a live cancerous growth. Ultimately, it was inner life threatening to become non-life—fetus as inanimate doll! To make matters worse, even as an illusory doll, it had never received its confirmation from a dying mother, and hence was in danger of being aborted and discarded as an unacceptable transitional stool.

In his essay on a doll phobia, Rangell (1952) found a link between a male patient's fear of dolls and that same patient's fear of forbidden erections. In a postscript to his essay, Rangell (1953) imputed the patient's terror of being broken like a fragile doll to that patient's femininity complex. With Lilli, the linkage between doll and pregnancy seemed even deeper. Her childhood had not only been marked by a tomboyish masculinity complex, but by a conflict centered around problems with time. The super-imposed reality of genocidal gas chambers compounded this negation of time. In her transitional symptoms Lilli was attempting to control time, to thwart the encroachment of transience by her biological compulsion to bring forth new life. On liberation, she was not prepared for the compulsive "growing pains," the pregnancies that for Lilli had become conversion symptoms, unsanctioned as these conceptions were both by the self and the outside "public." Just as Rangell's patient was fearful of his forbidden erections, so was Lilli fearful of her forbidden conceptions. It is not surprising that the births of her first two children were premature, the first after placental separation, the second after Caesarian section. What was surprising was that Lilli could give birth to new life at all, considering the ominous aspects of a transitional regression that had threatened psychologically to transform a live baby into a doll—and beyond that into excrement.

V

The Creative Passion for Timelessness

The quality of the transference in which Lilli engaged me could be described as sadomasochistic; it largely reflected her cynical convictions that people in general, her analyst included, were basically untrustworthy and deserving of both her suspicion and derogation. Such a premise indeed justified her perpetuating her illness. Whereas her drug taking reflected the oral aspects of her regression, I soon came to realize that her sadomasochistic seductiveness was a form of chronic procrastination which carried the stamp of the anal period of development.

According to criminologists, a frequently overlooked clue to a crime is the telltale excrement deposited by the criminal at the scene. Freud (1918) read into this type of anal act both a devil-may-care impudence and an infantile effort at restitution. Reik (1945) held that the fecal product represented the culprit and served as a symbol of confession and self-betrayal unconsciously motivated by the wish for self-punishment. My own view is that the *grumus merdae* symbolically reflects an unconscious gesture of restitution of both the transgressor and his victim, a motivation identical to that which operates in the criminal's compulsion to return to the scene. Mindful that many individuals took refuge by ensconcing themselves in processes derived from the anal period of development, at this juncture in Lilli's analysis I decided to be on the alert for all possible mechanisms that might be related to achieving a sense of timelessness. I decided to emulate the deportment of the diligent criminologist by following the clues, even when their trail led me to the excremental.

A protocol in this regard was long ago established by respected researchers, not only from the field of science but from aesthetics. Certainly rigorous training in medicine teaches the student a respect for the eliminative functions, insofar as the waste products of alimentation are as important in diagnostics as the raw diet. The good surgeon will always underline the dangers of omitting the rectal examination in gathering evidence that might alter the course of a patient's therapy. So it was with a minimum of self-efacement that, like the proctologist, I found myself wandering the corridors of the human bowel for the answer to the riddle of timelessness, especially since I knew that there are few activities peculiar to man more readily at his service toward a killing of time than his pastime of sitting at stool.

Anality and Timelessness

My readiness to explore anality was based on the realization that, until now, my investigation had largely reflected the human hunger for stopping time through oral efforts at reuniting with the maternal breast. It made sense that failure to achieve this reunion would in no way deter an individual from prolonging the quest through the agency of his bowels, particularly considering the important role of the mother in the early rhythm of sphincter functions. In his definition of time, Fliess (1961) not only made reference to the significance of orality, but specifically allocated the first subjective sense of time to the borderland between the oral and the earliest anal-sadistic phase of human development.

Up to this point, my overview of time as a trauma had been conceptualized in largely oral terms, the mouth of the child in search of union with the breast being the model for the recapturing of a timelessness. Yet it only made sense that the child's anal functions should likewise become drawn into such a quest. And, as with the oral phase, where the trauma of time called for a sufficient sense of a self for trauma to be experienced as such, it seemed only logical that in the toilet-training period, when the child first begins to achieve the capacity for volitionally offering the gift of stool to the mother, that such a situation could become another means for the child to fulfill a sense of timelessness. I speculated that the mother's smile acknowledging the excremental gift of her offspring to some degree compared favorably to the bliss and ecstasy of the nursling at the breast.

It is not difficult to discern how humanity strives, first passively in fantasy and then actively, to compulsively recreate a state of timelessness while engaged in the rapture of enthronement on the toilet. In truth, from the standpoint of closely guarded privacy, being at stool for some is more than a match for the ecstatic world of genital sexuality. Saint Augustine observed that although we try to cleanse sexuality as a natural expression of love, it nonetheless retains its private and inhibited sinful image in the mind of man. In the maculacy of one's private bowel evacuations, the secrecy and the inhibition are even greater than in coitus. It is not only natural for children and adults to dine at the same table, it is a cherished form of sociability. Even group sex orgies, although still uncommon in our culture, are for some people quite acceptable. Rarely, however, does one find such communal expression translated into the realm of the excremental, although an exception can be found in the regressive circumstance of wartime, when the dung trench revives the rural "four-holer," and the vulgarities of latrine talk overshadow the ideologies of war.

The secrecy with which the healthy person performs his excremental functions primarily relates to his sense of smell. Even in lower species, the retention of a well-developed sense of smell promotes instinctual aversion reactions to excrement (see Lorenz, 1932, p. 45). In fact, Freud's theory of organic repression drew a direct relationship between man's susceptibility to emotional illness and his diminished sensitivity to smell (see Freud, 1897, p. 269); he compared the stench of one's memory to a stinking object, from both of which the human psyche (like the nose) turns away in repressive disgust. Later (1912), Freud reiterated the conviction that the disappearance of one's coprophilic pleasure in smelling is due to repression. And in *Civilization and Its Discontents* (1930) he observed that man's erect posture represented the beginnings of a cultural evolution, a civilized move toward cleanliness in which anal eroticism becomes organically repressed.

In the dichotomized relationship between excremental functions and sexuality, there is little doubt that, although nature has brought together the anatomy of the two zones (and their functions), the psychological need of man is ordinarily to separate them in the service of his sexual activity. Not that he is completely committed in this regard, as witness some individuals who find considerable pleasure in coprophilia, which apparently heightens rather than diminishes their sexual interest. For most of us, sexual activity is only possible when we have freed ourselves from the undue cathexis of the bowel. From the standpoint of emotional maturation, disgust with excrement reaches its peak with the dissolution of the oedipal complex, when the ego and the superego derived from the internalization of parental images contribute their moral judgmental elements to the coprophilic repressions that are part of the taboos of civilization (Peto, 1973).

Aesthetics and civilization notwithstanding, there are other significant reasons why human beings relegate excremental activity to a status of the unacceptable. The young child does not adopt this attitude from the beginning; in fact, the natural narcissism of the child allows him a serene sense of indulgence in his own bodily products, smelly as they are. Sometimes only reluctantly will he relinquish the creative play with his own excretions. Ultimately he comes up against an anxiety that relates to parental expectations of controls, demands that mark the beginning of his potty training. His world undergoes a transformation in the concept of self, as it did earlier when he first had to acclimatize to the withheld bosom of the mother. Here again we have a case for the struggle with time, yet another rhythmic problem for the child to solve, the rhythm of his bowels. It does not take long for the child to translate this new upheaval in his life to a series of psychological ploys that are precursors of new dimensions of power. The cultural derivatives of the struggle with stool cast a lasting imprint on his later character, whether expressed in the collecting of material possessions, in the passion of creative art, or in the day-to-day struggle for mastery and domination. As often as not, he will retain in adult life some of the more infantile expressions of his anal development, reflected in symptoms or in character traits.

The anal character traits of people enmeshed in a neurotic struggle with their bowels are particularly well documented in the psychoanalytic literature. Jones (1918) had offered a classic study of the anal-erotic character. Reminding us that the eliminative function is the most constant preoccupation of all animals other than man, he emphasized the obvious and significant modelling of our sexual functions on the earlier excretory mold. He properly connected Freud's triad of anal traits (self-willedness, orderliness, and parsimony) with their relationship to conflicts around time (procrastination, slowmindedness, and heaviness of thought), including the fact that anal people are notorious bores. The tendency of the anally disposed to maintain a vigilance over things being taken from them (excrement), harboring as they do a special intolerance for being cheated, is for Jones an expression of their deeper fear of being robbed of time. Indeed, such people are unduly sensitive to being burdened with trivia, imbued as they are with the compulsion to gain mastery over the sense of transience. Jones also described people with protracted interests in their flatus, whether reflecting a passion for propaganda, or for the dissemination of scientific ideas. There is little doubt, the repression of anal smells notwithstanding, that our culture still gives special emphasis to our backsides. Just like in the days of the "old West," we anticipate dire consequences if we make the mistake of "turning our backs"; fresh air from open windows is a menace if we sit with our backs to them; at night, we feel more threatened by someone following us than if we are accosted frontally. This outlook, stamped with its flimsily repressed conditioning from yesteryear, justifies our speaking of an anal group character. The psychoanalyst is no exception, with his special preoccupation with the reverse side of things—a classic derivative of anality. Perhaps even the founder of psychoanalysis was swayed by his anality (in addition to the logic of preventing distraction or affording comfort to his patients) when he chose a therapeutic position to the rear of his patient on the couch. What a provocative position for the patient, reminiscent as it is of the child sitting in the adult's lap! And small wonder that in many analyses, patients bring fantasies of "analytic air-

flight" with the analyst at the controls in the "rear cockpit."
Sometimes they bring fears of being buggered by their
therapist.

Abraham (1921) substantially contributed to the understanding of anal characters. Echoing Sadger's sentiment
(1910) that they are usually convinced they can do things
better than other people in their arrogant assumption
that everyone is dirt except them, Abraham made the
observation that anal people tend to relegate genitality to a
lesser status than the productivity of their bowel functions.
Taking notice of the renifleur, whose facial demeanor
carries the telltale tension of nostril and curled upper lip
that suggests an individual constantly smelling himself,
Abraham, like Freud, was impressed with a constitutional
factor in anality, which would explain why an entire family
often carries the stamp of this particular characteristic.

By far Abraham's most important contribution to
understanding anality was the parallel he drew in 1924
between oral character traits and their extension into the
anal phase, the origins of which are manifestly connected
with libido that was centered in infancy around the mouth
before becoming faithfully translated into the functions of
the bowel. Abraham suggested a kind of migration of
pleasure at work, where conflict from the sucking and
weaning spilled over to the muscle action of the anus, as the
anatomical arena for sucking and holding became shifted to
its new site. The sucking lips became the model for the
withholding anus, and the possessed oral object later
became the withheld stool. In Abraham's terms, the clinical
traits identified with the anal character are built on the
ruins of an oral erotism that has miscarried. The pleasure in
acquiring objects becomes repressed in favor of holding fast
to objects already acquired, as extra vigilance is mobilized
against losing the smallest part of such possessions.

The sundry neurotic and often health jeopardizing complexes that emerge from the anal period of development, blended as they are with residues of oral conflict, are well known to psychologists. Closely allied with the respiratory incorporations that commonly occur in fetishism, certain asthmatic conditions, especially those compounded by hereditary predisposition, carry ominous implications for the therapeutic task. One severe asthmatic manifested the nature of his conflict in his predilection for smelling toilet bowls immediately following their usage by his mother; his symptom persisted from childhood into his adult years. So symbiotically attached did he become through this vehicle of reunion (the bowl) that the overly punitive efforts of his father to disengage him from this preoccupation would invariably lead to severe asthmatic episodes (a symbolic castration, loss of the mother). Some attacks were characterized by a menacing exudation of fluid into the patient's lungs. A hobby in his adult life took the bizarre form of hunting rats in the cellar with a rifle; the patient even fashioned a ratskin jacket, which he likened to his mother's fur coat, against which he would nuzzle as a lonely infant. This "rat-man" had a hyperacuity for sounds emanating from a toilet anywhere, his "antennae" picking up the sound of a toilet flushing from remarkable distances. Indeed, the splashings and the piddlings of a woman on the toilet gave him the serenity and comfort that music lovers derive from listening to a symphony by Brahms.

Today's society pays an inordinate degree of attention to toiletries devised to alter the smells of our bodies. There appears to be a greater emphasis on aesthetics than on our health care. Commercial advertising tells us about deodorants and smell guards which afford us greater "protection" from our perspiring bodies than we enjoy from the dangers of disease or war. Though our lungs may be jeopardized by industrial pollution, we can rest comfortably in the knowledge that we are "safe" from smelly armpits. However,

man's disgust with bad odors, and the strenuous prophy-
lactic measures instituted against them, by no means cut
down our cathexis of their source—the bowel. Seldom do
we acknowledge the staggering amount of time spent one
way or another on our bowels. When we remember, however, that the child enlarges his imaginative world of
mental representations by "eating people" so to speak,
eventually incorporating all the various qualities into what
becomes the self, then it is indeed not so incomprehensible
why we should continue, even as adults, to pay attention to
one of the visibly tangible means we have for "taking roll-
call" on the people we have chosen to assimilate into our
bowels. In examining our stools we keep abreast of our
world of values, of aesthetics, and of ideologies. Novelists
have written on the significance that people attach to their
bowels for taking stock or inventory; for example, Jonathan
Swift (1726), whose Gulliver so colorfully explores this
human preoccupation. (The striking anality of Swift
himself is studied by Greenacre, 1955).

There are the chronically depressed who judge their
economic life by the impoverishment of their stools rather
than by their bank account, and tycoons who can tell when
they are about to be successful in a business deal by the
enormous stools they suddenly produce. Many people treat
their bowels like an accountant listing income and expenditure. Writers and novelists seem especially prone to bowel
symptoms, to "intestines loaded with creativity"; they
compare their sensations to having a baby. And there are
people again with a disorganized sense of self who suffer the
incapacity for passing a formed stool, a psychosomatic
symptom often associated with a profound disturbance in
internalization. There is also a bowel language, which is a
part of our everyday lives. Feeling low in self-regard, we
feel like "a shit"; a bad person is a "stinker"; an illegitimate
business deal is "smelly." We should be grateful to mar-

riage, if only for its capacity to legitimize our anality. In courtship the sound of flatus is a matter to be handled with shy reserve; after the honeymoon is over, it is often the only mode of communication.

The relationship between anality and sex is one of the agonies of the human condition, approximated as the anatomies of these two functions are in a grim joke that God or nature has seen fit to play on mankind. Whether this explains the intricate merging of the instincts of Eros and aggression is not easy to say, but it is uncontroversial that sex invariably becomes colored with aggression, just as aggression is usually diluted by sexuality. Earlier I made reference to the significance of the primal scene, which psychologists have emphasized as an important constellation in the development of neuroses. Ordinarily we relate the child's curiosity as to what goes on in the parental bedroom to his or her exposure to reproduction and coitus, and the resultant trauma to childhood idealizations of parental immaculacy. The disenchantment that causes the child to recoil and to compensate with aristocratic adoptive figures who have retained the immaculate imagery of the child's first heroes (his parents) is put down by many psychologists to a disgust with genitality. However, one can easily neglect a counterpoint in this disenchantment: the toilet, or its euphemisms bathroom or powder room, is also of primal significance. Just as the child recoils from overhearing the noises of parental coitus, so does he ordinarily deplore any exposure to the sounds of parental toilet droppings. Both excremental and sexual functions are definitely unacceptable to the ego of the child at one point in his development. No wonder that in evolving his family romance, the child shifts to aristocratic substitutes whose qualifications include, among others, immaculacy not only in sex, but in bowel habits as well. A tall order indeed, one might logically protest, but it appears that children find it

most difficult to acknowledge as heroes or heroines any who
exercise their genitals, their bowels, or both. The British
commoner is no more enthralled with the idea of the Queen
sitting on the toilet, than the average American is contem-
plating the President; such is the nature of the family
romance. The point here is that witnessing parental intercourse or suffering the pangs of jealousy at the birth of a
sibling rival are by no means the only natural traumatic
experiences of childhood. For years, psychological therapy
has been geared to give special attention to the primal
scene; then there was the introduction of the therapeutic
primal scream; surely someone could make a case for the
primal poop.

The human agony in surmounting the anal aspects of
life is especially heightened in those who, for one reason or
another, have retained a psychological connection between
their excrement and death. There are adults as well as
children who suffer from phobias surrounding their anal
activity; fear of losing their stool is one such phobia, felt not
only as a loss of power, but as a kind of dying. To mind
comes a novelist I treated who was particularly inhibited in
writing on the subject that interested him the most, namely
his bowels. He was fearful that by acknowledging his excrement, he would jeopardize the completion of his works,
which would go down the drain along with his anal
products. In this he is like the child who, on first discovering the fate of his stool (flushed), develops the fear (often
nocturnal) of falling bodily into a watery annihilation.

Freud (1923) originally conceived the fear of death as
related either to castration anxiety or to fear of losing the
love object; he maintained that the operative model for
such a fear was the child's experience of losing either the
contents of his bowel or his mother's breast. He rejected the
more popular view that the fear of death stems from a fear
of real annihilative traumata coming from the outside

world. Ultimately, when he perceived how the ego could become hated by the superego, he also came to equate the fear of death with a fear of conscience. Where Lewin (1950) emphasized the oral aspects of the fear of death, Brodsky (1959) highlighted the anal component in the idea that the memory traces of self-image extinction laid down in one's early childhood become merged with the psychic representation of discarded stool. Brodsky proposed that various childhood experiences leave memory traces of self-extinction, something easily accomplished in the fragile ego of the child who, in the face of loss of breast and stool, becomes subsequently dependent on muscular body ego for an assurance of the sense of self. Brodsky hypothesized that the blurrings of self-image from such losses reduce the cathexis of the child's muscular body ego in promoting the fear of dying. He cited Greenacre's (1952) observation that for the child, the stool is the very opposite to the lively, self-moving penis—in effect, something dead. In comparing castration to loss of stools, the similarity found between stools and death on the one hand and between moving penis and life on the other is what leads to the child's rumination upon life and death. Brodsky became convinced that the fear of death was associated with the child's unconscious fantasy of being turned into a stool (one of Lilli's unconscious fears for the fate of her pregnancies).

None of these authors particularly emphasized the significance of the mother in the equation of stools with death. In fact Heimann (1962) expresses the sentiment that the mother's role in the child's anal functions is completely dispensable, in that the child experiences no relationship whatsoever with the maternal object through his anal organ. Heimann also feels that the child holds his excrement in little regard, perceiving it as indeed valueless. I cannot agree with these views; to the contrary, I feel that next to the nursing experience, the mother plays the most signifi-

cant role during the period of toilet training. My reasoning
is based on my earlier expressed views of the transitional
process, in which the child not only values and cherishes his
anal product, but sometimes almost as much as he values
himself. This is simply because the child's stool comes to
stand for his first two objects—his own self (his mother's
baby) and his mother's extruded milk products (his baby).
If we then make the equation between feeding mother and
child's stool, it follows that the child's first fears of dying are
triggered by the separation of the stool, a loss which in turn
stands for the loss of a loved object (a milk-replication of self
and mother) which has been transformed into stool within
the child's body. The fear must go hand in hand with a
phase of incorporative, assimilative, and self-replicative
activity that first acknowledges the equation of absent milk
with an absence of a product with which to replenish the
loss of the stool (dying).

Heimann's emphasis on the importance of the anal
period in the development of mastery and the sense of will is
easier to support. The capacity for establishing sphincter
control as well as other forms of ego autonomy, has long
since been treated in the literature. There is a multitude of
phobias that have to do with loss of control over bowel.
Even adults carry residues of these struggles from their
childhood. Urination, too, becomes intricately bound up
with the whole process, and although urination might be a
more socially acceptable vehicle for expressing a passion for
mastery, situated as the urethra is near the sexual tract, it,
too, brings stigma and shame when control fails.

Just as the protective shield of the maternal figure plays
a significant part in the development of the child's early
sense of safety from internal and external stimuli, so does
the mother also become important in safeguarding the
child's developing need to assume control over his sphincter
functions and to employ them in an appropriate adaptation

to his environment. Failure of the mother's proper under-standing of her role during the toilet-training period can often lead to serious complications in a child's subsequent development; reactions ranging from infantile defiance to overcompliance can hinder the child's later bid for auton-omy. His battle of the will, developing as it does in the anal-urethral phase, ultimately becomes linked with sexuality. As Erikson (1962) points out, ego strength is intricately bound up with the establishing of something more than simply a reality concept of the world. The actuality of proving or disproving the trustworthiness of parental pro-tection gives meaning to the otherwise trite phrase, basic trust. Erikson quotes a teacher who observed that children who feel loved become more beautiful, making the point that this love cannot be found passively, but only by actualization. This has to include the mother's role in supporting the child's mastery of his excretory functions. Erikson describes an ego actuality as something achieved by an active ego even when one is asleep, where dreaming is more than a passive wish fulfillment, in truth, a process that restores initiative in those who search, on awakening, for the means of sharing their actuality with others.

Any discussion of the functions of the bowel that over-looks the symbolic meaning of the stool contained in the bowel, while accentuating the ego development of the sense of will and mastery, begs a major issue. Bowel functions are irrevocably linked with the theme of the struggle with time and timelessness, which we know is the struggle with possession of the primal object, the mother. I have already contended that the stool itself (transformed milk) becomes one of the first part-object representations of the incor-porated, assimilated, and accommodated mother image; its loss must, therefore, represent a serious threat to the child's self-representation. It behooves us to attend to yet another foible of man, where, in his struggle for timelessness, he makes strenuous efforts to block his observations of his bowel function in a failing effort to retrieve that period of life antedating the establishment of a sense of self. In line with Fliess's suggestion in his concept of time, such a blockage of self-observation, partial though it may be at the anal level, nonetheless represents another attempt at assassinating time. One might theorize, then, that the struggle of man to transcend the anal period of development in a thrust toward genitality is energized not only by the elemental force of individuation and the compulsion toward a biological procreation of the species, but by a force in the opposite direction, a passion which, when aided by a blockage of self-observation with respect to one's excremental functions, is in the service of re-establishing a timeless coalescence with the maternal breast.

Tarachow (1966) cited clinical cases, one involving a patient's masochistic fantasy of being prevented from evacuating his bowels and bladder, and another in which ideas of "eternity" were linked up with the desire to indefinitely postpone bowel movements. Tarachow drew definite connections between time and stools, observing that even the nuances of language may derive from flatus and stool. He compared obsessively monotonous speech to a bowel movement without the activity of the subject and without the sphincter action that segments the stool; he suggested that time limits for some could be seen as the command to defecate, whereas the feeling of the stoppage of time could be equated with the postponement of a movement. Obsessive procrastination, suggested Tarachow, stemmed from the struggle against giving up the stool, while rumination was a matter of playing with one's stool.

For Tarachow, a person's stool represented a parent in part-object fashion, an object relationship of fetishistic quality. He observed that because there were two models of object relations, the separation from the mother's breast and the separation from the excreted stool, then one might regard mouth experiences as repeated motions of restoring one's lost infantile narcissism, in contrast to anal experiences, which are forever going through the repetition of losing something. Tarachow perceived the anus as the organ of loss, depression, and rage, and the mouth as the organ of repeated repair. He, too, saw the stool and the transitional doll as related, the doll serving the illusion that a part of one's body has not been lost. Through the doll as transitional object, the child reunites with her stool, which, for Tarachow, is the child's way of achieving independence from external objects. Perhaps Tarachow overlooked one fact, that the formation of the child's stools are indeed dependent on a steady supply of nutrition (milk).

In Lilli's analysis I had to bear in mind that the anal phase often becomes an important stage for the enactment of developmental complexes ordinarily attached to other stages of psychological development (Heimann, 1962). I agreed with Heimann that, logically, there could be an anal version of the Oedipus complex. For many people, moving their bowels certainly becomes a major sexual or aggressive experience in which a host of images can be conjured up in the reactivation of conflicts that have neither been solved at the oral phase nor evolved to the genital level. For some, sitting at stool represents an elaborate exercise in power, indeed in warfare and heroics. To mind comes one individual who in anal fantasy fought his way through the entirety of the Vietnam war (including the "final negotiations for surrender") while sitting on a toilet in Toronto; he would play out both sides in his "war-games," first employing "conventional weapons" and then, in moments of crisis, going all out with "nuclear warheads." On the occasions when this young man experienced loose stools (which he often did), he would grimly resort to "napalm" in a "wanton attack on civilians."

In the last analysis, my excursions into the excremental failed to support a premise that there was a direct anal road to timelessness, and I concluded that more derivative anal expressions were a more likely prerequisite. The treadmill elements of Lilli's sadomasochism hardly qualified in this category; the resistance she mobilized against progress was similar in quality to her fight against deeper regression. Either way her unusual sense of will was involved, the kind of resolve that becomes mobilized in all of us when signals first initiated in stomach and bowel trigger our lifelong battle with timing and time.

The Transcendence of Time

Neither Lilli's early familial exposure to religion nor her grandmother's later influence managed to provide the kind of solace that religion has offered to man in his quest for a state of timelessness. Perhaps religious systems are the most universally shared expressions of man's many efforts to transcend his sense of transience; although it is not my intent to elaborate on them here, they have to be included among the ego's most important constructs in dealing with time. In regression the ego's boundaries are prone to dissolving into the relatively undifferentiated timelessness of oceanic feelings or mystical states, whether associated with sexual expression or the use of chemicals; a similar result is often accomplished through the ecstasy of religious experience. Fraser (1975) postulates the operation of an instinctual drive in the achievement of these states, in which one experiences a sense of some overwhelming unintelligible power. He cites Brandon's (1966) view of religion as the expression of man's instinctive defense against the consciousness of time, although for Fraser religion is an acknowledgment of the heavenly beatitudes, a function of the higher levels of temporality in the realization that symbols outlast the individual.

The Freudian position explains man's universal need for God, as derived from the relationship of the child to the father, in keeping with "the great man" thesis (Freud, 1913). Originating in the ambivalence of humanity toward the primal father, expressed in his murder and subsequent deification (submission to authority), religion for Freud was conceptualized as a compulsive outgrowth of man's helplessness in his quest for an illusory rescuing father (Freud, 1927a). Mann (1964) reports on a panel of psychoanalytic thinkers trying to explore the psychology of religion: Serota, for one, defines religious belief as an externalization of the internalized father via the formation of illusion, perceiving religion as a respite from guilt, tension, and aggression against the self, and as a means of effecting a restoration of the harmony between self and self-ideal. According to Serota, the process promotes transcendent images through efforts at living up to higher ideals. For Mann, the excessive idealizations of religion are but the reflections of a need for greater reassurance in the face of unresolved ambivalence. By externalizing superego onto a deity and by assuring a permanence of idealization, religion offers a constant harness for the aggressive component of the ambivalence; by contrast, the non-religious individual externalizes his aggression onto living objects, placing himself as a result in greater danger of object loss. As an antidote for helplessness, however, Mann perceives religion as a failure, in the long run, no more comforting in the search for truth than reality testing. According to Ross, most religious phenomena originate from a fear of object loss and from the need for immortality, insofar as loving a viable object involves greater risk than loving a perfect god. In Ross's view, the mystical experience, an overwhelming conviction of contact with an external divinity (the noetic experience), reflects the desperation in mankind's need to love such a perfect object. Tarachow, by contrast,

perceives religion as prompted by fear of loss of ego boundaries, and although he concedes that the aggression stemming from man's ambivalence is unresolved by religion, he
is doubtful (as I am) that man is sufficiently rational as yet
to profit from disbelief in religion.

In Lilli's case her camp experiences were too overpowering for her to find succor in religious belief; she was
unable to convince herself that God would have allowed
the human bestiality to which she was witness. There are
psychoanalysts who perhaps would offer a deeper explanation for Lilli's impoverishment of religious faith. For
Klauber (1974), faith is not a belief in religious myth, but
rather the consciousness of a force within that ensures that
the individual will withstand traumatic instinctual frustrations and tensions within the ego without recourse to
murderous attack upon that ego by the superego. In effect,
Klauber's faith is in the indestructibility of those good
internalized objects that afford the child the conviction that
all dangers are illusory. Klauber's view may explain how so
many found it possible to walk into gas chambers with a
prayer on their lips and with faith in God. Malev (1974)
believes that in certain critical situations, only by regression
to some faith can there be hope. He reminds us, however,
that the state to which one regresses is by no means identical
to the one left behind, since in every regression one carries
elements of the stage already attained. Although passivity
may mark the regression, fate becomes transformed into an
old prototypical object—the benevolent parent internalized
in childhood and projected outwardly in time of crisis as an
illusion of Divine protection against misfortune and death.

Perhaps the attitude toward religion on the part of the
sick and the dying affords an alternate to Malev's viewpoint. Many people afflicted with serious or fatal disease
have in their last hours bitterly lambasted their god! Blas-
phemous and irreverent as their invective might be, it

tragically captures the awesome mixture of aggression, love, and fear; although religiosity and irreligiosity are both often expressed in such railings, there is hope along with despair—a paradoxical undercurrent of an inchoate immortality of the spirit mingled with a mortality of the flesh. In the dying, not only is there visible evidence of the ebbing of life forces, but often displacement of aggressions inherent in the early ambivalent attitudes of the child toward a parent, now externalized onto an outer cosmic force. In addition to the faulting of God, there is an implicit acrimony against the parent who was unable to protect the offspring against the forces of nature or disease. The bitterness of some who lie dying, though apparently an expression of defeat, may in fact reflect the triumph of creativeness over the passive repetition compulsion, a more creative compulsion wherein the enemy called aging or disease becomes personified as God or as a parent against whom one can actively aggress. Indeed, one could propose that for some, both God and the father are personified substitutes for Time—the original unpersonified cosmic intruder between the infant and its mother.

THE CREATIVE ARTIST

A concept to be pursued toward the understanding of the arsenal of implements available in promoting a sense of timelessness is the secondary stimulus barrier (*Reizschutz*). Because *Reizschutz* by all logic bears a significant part of the burden of adapting to psychic trauma, I found it helpful to review the manner in which the intricate shift of accent (or cathexis) transpires within this barrier to offer a possible respite from trauma. I was, of course, aware that Lilli had scant opportunity for exploring the avenues of artistic creativity that some of the more gifted inmates found at their disposal; nonetheless I felt that a deeper comprehension of the *modus operandi* of *Reizschutz* might open up potential alternatives for Lilli's road to recovery. For example, I was aware that a love of music in her childhood had been particularly supported by her grandmother.

In his foresight, Freud (1915a) rather cryptically pointed a finger toward *Reizschutz*, or secondary stimulus barrier, as crucial to the theme of transformation. He described it as an outer protective shield which defended against traumatic stimuli coming from the external environment and offered even more important protection to the psyche than the perceptual apparati lodged behind that shield. He suggested in 1920 that the stimulus barrier in the case of the time experience was different from the one through which other stimuli permeated in order to reach perception. Further he saw this defensive barrier as supplied with its own cathexes, and enjoying a special capacity for transforming such cathexes in the face of external dangers. He felt that only via projection did the shield act as a last line of defense against internal reactions to trauma. Ultimately Freud (1940) came to view this stimulus barrier as a precursor of the ego, deriving his conceptualization from the principle of constancy (nirvana), the striving of the organism to keep stimulation at a minimum. He visualized a topography for *Reizschutz* that followed the development of the structures of the brain, perceiving an outer inorganic coat that was resistant to external stimuli and that eventually was drawn into the interior of the mind. Whereas he had earlier perceived the barrier as being capable of protecting the psyche only from outside stimuli, he eventually allowed himself to entertain the possibility that it could deal with instinctual drives as well.

Contemporary psychoanalysts have come to consider *Reizschutz* as synonymous with ego, vulnerable to prolonged pressure that in undramatic ways can promote its breakdown. Anna Freud (1967) offered birth, loss of an object, and loss of love as stimuli capable of traumatizing the barrier, an inventory in which Fenichel (1945) had already included the primal scene, birth of a sibling, instinctual damming, and early physical illness. Engel (1962) emphasized the passion involved in bolstering a vulnerable *Reizschutz*, observing that under conditions of external stress, even object cathexes became temporarily relinquished in the service of propping the barrier. Winnicott's (1963) holding-environment introduced the importance of the mother's role of auxiliary protection; inadequate mothering, he warned, allowed too many impingements to reach the child during infancy, thereby facilitating impairment of the child's development. He elaborated the significance of the holding environment in the development of the transitional process, including creative artistic adaptations. Keiser (1967) proposed that *Reizschutz* underwent changes during life, enjoying various degrees of effectiveness in the engagement of dangerous stimuli at different periods of development. He cautioned that an apparently benign incident for one individual could be traumatic to another, depending on the unconscious representation of the event and whether it was symbolically charged. Most significantly, he suggested that the loss of one function of *Reizschutz* might be compensated for by an alteration in others. Gediman (1971) perceives such a compensatory shift of attention as a mean of lessening the vulnerability of a *Reizschutz* menaced by other threatening stimuli, as, for example, in youth's quest for excitement. Gediman observes that either a particularly impermeable or a particularly permeable quality to the *Reizschutz* is an outstanding character trait in some people; the threshold for tolerating traumatic stimuli may be excessively high or low as the case may be, an exaggeration in some adults that is derived from their infancy.

A transformation or a shift of cathexis within the

stimulus barrier becomes plausible when one investigates certain aspects of the creative process. Earlier, Bergman and Escalona (1949) theorized that it was the variations in the artistic child's sensitivity to sounds that promoted special sensory endowments. To these authors, a thin stimulus barrier could pave the way to a constitutional gift of artistry, in which from initially bad stimuli the artist procured good stimuli for his own protection. Bergman and Escalona felt that only the child who suffered from noise was likely to become a good musician, and they extended this to artistic endowment in general. But they elaborated very little on the actual mechanisms involved in producing such a thin stimulus barrier and its subsequent compensatory devices. Certainly music and rhythm have always served those in search of timelessness. One's personal and idiosyncratic relationship to rhythm may well have its origins in the intrauterine environment of the fetus, as well as in the post-natal holding environment of the infant. Some children show early disturbances related to this holding environment, including the rocking of infancy. The literature reveals that such rocking commonly occurs in children of mothers who failed to provide an average expectable environment. In conjunction with Wolf, Spitz (1949) classified rocking as one of the autoerotic activities of children who have not enjoyed a particularly well-balanced relationship with their mothers. Spitz found such parents to be extroverted and impulse ridden, having a heavy hand in promoting social maladaptation in their children from earliest years. He described rocking children as engaged in autistic, objectless activity dominated by primary process and motivated toward the promotion of wild orgiastic discharge.

Tracing the dance to the autoerotic rocking of infancy hardly identifies the element of timelessness. The underlying basis of the dance has to go beyond rocking to a prenatal rhythm, to the carrying mother's body. It is not difficult to relate the early kinesthetic orientation of the fetus as it rests in the undulating uterus of the mother to the earliest imprints of what might be called "body time." I suggest that dancing is a derivative expression of this early maternal rhythmicity, a model that might cast some light on man's proclivity for surrendering to the timelessness of Terpsichore. Mooney (1968) even ascribes the peculiar gait of the composer Mahler to a prenatal kinesthetic identification with his lame mother.

Mittelmann (1954) prefers to trace rhythmic imprints to the manner in which the postnatal child is carried. In Western cultures, he observes, swaddling is prevalent, whereas in non-Western cultures, where crawling is discouraged, the cradleboard is substituted. He contends that restrictions in the infant's mobility resulting from close contact with the mother—as, for example when the child is strapped to the parent's back—have a later psychological relationship to rocking. Certainly the manner in which a mother embraces her child after birth (the holding environment) is a significant determinant of the child's later orientation to its motor apparatus, not only in relation to infantile rocking, but to subsequent aptitudes for the dance. The kind of solo dancing that society encourages in our youth today might well, with a stretch of the imagination, reflect a distancing in child rearing on the part of our present generation of mothers, perhaps promoted in part by liberation movements. If this be true, then one might expect that the pendular rhythms of hammocks and swings will more and more substitute for the holding mother in our liberated times.

On the relationship between creativity and time, Freud (1908) perceived that the artist's perceptions of time and the manner in which his imagination became enlisted in his

search for timelessness significantly determined the quality
of his art. Listing his ingredients of creative art, Freud
(1917) included a richness in daydreams along with an.
expurgation of the personal elements by toning and con-
cealing their origins. The *ars poetica* offered a yield in
pleasure commensurate with the lifting of the repressions. I
suspect that Freud's (1928) oft quoted maxim that the
endowment of creative artists is not analyzable has only
served as a challenge to prove him wrong. Particularly in
current times, psychoanalysts have plied their analytic
knowledge toward an ever deeper involvement in the
creativity of the artist. Greenacre (1957) speaks of an
empathic animation of the inanimate, combined with an
anthropomorphizing of nonhuman creatures, capacities
ordinarily lost in childhood, yet retained in the gifted.
Greenacre means gifted in the literal sense, since she is
convinced that the genius of artistry is God-given, although
it may be augmented by identification with a godlike
father. Greenacre's concept of the gifted child includes an
intense relation to the mother's breast in terms of warmth
and smell and touch. Not only are primary objects richly
invested, but there is a greater field of related experiences
than in those less endowed. Greenacre refers to these
experiences as *collective alternates*, forerunners of the
created objects that reflect the artist's love affair with the
world. Such experiences include awe of phallic tumescence
and of pregnancy, a capacity for bisexuality, and a particular fluidity of libido.

Greenacre (1960) explains women's limitations in
creativity on the basis of their traditional absorption in
biological procreativity. A lack of capacity for externalization related to the anatomical fact of recessed genitalia is as
inhibiting of creativity as the neurotic interferences stemming from female attitudes toward anality (the tendency to
identify vagina as anus). According to Greenacre, the

superimposed difficulties in achieving the bisexual balance necessary for creative work, perhaps out of fear of promoting flagrant imagery of the illusory phallus, has often led to chaotic reactions in women who particularly aspire to creativity. Greenacre (1964) emphasizes the importance of increased phallic pressures in promoting artistic thrust, pressures that are operative in artists absorbed in oedipal conflict and in efforts at outgrowing their family romance. Such people, she feels, have experienced unique disturbances in their sense of identity and of reality; their special ability for splitting, as manifested in the multiple characters they create in their art form, stems from narcissistic defects similar to those found in fetishists and addicts.

Felix Deutsch (1959) sees the creative artist as enjoying a perceptual exclusiveness from infancy, a development that unconditionally forces an autogamous synthesis of his feminine and masculine wishes. For Deutsch, the qualities of genius are not inborn, the trigger for the passion being either the loss of an object or damage to the body ego or to a sensory modality. The loss calls on the ego to make good for the narcissistic injury (felt as a loss of the self) through the regressive activation of a repetition compulsion wherein the artist creates himself in a transitional art form which carries an aura of suspended time.

Weissman (1971), like Greenacre, sees the forerunners of the creative process making their appearance in the latter part of the first year of life, initially in the form of transitional objects and then as collective alternates. Their development is spurred when the sense of reality first challenges the infant's illusions, thereby triggering the ego to develop its own imaginary objects for retaining those original illusions. Weissman agrees with Greenacre that potential creativeness lies in the capacity to elaborate transitional objects into collective alternates, and he suggests that the extension of mouthed external objects to nonmouthed peripheral ones is involved in this creative sublimation. Rather than being relegated to limbo like transitional objects, collective alternates persist through the lifetime of the gifted person's creative activity because of the underlying process that generates them. Mechanistically, Weissman proposes that in creativity there is a transient alteration in the state of the ego, a dissociation that desynthesizes an existing phase of development for its replacement by the next phase.

Niederland (1975, 1976) particularly emphasizes physical deformities that give thrust to the artist's search for repair. He cites the facial disfigurements of Jacques Louis David and Michelangelo, which he sees as partly responsible for their artistic passion for saving face. Unequivocally insisting that he has never seen a creative individual who did not have a serious and all-pervasive emotional conflict, Niederland lists as ingredients for creativity early history of trauma, feelings of bodily ugliness, loneliness, and easily excitable curiosity linked with unconscious birth fantasies, along with feelings of incompleteness and of physical frailty, real or imagined. The core of Niederland's concept of artistic passion is the thrust toward rebirth and perfection, where a defective self-representation demands intrapsychic completion in an unconscious recasting of the body ego.

The enthusiasm of some psychoanalysts for analyzing certain classic works of art, as well as the lives of their creators, has to do, I am sure, with the model set by Freud for this type of exercise. Recently, people like Heiman (1976) and Simon (1977) have offered analytic interpretations of creative artists, particularly those who have committed suicide. Such retrospective efforts to find prophetic indicators of the dire fate that awaited these artists must, of course, carry a strong speculative flavor at best. Van Gogh's *Crows Over the Wheat Field,* a painting interpreted as the artist's suicide note, is to Heiman a portrait of time and space meeting at the crossroads of oblivion. In a more modest presentation, Simon attempts to identify an artist's suicidal violence by appraising the movement in his art; she relates this in turn to the trauma of that artist's repeated exposures to the primal scene.

I believe there are two interconnected motives in creativity, the restitution of the lost object and the transformation of the self. I regard the work of art as the artist's efforts at self-replication synthetically interwoven with his symbolization of a redeemed object. The processes that lift this product above and beyond the level of infantile forerunners to creativity include the deployment of the artist's aggression in the service of dismantling his objects and toward a heightening of specific sensory components emanating from these objects (a form of caricature). Touched by the artist's giftedness, whether naturally endowed or learned, and processed by an ego engaged in sophisticated secondary revision, the resultant art is a pleasurable and aesthetic reward to both artist and his receptive audience. An aspect of the mechanics of this process is the artist's manipulation of narcissistic cathexes, which permits a recapturing of illusions derived from the transitional period, heightening the suspension of disbelief and promoting an economy that yields an extra bonus in pleasure. Not surprisingly, high on the list of rewarded products are those that provide an illusion of suspended time.

Whereas Winnicott and Greenacre suggest that highly intense and satisfying mother-child dyads make for a favorable climate for creativity, my own findings are more in line with those of Deutsch and Niederland, that severe narcissistic traumata are involved, related to an infantile impoverishment resulting from lack of good mothering, which produced an extremely fragile secondary stimulus barrier vulnerable to exquisite feelings of damage and self-devaluation. The hypertrophy of sensory modalities not ordinarily accentuated in the average individual gives further thrust to the artist's efforts at transforming his damaged sense of self, thereby restoring himself. Indeed, the capacity of the artist to validate something he considers unsanctionable, to give life, so to speak, to that which is ordinarily associated with death—that is a special gift of the creative artist. Many of the creative individuals whom I have treated suffered periodic bouts of depersonalization in which they felt lifeless, like excrement. What better support for an illusion of immortality than through the artist's salvage of excrement!

Weissman postulates a dissociative or desynthesizing mechanism of the ego, one that allows a transformation of the infantile illusion of the maternal breast into the transitional object. Such a mechanism, he points out, stands in opposition to Kris's (1938) concept of regression in the service of the ego. Weissman comments that in the less creative, where there is a failure to retain the illusion of the maternal breast, a fetishistic delusion of the maternal phallus is an alternate outcome. Weissman's (and Greenacre's) model for creativity is like that of the explorer in outer space or the scuba diver in the deep seas. Their capacities for exploration rest on their maintenance of a fundamental security that offers a flexibility for research; this emotional home base begins and ends with the primal object. By contrast, my model for the thrust of the creative artist has him burdened from the outset with a loosening of his moorings (from the primal object), in itself the primal trauma that invokes the artist's compulsive self-replicative reactions aimed at reinstating the primal binding. Hence I would define the prelude to creativity as the *anchorless* phase, one that demands a search for binding; one might compare it to the lost astronaut's attempts to establish a lifeline to his command module. I see the artist, in his attempt to secure himself, exploring and cathecting more peripheral objects and ideas (Greenacre's collective alternates).

The singular element of creativity, in my view, involves a mandatory rather than an optional *peripheral cathexis;* the artist has no other choice if he is to reinstate the lost object. Perhaps the most striking peripheral cathexis involves the artist's anality. Weissman refers to Greenacre's collective alternates as nonmouthed; Greenacre's gifted child is able to sublimate playing with excrement by finding substitutes; Niederland speaks of the creative artist's sense of ugliness of the self. Even Freud makes more than casual mention of the artist's obligation to hide the "repugnant" aspects of his personal world in order to achieve an aesthetic validity. I suggest it is *the artist's excrement, specifically its psychological derivatives, that plays a crucial role in the transformation of his creativity.* The stool, however, is ordinarily an extension of the self; to become a created object, a work of art, it must in some way become modified by the artist in order to no longer appear a derivative of that self. Vital to the transaction is the disengagement of the anal components of the art from the person of the artist. I suggest that to accomplish this, the stool is neither abandoned, left unmourned, or relegated to limbo, as the child abandons his first transitional objects, nor retained (in the form of a substitute) and used for sexual activity, as does the fetishist; rather, the stool is "brought to life" by the creative artist, not as a part of the self (something aesthetically unacceptable), but as the symbol of a mourned and now resurrected external object. Thus, the art product succeeds in displaying the object libido of the artist to advantage over his narcissistic self-cathexis; and in demonstrating the artist's renunciation of narcissistic aggressions, it captures the agony as well as the ecstasy of the art work.

Once a creative artist becomes successfully established in his field, he is thenceforth no longer burdened with having his art meticulously examined for public acceptance; the artist's signature alone, whether it be a doodle on a dinner napkin or a crayon sketch on a shirt cuff, is in itself sufficient to warrant a public acclaim. The explanation for this symbolization lies in the ultimate fate of the art, that of being dissociated from the artist. As Weissman has pointed out, the created object, unlike the creative process generating it, can under certain conditions be relegated to limbo, not only in the mind of the artist, but in the mind of the approving public. The stamp of greatness shifts from product to process, as symbolized by the artist's signature. The respect this insignia receives is commensurate with the homage society offers to those who have the artistic capacity to resurrect the dead and thereby earn a symbolic immortality.

To summarize, although I believe that creativity begins in the transitional period of infancy, it involves the later developing capacity for investing inanimate waste (excrement) with object libido (liveliness) towards the creation of a work of art that symbolizes the resurrection of a lost and mourned object. The response that such resurrection finds in a collective audience reflects society's passion for embracing this particular mode of expressing a transcendence of time.

THE COMEDIAN

When it comes to gleaning further evidence of the psyche's transformatory ability, the phenomenon of humor stands high on my list of such metapsychological processes, shedding further light on the compensating potential of *Reizschutz*. Since Freud (1905a, 1927b) comprehensively examined the process of humor, I thought something might be gained from exploring certain developmental aspects of individuals who are particularly prone to provoking it. Despite Freud's distinction between comedy and humor, the comedian might well be described as a humorist—indeed, a creative artist of sorts. Having had the opportunity to study several individuals who made comedy their profession, I did find one developmental denominator common to these individuals; part of their infantile "machinery" was experienced by them as malfunctioning from their earliest years right on through adulthood. They suffered an early deprivation of some crucial aspect of the maternal protection that psychoanalysts now refer to as the holding environment, which strengthens the infant's early reactions to otherwise disturbing stimuli.

According to Winnicott, the transitional process is encouraged and fostered by the responsive and protective good mother. Yet paradoxically, the comedians whom I investigated were exposed to potentially traumatic stimuli by relatively unprotecting and naive mothers, although there was no active discouragement of the animistic illusions on which so many children thrive in their early transitional period. Again, unlike the unquestioning trust of the secure child, these comics, as they grew older, without exception actively researched their simple and unprotecting mothers, worried lest they find that they were callously deprived of mothering or that mothering had been selfishly withheld (a potentially disastrous discovery). Their search, wherein they compared other children's relationships to their mothers, produced little evidence that any gift of some special powers had been held back. As in the case of Deutsch's handicapped or loss-burdened creative artists, where grief triggers an infantile process of mourning and restitution, so did these (future) comedians try to compensate for their loss (defective shield) by a hypertrophy of whatever adaptive and creative mechanisms they could mobilize. Unable to redeem the maternal shield through internalization, the comedians of whom I speak resorted unwittingly to *contriving their self-made Reizschutz*, a kaleidoscope of assimilated part-objects that substituted as a rudimentary superego. Their vigilant eye and ear for mimicry, a compensatory talent that afforded them a precocious image of a comical and imposturing quality, was described by Freud as the child presenting himself as a serious adult. In later life, this hoaxlike element became disguised by diverting the attention of their audience, a dazzle technique similar to the sleight-of-hand employed by the magician.

By juxtaposing Freud's metapsychology of the phenomenon of humor with the development (or rather maldevelopment) of the individual who inspires it, further clarity as to the psychology of the phenomenon can be gained. The elements provoked in society by the humorist which were particularly emphasized by Freud include the rediscovery of the familiar, the sense of contradiction and bafflement, and the pleasure inherent in degradation of and cynicism toward things normally exalted by society; as examples he offered caricature, parody, travesty, and unmasking. Freud perceived a rebellion in humor, the humorist gaining a certain superiority, but how this came about was as puzzling to him as the reason for the value placed by society on this form of pleasure. In comparing it to dream work, in that humor, too, is a contribution of the unconscious, Freud cited the brevity, the lifting of repressions, and the mechanism of psychic damming (derived from Lipps, 1898). As a substitute for the generation of distressing emotions, the kingdom of humor, according to Freud, afforded submission and control of previously unconquered emotion. Conscious distressingly painful ideas were able to remain unrepressed by the economic shifts of cathexis promoted by the humor, toward a regaining of the euphoria so typical of childhood when there is little expenditure in energy. Dynamically, Freud identified a redistribution of energy from ego to superego, which suppressed the ego's possibilities of reacting in much the same way that love affairs and persecution complexes become resolved—through the withdrawal of the attention that they were formally afforded. He concluded that operating through the superego, humor repudiated reality in the service of illusion. More significantly, Freud ascribed to the humorist himself a special gift (in Freud's mind a genetic one) with which he felt most of us are not endowed.

The personal analysis of the comedian offers a developmental blueprint of the transitional aspect of humor. One of my patients, a comedian in his late twenties, came to analysis not only for cyclical depressions, but for bouts of terror in which he experienced the foreboding that he was about to "disappear." He reported on the naive and unprotecting mother of his infancy as a key to his illness and as a provocation for his humor as well, although he was vague as to the actual connection. Although he afforded little significance to the role of the father, a rather nondescript businessman, it became clear that, as with the other comedians I had examined, my patient had spurned any meaningful identification with that parent, negating the brand of paternal guidance that ran the gamut from common sense to homespun philosophy. More significantly, this budding comic had cringed from the skeptical father's rejection of his displays of comedy. By his disinclination to trade in his mother's ignorance for his father's reality, he was left to his own devices, his distancing from his father leaving him without the traditional values that lead toward some conformity to communal standards. While companions became imbued with the burdens of a maturing, oedipally-derived superego, he was left unencumbered as he turned his attentions to his comical antics.

Working with his mind from earliest years as if he were playing with a gadget, and ridden with the fear of being overpowered by stimuli that other children seemed to take in their stride—loud noises, rough-and-tumble action on the sandlot, or even the passions of cinema, which so often afforded him acute distress—he resorted to efforts at dealing with emotions that arose in him in these situations. He would try to disarm feelings that he considered threatening, including fear of dying and bouts of shame for what he felt was his problem of cowardice. He was constantly guarding against ridicule and attack from the outside and against losing control from the inside. *Dabbling in a play of opposites* (unconsciously), a game of the mind which he translated to the classroom to the amusement of children and teachers alike, he would step with the left foot when others stepped off with their right, he would be absent when others were present and sleeping when others were awake. This behavior, however, was neither in negation of nor rebellion against family or society; it was an attempt to overcome feelings of being damaged, a strategy demanded by an inchoate sense of vulnerability that compelled him to avoid external stimuli that menaced him and to modify internal stimuli that might overwhelm him.

Freud could not understand why humor, beyond its capacity to transcend painful feelings, was so highly valued for its relatively subdued pleasure. Perhaps humor offers an even greater economy than Freud realized when he identified an affective savings through the blockage of painful emotions. He did discern that humor often promoted an economic illusion by projecting the burden of energy expenditure onto the comedian himself. In our present-day culture, this is no mean feat for a comedian to accomplish, since such an illusion is often in direct reversal of the facts. Not only does our society offer the professional comedian handsome financial acknowledgment, it exalts the meager

work output involved while continuing to stubbornly deni-
grate the services of those who earn their keep by the sweat
of their brow. This suggests that humor provides an additional economy in fostering the illusion that all of us, like
the comedian, can find compensation for avoiding the
tedious problems of maturation by having a sense of humor.
By presenting a playful picture wherein one grows to adulthood without full object relations in a bypass of effort (and
of superego development), perhaps the comedian achieves
an aggrandizement of immaturity. Such seduction of the
superego intensifies the illusion that man can indeed pawn
off his narcissism as something other than it is.

Freud speaks of humor as involving a hypercathected
superego. My patient displayed this hypercathexis, but of a
stunted superego, one that was heavily populated with the
mental representations of transitional objects. This helped
promote an illusion of a burdensome superego—in truth, an
inflated one which was coupled with a relatively non-
performing ego. Such juxtaposition of *inflation and deflation achieved a caricature effect,* wherein the reverse of
what man ordinarily hopes for was presented in the image
of this comedian as well as in his comedy. Where ordinarily
people long for that infinitely strong ego of achievement
coupled with a mature, yet liberal, superego that offers
promise of fulfillment of instinctual drives, my patient
presented a reverse caricature with which his audience
could empathize. Both physically and psychologically, he
presented the image of an individual with a large head
supported by a ludicrously small torso. Perhaps it was the
smallness (of body and ego) that helped desensitize his
respondents to the unmasking of the narcissism of the transitional process, which man so often presents as object
libido.

By manipulating opposing ideas, my patient could cast
an aura of festive omnipotence, as if everything were under

man's control (including the passage of time). The exaltation thereby achieved could be described as an illusory victory over Father Time. In the triumph, pregenital as it was, the humor appeared to supersede the communal image of the patriarch, a feature without which humor often suffers a lack of vital substance. However, to consider his humor emasculating in its depreciative attitude toward the father and to suggest that it rested on the liberation of destructive instinct (see Winterstein, 1934) would blur the distinction between his brand of humor, in which ambivalence toward the father was conscious and contained, and a hypomanic elation, where the self often remains unconscious of what it has failed to overcome.

It is not difficult to support Tarachow's (1966) observations that a child's stools can become his transitional object. In fact, I take this one step further by observing that both the mother's milk and the child's excrement (both physiological extrusions from the body) blend to give the cast to the infant's first not-me possession, commonly a soft cloth impregnated with milk-feces odors. The comedian I have presented here manifested a comedy that was stamped with the ingenuous quality of the transitional process of infancy, his art form (the humor) reflecting the mental representations of this process. In his own words, his head was filled with foreign bodies, a Disneyland of visual *caricatures* that seemed to have found their way to his head from his bowels through some magical channel of transformation. Inanimate until touched by his magic wand (narcissistic cathexes), they became animated and were communicated for the sake of some empathic response from an appreciative audience. Not surprisingly, his "black humor" could transform the ordinarily painful theme of death (immobile stools) into one of life (moving penis), a phallic illusion in which the uncanny was permitted a familiar and pleasurable return from the repressed.

In his mind, this comedian was transitional object to his audience; a negation of his humor by outside respondents would lead to the abortion of the creative product and to a bout of his "disappearing," in which he would abandon self and mental creations to limbo (a process commonly associated with nausea, gastric pain, or diarrhea). Such a letdown he compared to a woman suffering a miscarriage. Without exception, the comedians I treated suffered from gastrointestinal symptoms from childhood. Deprived of an adequate stimulus barrier in infancy, they were provoked to assimilate many part-objects in order to compensate for the deficit in the sense of self. In addition to compromising their ability to accommodate what they so ravenously assimilated, this resulted in failure to properly internalize object representations (the larger profile of a meaningful person).

Nutritionists claim that we are *what* we eat; in terms of psychology, it is more accurate to say that we are *who* we eat. Certainly no one will argue that, to a degree, who we are is derived from whom we internalize in our psychic representations; the process of internalization even has a bearing on our physical configuration, on how we move and speak and gesture. Our facial expressions and body posture reflect the people with whom we live, our parents, our siblings, our marital partner. It is an observable fact that after years of living together, a husband and wife take on similar facial expressions; it is not wild to suggest that psychiatrists look as much like their patients as their patients look like their psychiatrists. Even our jobs and leisure activities have an effect on our physiognomy, although part of this is our anticipatory projection of how people in certain jobs or professions should look.

Instead of adequately internalizing, the comics I treated had to "chop up" what they devoured in an effort to construct a sense of self. As one comedian put it, "I can only take in pieces; and when I put together parts that don't belong to each other, I come up with a monster." This particular comic's difficulty in accommodation and in subsequent internalization was reflected not only in his foreboding sense of impermanency, but in his digestive processes, in his malformed stools. He had *problems in developing phallic structure* similar to his difficulties in his pregenital development. Disturbances in body imagery, in sexual identity, and, of course, in object relations were the result.

Every so often, he would suffer a glut in his part-object assimilations. His dependency on maintaining his "exalted superego" by the incorporating of newer part-objects in pace with the times would result in repetitive crises in accommodating the heavy meals so capriciously imbibed. The danger of loverload called for *cyclical evacuations* of a malformed and stunted *superego* that had attained a state of glut tension. The result was a deflation and a house cleaning. These bouts, approximating a complete drought in humor, posed serious identity crises. After a period of letdown or depression, sometimes associated with the feeling that he would completely disappear, he would rally his forces, and the process of rebuilding internal part-objects would gradually bring recovery.

Although Freud (1921) suggests that it is the vacating of the superego in reaction to undue prohibitive periods of depression that accounts for the narcissistic festivity and elation that follows, with this comedian things worked in reverse: *it was the vacating of the superego that yielded the depression.* Only through the activity of a "busy" superego, not through instinctual fulfillment from ego performance, could he restore self-regard. In sacrificing instinctual life for the sake of acknowledgment from society, he could, like the creative artist, be described as having a love affair with the world. In his comedy, he undid the losses experienced in his infancy by structuring a *Reizschutz* with hypertrophied modalities not customarily accentuated in the average individual; his capacity for illusion, for paradox, and for skewed thinking replaced objectivity and ego performance. In line with Freud's view of humor, he had chosen to cathect his superego, which though transitionally maldeveloped, carried an illusory image that approximated the artlessness of the child, an image which his admiring respondents could empathically exalt.

The childhood of the comedian raises the question of whether everyone with a sufficiently damaged *Reizschutz* in infancy becomes a comedian of sorts or a creative artist. One can only suspect that in pace with other natural endowments, in one degree or another, those so victimized do derive a creative thrust from their deprivation. This in turn suggests that the more mature and healthy are doomed to impoverished creativity, that an individual with a resolved oedipal complex would probably not remain particularly invested in comedy or humor. Ordinarily the activity of a mature superego should force one to acknowledge by the sweat of one's brow that comedy is basically a narcissistic balm for the frustrations of earlier deprivation. Freud (1905a) accounts for the variety of creative and inventive devices found in wit and humor by an entrusting of preconscious thinking to unconscious elaboration. One might well argue that this tendency should be less apparent in the fulfilled and the mature. To put it in Greenacre's terms (1964), the individual who has already achieved wholeness of identity is less likely to be creative, and Coltrera (1965) implicitly supports this concept in his observation that creativity in children seems to disappear at the age of five or six with the abatement of the Oedipus complex. Perhaps it is logical, then, to conclude that the mature among us, rather than having the capability of provoking humor, are more apt to appreciate the humor-provoking capacities of others, of those who continue to languish from (or thrive on) transitional efforts in transformation.

EXHIBITIONISM

The profile of a comedian exemplifies the importance of "show and tell," the yearning to be legitimized by gaining acknowledgment from society. Such a need for self-validation has been traced to the transitional process, to the infant's first quest for maternal corroboration of an only partially internalized sense of self. One might say that when this need to display becomes a compulsive phenomenon demanding the attention of society, it qualifies as *exhibitionism*.

Surprisingly, psychoanalytic literature predominantly orients itself to the subject of exhibitionism in relation to the perversions. The themes of nakedness or at least undress are emphasized, as well as the paired component instincts of wishing to see and wishing to be seen (scopophilia and exhibitionism) first introduced by Freud (1896, 1905). Postulating exhibitionism as a direct offshoot of libido and as a passive partner of scopophilia, Freud traced these "perversions" to infantile sexuality, pointing to phylogenetic roots originating in the earliest delights of the human society in the natural exposure of the flesh. Human narcissism was perceived as the autoerotic motif underlying exhibitionism. By dint of willful inhibition, the exhibitionist's libidinous compulsion was perceived as censored by the ego in the service of a conflict of will. The only reference in Freud's writings to exhibitionism as something beyond frank sexual display is a reference to "innocent jokes" aimed at displaying one's cleverness (Freud, 1905a). Although he chose not to emphasize it, obviously Freud (1915a) was aware that the wish to exhibit can undergo a host of transformations which in themselves can hardly be considered perversions. It does not seem helpful, then, to describe these transformations as perversions; it is more a question of the maturity or immaturity of the psychic development of the individual engaged in their display.

One might even quibble with Freud's tracing exhibitionism to an autoerotic display of the flesh, since the infant's first transitional object is sometimes its own excrement, something to be applauded by the mother as it lies like the crown jewels resplendently on display in the bowl. I would argue that exhibitionism is derived from the wish to be loved, beginning with feeding and with the child's first demands for the attention of the mother: "See what I ate—love me."

Siegman (1964) sees exhibitionism as an active form of the infantile state of fascination, perceiving a gain in narcissistic satisfaction in the exercise of magical influence on an audience. To Siegman, to fascinate means to actively reproduce in an audience what had been passively experienced by the exhibitor in his childhood (the active recreative repetition compulsion). Allen (1974) found that his neurotic patients who demonstrated exhibitionistic trends had been largely thwarted in establishing a gratifying relationship with their mother, whom they secretly resented out of fear of rejection. Where Allen speaks of the wish *to see and display*, and where Siegman speaks of an aim *to fascinate*, I believe the root motive of exhibitionism lies in *self-validation*. Allen ascribes the trigger for exhibitionism to traumatic incidents of the phallic phase, where looking and showing were severely reproved by a mother threatening loss of love. Siegman does not commit himself to an originating phase, but offers the suggestion that although exhibitionism is predominantly visual, it may well have its origins in something nonvisual. Obviously the implication here is of prephallic origins.

It is difficult to delineate exhibitionism from normal display. All of us are familiar with the lengths to which people go for the attention or the notoriety that comes from showing off. Clinical psychologists and psychiatrists encounter many bizarre examples of this human hunger. In childhood, showing off manages to have a certain charm, but later the behavior is far from attractive, exposing the human foible in pathetic and sometimes ludicrous tones. The "life of the party," for example, at first so adamant in his refusal to perform, later requires physical force before he'll shut up. A "suicidal" exhibitionist suffering urges to leap from balconies while attending theater turned out in analysis to have an inordinate craving to be one of the lead actors on stage. Then there are the attention-seeking individuals who hang around police stations ready to confess to any publicized crime. Even love-making qualifies as a vehicle for exhibitionists; every social clique has at least one couple devoted to displaying their passions in public, frigid as they often are in the privacy of their homes.

It may be concluded that exhibitionism is pathological when it reflects some aspect of the exhibitor that has failed to become transformed into something acceptable to the society whose acceptance is sought. In these terms, normalcy involves adequately disguising the origins of the product on display; there has to be some creative synthesis that will permit the production to find meaningful appreciation in a significant segment of society. This begs the question of what is meaningful or significant; for example, we might well applaud a striptease, but whether it qualifies as an art form or simply as a piece of exhibitionism depends on the values of our ever-changing society. Nonetheless, whether we speak of a display that is applauded or of one that is censured, it is fair to say that the urge of mankind to externalize or exhibit has its roots in the compulsion to be validated by the outside world, a fulfillment that offers a rescue from anonymity in the face of the trauma of time.

VI

A Voice in the Crowd

One of the common pitfalls of psychological treatment is that it often affords temporary relief from the manifest symptoms before the underlying problem is resolved, fostering thereby a false sense of security—not only in the patient, but in the physician as well; wishful thinking simply gets out of hand. In Lilli's case, although I knew she was still sneaking drugs and by no means in good faith, as proven by her failure to report on this matter, nonetheless, I began to be influenced against my better judgment by her outward signs of improvement. During the early stages of her analysis, there had been a morbid undercurrent of depressive brooding which went along with the way she carried herself and the way she dressed, signs that left little doubt in my mind that she was seriously ill. Then came a lengthy period of overt feelings of relief. She began to manage the occasional smile on leaving her sessions, colors began to creep into her dress, anecdotes demonstrating that she was deriving enjoyment from her children were brought to her sessions. She spoke of her husband in more positive terms. I became impressed by what I considered to be strides toward recovery, particularly when she had been able to mourn the death of her grandmother, who had been

such an important figure during the dark days of Auschwitz. With her brightening outlook I pushed aside a sense of
unease that related to her perplexing lack of feelings regarding her dead mother; the theme never really made an
appearance. Only later did I realize that this omission was
largely due to Lilli's heavy intake of drugs, one of her ways
of not only searching for timelessness, but of perpetrating a
flight into health.

A Crisis of Therapy: Melancholia

It is easy to overlook the effects of outside events on the
mental state of patients in psychoanalysis. In Lilli's case,
however, it was impossible to ignore the obvious, so
dramatic was the trigger and so flagrant the patient's
reaction. The manner in which she presented herself in my
consulting room the day after the press reported the capture
of Adolf Eichmann and his abduction from his South American hideout is still vivid in my memory. She appeared in a
state of dishevelment; obviously she had not slept the night
before. Noticeable sores were already beginning to form
about her mouth and cheeks and she seemed flushed and
weak. From the moment she lay on the couch, frightening
images emerged in her communications. She perceived her
body as a gas oven consuming Eichmann's flesh. Once
again she brought memories of rotting corpses impaled on
barbed wire ... odorous flashbacks of cremating human
flesh ... memories of fevers and diseases she suffered
during her camp incarceration. She recounted how shortly
after her liberation, on hearing of her father's sanctuary in
America, she developed a similar illness, although not as
severe as illnesses in the concentration camps. It was diagnosed at that time as an infection of unknown origin. Now,
as she once again spewed forth her morbid recollections of
the Nazi gas ovens, I realized that not only had Eichmann

and her father come under her indictment, but the transference had taken a negative turn as well.

Lilli's condition quickly worsened. She became not only severely depressed, but febrile as well. It was obvious that she required immediate hospitalization, which was quickly accomplished. As in her earlier bout of similar symptoms, medical work-up again failed to reveal a specific organism that might explain her fever. The physicians who looked after her could not make an organic diagnosis, although they speculated that drug abuse might be involved. After a week of exhaustive investigation, during which the fever had slowly subsided, her physicians, concerned about her depression, felt that resuming her analysis offered the best prospect for recovery, and she was released to my care. On her return to analysis, her emaciated and profoundly melancholic state immediately heightened my concern for her. Soon I wished her back in hospital, undermined as I was beginning to feel in my ability to pull her out of her deep depression. Yet I recognized the value that insight into her all-consuming psychological process might afford her in this crisis. There was a dramatic change in the analytic content. Where her betrayers (Eichmann, father) had initially been external targets for her condemnation, now, weeks later, Lilli had become in fantasy the target of her own prosecution. Eichmann now seemed inside her, and the full brunt of her aggression had turned against herself.

Freud (1917a) first differentiated between mourning the loss of a meaningful object and the more pathological form of melancholia involving a withdrawal of love from the object to the self, and associated with a fall in self-esteem. He clarified the mechanics of this drop in self-regard (Freud, 1923) as a regressive, narcissistic, instinctual defusion which allowed a liberation of the usually fused sadistic component. The defusion restored the infantile split of good and bad objects, the bad being internalized into conscience (superego) as a punitive, self-critical force. This, along with a lowered self-esteem, rounded out for Freud the clinical picture of the illness. Jacobson (1953) further refined the dynamics of melancholia by offering the clinically confirmable proposition that what is introjected into the victim's conscience is the part of the mourned parental image that was originally considered good, and hence entitled to assume a punitive and attacking posture. Jacobson's corollary was that the bad or worthless part of the object, the part deserving attack or punishment, was also taken in by the melancholic, but as a part of the self. For Jacobson, then, the condition consisted of a good conscience attacking a bad self.

Lilli's melancholia was triggered by the exposure of the whereabouts of Eichmann. For her, this meant that Eichmann (father) was no longer in limbo, he was alive and real—and a most definite target for the retaliation of the people he had victimized. On first interpretation, I took Lilli's melancholia as a decompensation of her defenses against the hatred she harbored for her father, toward whom she had always displayed ambivalent love and hate. I felt that in her need to punish her father, she had identified with Eichmann (identification with the aggressor), incorporating this persecutor into her conscience as an attacking and punitive figure whose role was to psychologically mete out the same sadistic punishment to her father that had been suffered by her beloved grandmother (the gas ovens).

Had Lilli been emotionally capable of such an attack against her father, perhaps a melancholia would not have developed at that time. In fact, quite a different story emerged to adequately explain the melancholic regression. It also clarified why there had been a dearth of material in her analysis about her deeper relationship with the sickly mother who had found it so difficult to fulfill a child's need for love. It now became clear that the mother had early on become a rival in Lilli's mind, particularly since the grandmother had taken over the maternal role so early in Lilli's life. Her envy and hatred of the attention that her mother, in illness, had received from her father accounted in large part for the defensive solicitousness that Lilli had learned to adopt in matters pertaining to her mother. There was also an identification that allied her with her mother against a common scapegoat, the unfaithful and betraying father. As a target in limbo for Lilli's aggression, this enigmatic paternal figure, "neither alive nor dead," whereabouts unknown, served much the same defensive purpose as a transitional object or an imaginary companion. Once symbolically apprehended and identified, however, this father image, now a live target for punishment (Eichmann), no longer served as an adequate buffer against the concealed aggression that Lilli still harbored for her mother. Her libido, which had been unable to flow outward in a cathexis of her husband or her children, became subsequently withdrawn to a position prepared by her identification both with a mother who had deserted her in sickness and death, and a father who had deserted her in escape. It now had no other direction in which to move but toward an investment of the self. As in Helene Deutsch's (1930) graphic example, Lilli's subsequent regression to an oral incorporation of the sickly mother led to a further shredding of self-esteem, to an instinctual decomposition that promoted a disappearance of the boundaries between Lilli's ego and the psychic representation of her mother. Her melancholia could be said to consist of a sadistic conscience (the introjected father identified as Eichmann) attacking a bad self (the incorporated mother now fused with the self).

Looking back, I must have surely reactivated my own family romance during Lilli's melancholia; not only did I

feel like a lifeguard diving into deep water to save a drown-
ing victim, but in some ways, I felt like I was saving myself.
I realized that despite her self-flagellation, she had managed to spare part of me (and part of herself) from her
destructive vengeance. She had placed the two of us "in the
glass cage" to plead a case against her scathing attack
(projective identification). Neither Eichmann, her father,
her mother, nor Lilli had an adequate defense. Only I was
able to speak up for myself, and this I did in my interpretations of her struggle. Yet during those stormy days, it was
my faith in myself as a therapist that faltered, rather than
my outlook on Lilli. Unresolved aspects of my own psychological life became reactivated as I allowed self-doubts to
come to the foreground, qualms which I knew were partly
countertransference, but which nonetheless made inroads
into my sense of adequacy. There were periods when I felt
somewhat like an impostor, and these feelings spilled over
to my profession as a whole, an experience many psychologists have from time to time in their practice. Only later
did I realize the degree to which I was identifying with my
patient's self-critical attack.

THE IMPOSTOR

One of the most burdensome problems of those who
treat emotional illness is the impostor complex. In the
psychoanalytic literature, the major emphasis on the
subject of imposturing is related to problems within the
patient; little attention has been paid to such a tendency
within the therapist. The inference of such disregard is that
the therapist has resolved such a problem; however, this is
not always the case. Indeed if he has, relapses can occur
nonetheless, since imposturing can easily become reactivated by crises within the therapy. We should acknowledge, then, that problems of imposturing not only occur in

patients, but in psychoanalysts, as well as in members of society at large (even in our leaders). Let us first attend to the problem within the patient.

Traditionally, gross imposturing, as compared with affectation or pretentiousness, is considered clinically pathological, in fact, a form of sociopathy. Helene Deutsch (1955) elaborates on a case of imposturing in a young man. His father was a successful businessman of dignity and stature in the community, sincere and altruistic, and ostensibly free of pretense. Deutsch hints that his role as father was marked by a certain austerity. The mother was a simple woman, neither gifted, beautiful, nor talented, her husband's obedient bed companion and housewife, whose endless indulgence of her son encouraged the development of his imposturing. The death of the father during the boy's puberty triggered an outbreak of anxiety and delinquency which later flourished into forgery, affectations of creative genius, and would-be military heroics in army service. Ultimately panic, malingering, and mental breakdown resulted in discharge from basic training. Quick-change artistry from gentleman farmer to creative writer, and from movie producer to inventor, led (with the help of treatment) to a college degree, but not without considerable hoodwinking of teachers.

Deutsch offers the combination of indulgent mothering and severe fathering as conducive factors in her patient's pathology, since paralysis of activity through premature compliance with maternal emotional overindulgence produces the same heightening of infantile narcissism as results from maternal emotional deprivation. The fatal illness of the father was the final blow to the crippled ego of the developing impostor, an ego too fragile to endure the loss. The patient was fatefully vulnerable to identification with his father, as displayed in the hypochondriacal symptoms provoking military discharge. A factor emphasized in the study was the patient's narcissism, as reflected in his disdain for being anything short of unique, despite his incapacity for prolonged creativity, denial of an identity he secretly regarded as inferior, and emptiness in emotional life and moral structure. Deutsch concluded the world is crowded with impostors, to be found among her friends and acquaintances, including herself. She also suggested that only saints, geniuses, or psychotics manage to achieve their ideals, whereas the rest of us, who are not completely fulfilled from within, must settle for the pretense that we are what we wish we could be.

It would appear from Deutsch's treatment of the subject that imposturing is a sickness of the mind fed by narcissistic trends of uniqueness, pretense, and deceit, all encouraged by family indulgences. Perhaps the influence of overindulgent mother and severe (and one suspects imposturing) father was not the only major factor that nourished the imposturing elements in the superego of Deutsch's patient. Other factors might have included the images of communal figures (teachers and others), whose paradoxical values may have helped affirm and legitimize the hoaxlike aspects of his family. It is a fact that our culture, like past cultures, reeks of hoax, fraud, and corruption, and the standards of the communal conscience are easily bent to service the needs of the masses. Individual conscience, as well as the conscience of small groups, follows the pattern of a nation in compliance with the mood of the times.

I would, then, broaden the causes of imposturing beyond the confines of immediate family by giving equal emphasis to the hoaxlike elements in society at large. One particular characteristic everyone in our society has in common, to some extent, is that we are all "experts." In such self-styled virtuosity, we manage, with considerable encouragement from our fellow man, to value the kind of individual audacity that helps belie the otherwise shaky ground on which we base our presumptuous posturings. Earlier, I touched on some of the positive aspects of human impudence as related to the humorist, proposing that a search of the mother's superego for a nonexistent "secret" was prerequisite to legitimizing the audacious stance taken in the humor. I suggest that the more tragic (yet often comic) figure whom we label the impostor searches the communal as well as the parental superego to justify and legitimize his solution of imposturing, and that relatively speaking, in so doing he is by no means operating on a faulty premise.

I think it is indisputable that, like the comedian, the impostor is empathically supported by large numbers of people who can easily identify with the elements of imposturing—the time-saving shortcut, the rebelliousness against authority. Certainly there is a transformational element in imposturing, as in humor. An illusion of timelessness is sometimes achieved by the impostor's bypassing of long-haul effort. Like the humorist, the impostor deceives a society still prone, like the child, to an animistic world of magic, where something can be made out of nothing, and nothing can be made out of something. Just as the humorist plays with transitional illusions of omnipotence, so does the impostor charm society by a borrowed costume reminiscent of the child's dressing up in parental clothing. The delight of the approving audience adds to this telescoping of time where, in the transformatory illusion, the world can be magically re-created in one's childhood imagery. Like the comic, the impostor in his procrastinations offers to all who vicariously empathize, the avoidance of painful emotions of separation as well as a respite from fear of castration.

As with humor, there is even an element of creativity in imposturing—perverse, deformed, or abortive though it may be. In both, there is a struggle toward a transformation of the unacceptable into the more acceptable. At an instinctual level, imposturing may reflect an infantile manifestation of imitation, a filling of the shoes of a parent in a precocious exercise in adult performance. Greenacre's (1958) view of the impostor emphasizes a protracted family romance and a disturbed sense of identity, as well as a struggle within the superego. Although she perceives a "killing" of the rival parent, a dynamism reinforced and sustained by the intoxication of the limelight and the adulation of the public (originally the mother), she also diagnoses a persistent and repeated attempt at reclaiming the role the impostor might have glimpsed in earlier years in a parent or a sibling. For Greenacre, the imposture is an attempt to achieve a sense of reality and competence (I have suggested legitimacy). Significantly, Greenacre allows the possibility that gifts or talents stifled and unacknowledged by family or society may be prompting factors in deforming the creative potential of the impostor. She, too, mentions the confirming audience, which offers the impostor a sense of false self that "strengthens" rather than weakens his sense of reality and identity.

One might say that the rules of propriety in our society are based to some extent on one individual's trust of another. Certainly we try to establish laws to deal with failures in trustworthiness. One might trace the origins of trust back to the age of innocence, when the infant or child develops a sense of confidence (Benedek, 1938) or basic trust (Erikson, 1950), which plays a significant role in the ultimate development of the capacity to discriminate between trustworthy and untrustworthy people. A disturbance in those early formative years can lead to gullibility, a readiness to believe that what is wished for, often unconsciously, will come true despite its unlikelihood, a gullibility that can be described as a readiness or a desire to be deceived (Isaacs et al., 1963). These authors point out that an untrustworthy parent will lead to a defect in the child's developing sense of trust, insofar as trust is directly related to superego formation. The same authors also observe that an individual (or society) usually develops a pathologically misplaced trust in direct proportion to the gullible person's (or society's) unconscious guilt for wishing to deceive others. In effect, an impostor or hoaxer is a most likely victim of someone else's imposture or hoax.

Rarely, in my view, is society an innocent victim of imposturing, whether it be perpetrated by an amateur bunco artist, by a smooth professional, or by a political leader reading the mood of a nation. I see a good segment of humanity caught up, in one way or another, in imposturing. It is part of our way of life, something built into the fabric of our culture and into the core of its conscience. Even our politics offers us leaderships that reflect imposturing, leaders who not only engage in hoax in the daily exercise of their office (see Rangell, 1976), but who, like the confidence man, the magician, the entertainer, and the humorist, are applauded if their performance is professional. Finkelstein (1974) observes that the relation between audience and impostor is similar to that between followers and their charismatic leader. He, too, emphasizes the importance of the supportive external factor in perpetuating the sanctioning of hoax. We have all experienced the exquisite delight in someone's smoothly perpetrated fraud, especially if the victim is some large bank, a central intelligence agency, or some other police institution. Implicit in this paradox is the relish we all have in seeing the overthrow of the agencies of superego in a rebellion against an overpowering world. Again, like the humorist, the impostor becomes our proxy with whom we can vicariously identify when he succeeds, and from whom we can dissociate when he fails. We privately applaud his brash courage while publicly deploring our kinship with him. Through his challenge of communal values, we hope to see those values transformed into those more commensurate with our own inadequacies, where the long haul can be bypassed, and where the illusion of postponed transience prolongs remembered pleasures of childhood.

I have suggested that the impostor requires an empathic response from parents and teachers, and from society at large in order to legitimize the illusion of adequacy. I have also suggested that most of us, and this certainly includes the psychoanalyst, are to some degree impostors. There is a discrepancy between the investigative instrument of psychoanalysis and the practitioner who uses it, burdened as he is with imposturing. We are on shaky ground when we try to quantify the phenomenon for labeling as psychopathy, just as we are when we try to identify those reflections of narcissism we should call abnormal. If most of us are impostors to some degree, at what point do we begin to label imposturing psychopathy? Perhaps this should depend on the degree to which the impostor is capable of inflicting harm to himself or to others.

Writing about the psychologist's internal struggles in his daily treatment of patients, McLaughlin (1961) observes that with the burden of lofty Hippocratic ideals demanding maximal instinctual renunciation, the healing therapist is often vulnerable in his inhibited and masochistic nurturing role, which McLaughlin considers a negative aspect of the physician's commitment to a Hippocratic ideal that tends to stifle capacities for exploration and discovery. Perhaps McLaughlin unduly spares the psychologist discomfort in downplaying another aspect of the therapist's role, where exaggerated elements of imposturing foster exploitative tendencies under the guise of "lifeguard." Unquestionably a gullible segment of society is disposed to collusion in such therapy, and one can only speculate as to how many people are unwittingly seduced into empty aspirations to creativity, or how many valid creative potentials are undermined by such healers. On recovery (from their treatment), few suspect that they participated in a hoax.

One of the main reasons for a therapist's impostor complex (aside from the obvious possibility that the therapist is really an impostor) lies in the nature of the work. Dealing with the human mind is a much more abstract activity than investigating the functions of the human body. In comparing the therapeutic validity of psychological treatment and physical medicine, although neither can be classified as an exact science, the predictability of cause and cure is far more accurate in the realm of organic disease. Psychoanalytic treatment often involves intuition and clinical speculation, and it therefore becomes easy for the therapist to develop doubts regarding his work. I am sure that in any given day of office practice, the incidence of bouts of depression from lowered self-esteem, even among experienced psychotherapists, would prove relatively high.

Paradoxically, young and inexperienced therapists, the zealots of the profession, are the ones who, despite their difficulty in formulating accurate diagnoses and in prognosticating the course of a patient's illness, are the least likely to be burdened with depression from an impostor complex. The complex is motivated in part by the patient's psychology, which is often infiltrated with the elements of illusion typical of the transitional process. This same process has shaped some of the neurotic features of the therapist, features that are especially vulnerable to reactivation during the heavy going with regressed patients (this is an occupational hazard of which the analyst is usually aware). A life work that consists predominantly of helping people separate fact from fiction is prone to lift repressed elements from the analyst's childhood into consciousness. As a result, it is not only the patient who is troubled during treatment.

Relapses and acute crises in patients are the common

triggers of the impostor complex in therapists. The regressive disintegration of suicidal or homicidal people is always frightening to an involved physician. It is inaccurate to say that only the more experienced will be quick to hospitalize a patient under these conditions; impostors may act quickly, too, so that it is sometimes difficult for the therapist to be sure whether he is an impostor or experienced old hand. I doubt that any psychoanalyst relishes the suicide of a patient. Even if he were outrageously callous, he would not want it to happen on his doorstep. Even the less vain feel piqued at impulsive acts of patients, particularly if the therapist's work is exposed to the community in a bad light. Most psychologists have had patients who, in their negative transference reactions, purposefully did things to tarnish their doctor's reputation. Some physicians are so intimidated by the public antics of vengeful patients that they have resolved only to treat the healthy. A show of illness, and the patient is discharged! Likewise, there are doctors who refuse to drive a car with medical license plates in order to avoid involvement with street casualties for fear of a lawsuit.

Even when a patient does well in treament, it is often sufficient a mystery to provoke an impostor complex in some psychotherapists. One is left with the suspicion that one had very little to do with the result; perhaps it was simply a matter of time, or of the patient's innate strengths —or maybe outside social influences promoted the recovery. In effect, in the field of psychology, it is not easy for any therapist to take credit for good results; he is, however, invariably given credit for cases that go sour, whether he likes it or not. Often I have tried to convince myself that I was crucial to a patient's re-creative reparation because of my interpretations, that without my mutative feedback, Lilli, for example, would never have been able to transform her sense of self or her conception of her trauma. Yet interpretations cannot be compared to antibiotics; you don't get the immediate response, like the sudden drop in fever. Paradoxically, one of the operative factors in triggering the therapist's impostor complex is his sense of reality, his inability to be as free in his illusions about himself. On many occasions I have felt like an impostor when, after leaving my office at the end of a laborious day instructing my patients, I found I was doing the same neurotic things they did.

The military bluff of Deutsch's impostor was, I am sure, inspired by society's long tradition of worshipping the uniform; the adulation it bestows on the fighting hero, the awe with which it pays homage to "true grit" is a characteristic which perhaps reflects some of the deeper reservations most of us individually harbor about our own personal capacities for courage. I can single out from my list of favorite impostors one whom I challenge the reader to indict, since he illustrates the phenomenon in a style with which many of us can empathize. Particularly in time of war, society, hungering for leadership, often reaches out in desperate trust, sometimes even to impostors—the way some of us reached out to "the Major": It was World War II, and we were about to embark and set sail for enemy-occupied territory. I recall how the rays of the North African sun bounced off the ship's turrets, a dazzling relief from the prevailing mood of fear. Missing was our morale-booster the Major, an expert in logistics, and one of the few among us who seemed to take things in his stride during the grim preparations for embarkation. His absence left us spastic with anxiety, including the noncombatants such as myself. Then the heartening voice of our Major! You could feel his reassuring presence as his lusty military vibrato rang out along the seaway: "On the double—go!" His order carried total authority. Swiftly we embarked at his clipped command. I remember that last look at the mainland, and I can still see the Major—short, stocky legs in military stance, arm pumping in brisk salute—as he stood on shore while the rest of us glumly set sail. From the obscurity of his fierce mustache came his parting battle cry: "Gung-ho!"

THE CROWD AND TIMELESSNESS

Energetic interpretations, together with my obvious concern for Lilli's welfare, I am sure contributed to her slowly working her way out of her depressive state. There were several weeks during which I was acutely mindful of the risks attending the recovery of melancholics, particularly those who get carried away by regressive psychological attempts at extricating themselves from their suffering. I knew that self-destructive acts associated with manic episodes were not uncommon and that Lilli might try to effect a resolution of her problem through means other than restoration of self-regard through psychological growth. Freud (1921) first offered periodic rebellions against the self-flagellations of melancholia to explain the festival of the ego known as mania, and Rado (1928) perceived a fusion of self with conscience in a reactivation of the euphoria of the suckling. Helene Deutsch (1930) remarked on how the periodic fluctuations of depression and euphoria even in normal life corresponded to the more pathological processes of melancholia and mania. Fenichel (1939) described two kinds of mania, an active one characterized by overthrow of the superego and a passive one reflecting an identificatory surrender to that agency. Lewin (1950) saw mania as the denied, displaced, distorted, and revised wish to be devoured and to sleep, which resulted in the hypervigilance and insomnia so characteristic of the condition.

Lilli did not go on to mania, although relief from her profound depression brought a mild reactive euphoria. In retrospect, I realized that she had taken on a significant alliance with her therapist in bringing about a necessary reshuffling of elements within her sense of self. The more stormy aspects of her transference involved identifying me in part with both her father and Eichmann; in her projective identifications within the transference, she saw me alternately as a coward (father) cringing from the enemy and as a sadistic camp guard. Of course, I became quite active in my interpretations of these transference images. I used the leverage of the therapeutic alliance to get her to see that psychic growth was possible and necessary, that new attitudes toward herself and toward others might promote some alterations in the archaically vindictive aspects of a conscience that needed a strong infusion of new reconciliations.

Recovery from melancholia meant more in Lilli's case than simply feeling like her old self again; the analysis of her melancholic process allowed a considerable degree of resolution of her previously unconscious symbiotic attachment to substitute mothers (such as her analyst), leaving her much freer to invest her interest in the outside world. This is not to say that she immediately resolved her personal relationships with men, and she still struggled to appropriately involve herself with her family. Nonetheless, her ability to disengage herself from her former self-absorption through an interest in community affairs was a most welcome sign. She recalled being one of a group in Theresienstadt, where she and some other inmates had tried to capture the aura of kibbutz living, imagining themselves to be training for a new life in Palestine. It was bizarre that a concentration camp should have been the setting of Lilli's first real taste of group life. Not that this sustained her later during the darker trials of Auschwitz, when the Nazi psychology was to keep the prisoners scattered and in a state of helpless fragmentation.

On emigration Lilli had avoided any group persuasions. Aside from attending opera or ballet, she kept her distance from organized groups, including the youth cults that were beginning to spring up in a postwar world still fearful of the domestic responsibilities that went with peacetime. Although many people hungered for altruistic escape into the kind of group psychology they had enjoyed in wartime, for Lilli the very thought of a group brought a chilling reminder of Hitler's worshippers gathered en masse. Even after marriage, except for school affiliations in the interests of her children, she remained programmed against membership in organizations. Actually, she did maintain some interest in a group composed of survivors of Theresienstadt, who had been scattered all over the world following liberation and who, through correspondence, arranged to meet once a year in a renewal of their common bond. In some ways one could compare this with the need many young people feel for membership in a cult. The phenomenon of cultism was tailor-made for those with postwar alienations or traumas, group situations particularly geared to individuals struggling with time.

It should be emphasized that the hunger for timelessness is by no means unique to those suffering holocaust or war neuroses. It is, for example, a part of our whole drug culture, where youth seems compelled to precociously reach out for sexual expression on the one hand, while making desperate efforts to ensconce themselves in the dependencies of their childhood on the other. Philosophically, one might link the search for timelessness in such young people with an aversion to death. Cohn (1957) speaks of narcissistic time, which is entirely unconscious and the equivalent of immortality. Georges Abraham (1976) relates all psychopathology to a struggle with time: He sees in conversion hysteria a flight from time, the impelling force being a narcissistic past transposed into the present. In hysterical phobia, he sees the past disguised as the future (the fear of tomorrow), and in obsessional neurosis, he sees a premature sense of the flight of time, with a compulsion to master it amidst fear that there may not be enough time to do so. No doubt Abraham would describe Lilli's sadomasochistic flashbacks as handmaidens of the death instinct, unconscious repetitions imbued with timelessness. According to Abraham, even the superego, being largely unconscious, is engaged in the recovery of timelessness. E. M. Stern (1977) perceives narcissism in general as a defiance of or a denial of time, particularly in mania, where the patient's aim is to retrieve a primary narcissistic omnipotence. He views narcissism as the playacting of time-defying roles, in contrast to schizophrenia, wherein time is denied through an overinvestment in primary process.

Myerhoff (1974) describes the Huichol Indian peyote hunt of North-Central Mexico, a cultural ritual involving a negation of time. It is a ceremonial group journey to a mythical ancestral land where the old defer to the young and where goodbye is a greeting and hello a farewell. The entire ritual is a time-out for everybody, a pause that reinforces a feeling of continuity and a sense of cultural identity. Perhaps it is a confirmation of Freud's view that mankind's time distortions may be its way of preserving the continuity of the individual (see Calhoun, 1976). The peyote hunt can be compared to the ritualistic manner in which other, more primitive societies deal with their perceptions of transience. Masler (1973), for example, reports on the Trobriand Islanders, who hold to the belief that people remain physically unaltered with the passage of time; they negate actual bodily changes by decreeing that the aging person no longer exists, and he thenceforth is invested with a new identity.

The remarkable infiltration of cults and cultism into middle America during the past decade is testimony to their popularity, particularly with certain segments of the disenchanted. Where the motorcycle gangs, the "rock 'n roll" groups, and the drug cults of the sixties catered to the pleasure principle, today's Babas, Krishnas, and Moonies embrace asceticism and the altruistic surrender to charismatic gurus. Sociologists, such as Zaretsky and Leone (1974), attribute the hybrid vigor of cults to a capacity for inventing, borrowing, and welding together ideas that are ordinarily incompatible with each other. These authors emphasize the importance of women in cult life, where they are allowed a power they cannot easily acquire in ordinary society. Defining a cult as a loosely structured, transitory group composed of people sharing a unique negation of traditional values, Eister (1974) identifies its sociological role as an aid, particularly to young people, in coming to terms with time. According to Prince (1974), the emphasis that cults place on altered states of consciousness derives from the subjective sense of timelessness and from the flashbacks of primal experience that the regression to such altered states makes possible. Prince claims that without the use of drugs, the regression heightens reality far beyond the psychological scope of those engaged in routine living, since to attain these altered states requires that memories be subjected to a different mode of consciousness.

A passion for timelessness is particularly embedded in the theme of the occult. We are witnessing a revival in man's age-old fascination with witchcraft, satanism, and mysticism, not to mention his continued absorption in mind expansion. One might well argue that as long as there are things unknown to science, occultists will have a legitimate claim to the importance of their beliefs. Truzzi (1974) observes that matters considered occult yesterday have been incorporated into the science of today. He argues that, although in large measure occultism stems from mysticism and antiscientific philosophies, it nonetheless serves a function for science, as data repository or as a reminder of the existence of anomalies. He cites the role of hexing in psychosomatic disorders, as well as the remedial aspects of herbs long used in witchcraft.

Helene Deutsch (1926) observed that man's inclination toward the occult was one of the manifestations of his eternal desire to break down the barrier between the self and the world. She pointed out that by projecting his psychic forces outwardly, he evolved a belief in the supernatural, which kept his animistic psychology alive in the guise of occult experience. Using Freud's definition of telepathy as the reception of a mental process by one person from another by means other than sensory perception, Deutsch saw the psychoanalytic situation as providing the greatest hope for discovering how an individual's emotionally colored recollections are transmitted through extrasensory perception to provoke a response in another. One must suspect, Deutsch commented, that the condition for this transfer consists of a certain unconscious readiness on the part of the receiver, and she concluded that if we do not deny the powers of the repetition compulsion, then we must accept psychic predestination and acknowledge its constructive force as one of the sources of prophetic inspiration.

I would observe here that anyone who has experienced the psychological interaction between patient and doctor (as in the psychoanalytic setting) can attest to the often occult manner in which one reads the other's thoughts (phylogenetic empathy). This kind of empathy must surely transpire between people in many kinds of situations, and although some would attribute it to brainwave communication, one must anticipate the likelihood that intrapsychic processes common to both sender and receiver are sympathetically (and unconsciously) at work. I have offered the human passion surrounding the riddle of time as one such common bond.

The Primal Sound

Persons reared in an average expectable environment somewhere along the way usually experience an altruistic surrender to an organized group cause. I would have been greatly relieved had Lilli made a move in this direction. However, she simply was not taken with groups, an indicator of the disenchantment and cynicism she harbored toward people gathered en masse. One could hardly blame her for being frightened by the imagery that she continued to conjure up with respect to groups. In fact, she struggled against the urge to become caught up in the group of former inmates of Theresienstadt. At first this seemed to be in defense against remembering, but later was recognized as a reflection of her resistance to becoming more deeply enmired in the masochistic aspects of the identification.

In his theory on group psychology, Freud (1921) derived his conclusions from the contributions of investigators such as LeBon, McDougall, and Trotter. He emphatically differed with Trotter (1916) on the bonding factor in group life. Freud believed that man's social instinct originated in the family at the level of individual psychology, rather than in some irreducible herd instinct reflecting a biological continuation of the multicellular character of all higher organisms. Freud was not convinced that LeBon's (1895) collective mind, derived from a racial unconscious, did, in fact, afford the group its unique characteristics of hypnotic suggestibility and contagiousness, although he did acknowledge surrender to prestigious authority as primal. Closer to his ultimate thinking was McDougall's (1920) principle of emotion induced through numbers, which gave structure and continuity to those bonded by an idea.

Freud's main contribution was his proposal that the suggestibility and contagion within the group were founded on a common bond of reciprocal love, as well as on a common hatred of those excluded from the group (strangers). His concept that egoism becomes transformed into deference to a leader serving vital needs was elaborated by Anna Freud (1936) in her description of altruistic surrender as one of the several defenses of the ego against narcissistic mortification. In vicariously fulfilling one's wishes through others, there is a liberation of inhibited activity and aggression ordinarily reserved for one's own fulfillment, but capable of expression through the fulfillment of others. An example is the parent who supports a child's instinctual demands. She emphasized the need for defenses against the *quantity of instinct* mobilized in infancy, and reactivated at puberty and at the climacteric, when strong instincts confront a weak ego and the outcome of the conflict in each instance hinges on the transforming capacities of the ego and the superego (like the naughtiness of latency becoming transformed into the delinquencies of pubertal life). For Anna Freud, the asceticism of youth was the direct result of a primary phylogenetic tendency in man to repudiate his instincts. Through intellectualization, whereby ideas become attached to these threatening instincts, some control over them was gained in the face of a rupture in the ascetic adolescent's superego (overthrow of parental influence), a happening that mobilized anxiety and threatened a regression to more flimsy identifications of a fickle and self-centered nature.

Offering the model of a thwarted love affair, Freud (1921) equated the cannibalistic reaction of the primal horde toward their leader with the jealous rage of thwarted lovers. In individual love affairs, a specific trait of the object is often selected by the lover as the focus of his adulation and identification; Freud perceived this same phenomenon transpiring in groups, where a single trait of a leader—his courage, for example—could become the pivot of the group bond to that leader. He felt such a dynamism to be symbolically apparent in the ritual totemic meal of aboriginal tribes. I have suggested that in group psychology there is an additional element in the group regression, one that has a less primitive and more transitional quality, which is reflected in the strong attraction to religious cults on the part of young people seeking a detour from maturation through a fascination with the charismatic and the occult. On a more concrete level, group movements mobilized to censure the human dissipation of ecological supplies appeal to young people who particularly deplore waste. Paradoxically, the asceticism and the rebellion against materialism that keynote some modern cultist movements (like collecting for Krishna) depend on the very pipeline of material supplies that they ostensibly disdain.

Returning to Freud and his model of a love affair, he observed that the idealization of love is reflected in group dynamics, in that the leader, like one's personal love object, comes to replace the ego ideal of the individual members of the group. Because sexual satisfaction is excluded (as in hypnosis), latent or overt homosexuality is a more likely group expression of sex than heterosexuality—a remarkable fact, Freud points out. For him, the group's multiplication of the hypnotic dynamism, embellished with the regressive identification of its members, is the phylogenetic core of infectious group bondage to a leader, something from which lovers and neurotics are excluded. In offering an alternate and more anarchistic dynamism to explain organized group life, I have introduced the appeal of cultism to young people searching for a defense against the relentless encroachment of time. The fear of sustaining a genitality without adequate narcissistic supplies causes them to seek group activity for sharing responsibilities of marriage and family as well as the burden of severance from the sustaining mother. Such a rescue involves the extension of the personal family romance into group life (communal family romance), where the young en masse, disenchanted with both familial and traditional communal figures and institutions, seek a more charismatic aristocracy to temporarily idealize. Because the common bond is severance, then underlying the conflict with the oedipal parent (Freud's patriarchal leader), there also machinates the age-old search for a timelessness which paradoxically demands sufficient time for youth to gain the power to make a successful bid at reclaiming a personal love object.

The psychology of a group is directly related to the degree to which it is structured. Groups range from highly structured organizations, such as the army, political groups, and the major religions, to disorganized crowds and mobs, some loosely bonded, as at sporting events, others more deteriorated and chaotic. In assessing the dynamics operative in these groups, great emphasis has traditionally been placed on the presence or lack of a common bondage, on the depth of the mass regression, and on the degree of individual merger with the crowd. For example, Greenacre (1972) feels that the individuals in a crowd use multiple contacts with those around them as a collective mother with many faces. I view the complementary faces of the crowd as siblings, all searching in common for an abstract pivotal mother. I believe this conceptualization particularly applies when the mass rally is attended by figures in high positions —presidents, prime ministers, or royalty—prestigious figures who help fulfill a communal family romance. In the absence of such figures, a national flag or a portrait of regal stature is fittingly substituted to symbolically exalt the conclave as a prelude to the subsequent hunger of agitated citizenry, ready to become infected with the group contagion.

I offered a theory of group bondage (Schiffer, 1973) that differs somewhat from the one Freud (1921) put forward in his concept of the group tie to a patriarch. I perceived the group as sharing a common struggle against the trauma of rupture from the primordial mother. The patriarchal leader was viewed as an invention of this earlier group aimed at harnessing their reactionary aggressions in a rescue of the self-regard of the first human family. The role of the mythical patriarch was to ensure that every individual could borrow the power and the tools to successfully reclaim the mother. Other writers, such as Saravay (1975), have become equally attentive to the pre-oedipal matriarchal undercurrents in groups. Saravay goes even further, hypothesizing not only an instinctual regression, but one giving way to primitive part-object relations. He ascribes the merging of identity among members of the group to the contagious suggestibility and imitation that replace the moral and rational considerations of the individual. He disagrees with Freud that the heightening of emotions and the progression from narcissism to object love is inspired by the leader; instead he favors LeBon's view that there is a disappearance of conscious personality structure in deference to the common instinctual foundations of the group.

My own concept differs somewhat from Saravay's, just as it did from Freud's. I join Bion (1961) in the opinion that neither the leader nor the collective following has the last word in group dynamics; an individual psychology still permeates all groups. I suggest that only the few who aspire to leadership, including close party followers, become fully caught up in the dynamics put forth by Freud. Saravay's pre-oedipal regression seems to me to be more in the service of the ego than Saravay is willing to acknowledge. Rather than perceiving the crowd as a conglomerate of potentially regressive lunatics, I see individuals seeking *to rescue timelessness en masse,* while clinging to individualistic exercises in anarchism. This is complemented by the controlled illusion that captures Saravay's interest, a cover impression of more primitive disintegration. His dynamisms

stand in conflict to each other in much the same way as
Freud's; he speaks of regression to part-objects, yet he
allows for a concept of idealization which certainly is a
post-object development. Saravay assumes, as does Freud,
that the manifest behavior of the crowd is a reflection of the
operative dynamics, rather than their cover. To me, every
mob, crowd, or group—structured or unstructured, with or
without a leader—has one unshakable narcissistic psychology. In the structured group with leader, narcissism is
rescued through idealization; in the unstructured mob
without leader, the masses rescue their narcissism by
ordaining some proxy or representative to effectively lead
the rescue. Regardless of the situation—unstructured or
structured, led or leaderless—in my observations individuals in a mass rarely succumb to the level of regression
that Saravay suggests; the degree and quality of the regression of the masses depend on the idiosyncratic structure of
the individual, as well as on the degree of the operative
suggestibility.

As to the dynamics of merging with the crowd, I have
suggested that the controlled illusion of mass bondage offers
a necessary cover for the private rivalries of individuals.
What more appropriate camouflage than a "just society,"
an altruistic mob with a chauvinistic *esprit de corps!* Such
an ostensible merging under the banner of equality for all
fails to hide the self-centered currents underlying the
posture of altruism. Object regression, in my view, does not
occur that much more frequently in mobs than in structured groups, and instinctual regression is not necessarily to
deep oral levels. Sometimes, object constancy is even
strengthened rather than weakened in crowds, except in
people who become fragmented in such an atmosphere.
One could argue that such individuals tend to avoid group
situations because of their particular vulnerability. I think
Freud was correct in seeing the progression of secondary

narcissism to love of a leader as a replacement for the ideal of the commune. However, I take issue with Freud's notion of the patriarch as that ideal. By ignoring the pivotal mother, he was deafened to the sounds of anarchy and to the "drums of the restless natives," who are always in preparation to undercut the "great man" in favor of the matriarch. Losing oneself in the crowd, then, is but a group posturing, one that facilitates borrowing the tools and the magic to achieve individual fulfillments. Suggestibility in a crowd, a phenomenon ostensibly shared by mankind, for me has the make-believe quality of hypnosis, where a display of homage to external authority by no means represents a deeper relinquishing of what is good for oneself.

Earlier I described the mechanism of projection, wherein our own attitudes, including those dealing with time, can be externalized. As members of the mob, and through the use of an agent acting on our behalf, we can rest complacent in our expectations that this designated proxy will help us kill off time. Just as the political leader becomes a pivot acting for the masses in matters of state (sometimes an illusion), so, in the competitive arena of sports, for example, can we anticipate that some proxy on the field of play (the referee) will help us recapture a state of timelessness (by hindering the play). The cultural origins of this umpire (or timekeeper) might historically be traced to the days when the warlike aggressions of man necessitated arbitration for sheer survival. Communal conscience outwardly motivated by a concept of fair play might have been the surface factor, but one must suspect that in addition, the task was then, as it is now, to slow down the action on the field of combat to offer the spectator more time to play. It is amazing how a man with a toy whistle, prancing about in an awesome display of time control, can reduce a charging horde of athletic giants into a whimpering brood of misfits. And just as he can transform peaceful spectators into a rabble on the fringe of lunacy, so can he incite the sports fan at home by the television to bizarre acts of violence. It is only partially true that the outcome of the match is decided by the athlete on the field of play, since it is the referee whom we ordain to "kill the clock." When he fails in his appointed task, we pelt him with beer cans or with a rubber chicken; by chanting "kill the umpire," we symbolically get rid of time and timekeeper as we create en masse our version of timelessness.

I have often wondered how many people in their youth hovered outside a sports stadium, as I did, listening to the roar of a crowd. At the time, I did not fully comprehend this unique excitement; all I knew then was that reality seemed altered when I heard the swelling crescendo of human sounds. Certainly the size of the crowd is of particular significance in assessing its capacity to induce an aura of timelessness. A mass rally takes on heightened contagiousness with the mounting of its numbers, and the success of a sporting event, beyond the actual skills of the athletes, depends heavily on the numerical support of its spectators. Crucial to the very legitimacy of the play is whether the stadium is jammed to the rafters, and one's own validation as observer is especially secured if he is in attendance and contributing to the noise.

Curiously, however, when one listens to the sound of a crowd without visual access to the play, one can conjure up imaginative images that are not at all forthcoming when one is provided with the visual picture. By contrast, the imaging of sounds when presented only with the visual is a more difficult task by far. It seems that elimination of the modality of sound more profoundly interferes with one's sense of group participation than deprivation of other sensory stimuli. To explain this observation, one might theorize that the average stimulus barrier requires superego nourishment of an auditory nature in order to compensate for sensory deprivations in other spheres that might have transpired in one's earlier years. The corollary is that it may be more difficult to compensate for deprivation of sound in the formative phases of the stimulus barrier than for other sensory deprivations. Isakower (1939) pointed out that the sensory organs of equilibrium and orientation in space are closely associated with the organ of hearing; both embryologically originate in a single tissue, and both are anatomically and functionally bound together. I would extend this conjunction to include their connections with memory and with time, since both our memory libraries and our neurological pacemakers are lodged in our temporal lobes. By linking these, in turn, with Freud's (1933) view of the superego, Isakower further accentuated the importance of that agency's psychological contribution to the pacemaking functions. Probably hearing, sense of smell (despite the olfactory repressions in man), and sense of position in space are of considerably greater significance than vision in the earliest phases of infantile development, particularly in the prenatal period. This may explain their peculiar ability to augment an aura of timelessness. Sontag (1948) has observed that responses to sound can be elicited even in utero during the last few months of pregnancy, and Fodor (1949) perhaps should have included the sounds of maternal peristalsis as one of the eidetic imprints of fetal nostalgia.

Sound is particularly vital to the humorist, who derives the comforting confirmation of being legitimized from the laughter of a responsive audience. Kris (1940) proposes that collectivity rather than common stimulus is the trigger of such group laughter; certainly those in the entertainment media take this into account when planning the canned laughter that is so crucial to modern television. Canned laughter provides artificial confirmation of group acceptance by creating an illusion of humor simply through the infectious increment of artificial sounds. Knapp (1953) emphasizes that sound as a primary modality brings fusion with the primal maternal object. The rhythm and the sounds of the carrying mother bridge the infant's sense of time and timelessness. Indeed, when an infant is deprived of maternal sustenance, one must wonder which comes first, hallucinatory visions of the breast or hallucinatory sounds representing the maternal rhythms. According to Knapp, vision is related to the future, whereas sound, a more passive modality, is related to the past and the present. From my point of view, sound is especially significant to people suffering from the passive repetition compulsion.

Sounds of the crowd may recapture elements of the primal scene (the primal sounds of parental coitus, whether real or imagined), with the undercurrents of human phallic aggression adding their particular dimension to the aggregate display of noises reflecting our common bond with the animal. In analysis, all kinds of sounds have been clinically traceable to primal scene noises; for many, even the sounds of mob violence or the explosions of war carry an aura of sexual excitement. Whether these sounds be pleasurable or anxiety provoking, Peto (1975) suggests that their linkage with the emergence of superego functions structuralized in the earliest years of life accounts for their effect on the mob. According to Peto, the oscillating and disorganized quality of the noise of a leaderless crowd contributes to the confusion, furthering loss of control even of one's body equilibrium. For Peto, even organized, rhythmic auditory stimulations activate the commands that came from parental figures in childhood, thereby promoting regression to sadomasochistic fantasies of annihilation. Peto fails to acknowledge the sedative effect of organized group sounds which, like the drums of a marching band in wartime, can transform an individual from misfit to sanctioned member of the human species. Being a member of the vocal mass affords an extra dimension of actuality, as well as additional credit for co-producing the sounds. I suggest that in the rhythmic roar of the crowd there is a reactivation of the archaic undulations of intrauterine life, which justifies the conclusion that *the sounds and the rhythms of the crowd are primal* in their inspiring capacity to re-create an illusion of timelessness.

VII

The Return to the (Primal) Scene

THE FAMILY ROMANCE

Like the criminal who returns to the scene of his crime, so the investigator of the killing of time is ultimately drawn to the act of coitus and its *anlage,* the primal scene. Freud emphasized the threat of oedipal castration as a damper on the ardor for sexual consummation. I stress the infiltration of transitional illusion into man's phallic development toward a tenacious postponement of the acknowledgment of time. To introduce the nuclear psychological happening known as the primal scene, I would place particular emphasis on a derivative expression of infantile omnipotence known as the *family romance.* A complex characterized by fantasies of noble birth and commonly associated with the conviction that one was adopted in infancy by "commoners," it makes its appearance much later than the Oedipus complex, commonly toward the end of latency. Nonetheless, it bears a direct relationship to oedipal frustration, which often provokes accentuation of this complex; the family romance, in turn, often causes adequate phallic resolution of oedipal conflict to be postponed. Although

193

some feel that the family romance primarily occurs in the emotionally disturbed or in creative artists, most psychoanalysts have discovered extensions of this complex in the everyday life of humanity at large. As Chasseguet-Smirgel (1976a) has observed, at the heart of all activities, the omnipotent dreams of mankind are to be found—transformed, but nonetheless irreducible.

Clinically, I have encountered two different types of family romance, a benign form and a more pernicious or aggressive one. I emphasize this because it helps clarify the aggressive manner in which the narcissism of the transitional process infiltrates the phallic strivings of adolescent life, as reflected in fetishism and the various perversions of this stage of development. One of the problems with which my patient Lilli had to contend, both within her transference and in her difficulties with her husband, was a congealed aggression, which Greenacre first decribed in fetishists. I feel this aggression keynotes the more pernicious form of the family romance, notwithstanding the simpler emphasis on disappointments and idealizations, which are traditionally offered as the main features of this complex. Overall, the patients whom I have treated have led me to conclude that the benign form accompanies more routine dissatisfactions than the pernicious—discontents usually involving sexually defined parents who provoked relatively innocuous primal scene imagery, which in the main was helpful to their child's sexual development. At the same time these were parents who fostered a sense of ordinariness sufficient to inspire in their children a hunger for a different heritage, usually one involving loftier parental idealizations. By contrast, the pernicious form that some of my more narcissistic patients displayed was linked to more disturbed parents, some whose sexual identity was questionable and whose primal scene imagery only brought confusion and a sense of sordidness to disappointed offspring experiencing a revulsion toward sexuality in general. A more marauding character pervaded the aggressivity of these patients, sometimes involving ghoulish necrophilic fantasies. Whereas the benign form was usually directed toward the search for idealizations and identifications with adoptive communal parents of lofty station, the pernicious form involved the more regressive aim of replacing their adoptive victims.

For Freud (1909), the family romance stemmed from the child's observations of defects in the parents. He regarded the complex as a primal universal fantasy serving the defensive function of disguising or avoiding forbidden sexual activity (incest taboo). Rank (1909) perceived the complex as an expression of the child's need to rescue his self-esteem, particularly in his dealings with his hostility to his father, a theme later elaborated by Sterba (1940). Helene Deutsch (1933, 1937, 1942) stressed the child's frustration in the oedipal conflict and the falling back on a secondary narcissism that required bolstering from the family romance. Like Freud, she, too, felt that the complex originated with the child's first awareness of parental maculacy, compounded by deprivation inflicted by negligent parents. Frosch (1959) observed that although the florid rescue fantasies usually subsided after adolescence, often there were more subdued expressions that lingered into adult life, particularly in people with problems in sublimation or in those suffering from narcissistic injuries. An example is the search for "an identity by association."

Although ordinarily the family romance involves an exchange of one's paternity for a more exalted model, there was every indication from Lilli's defensive secrecy and ultimate melancholia that it was her disappointment with a mother who had been too sick to care for her (and perhaps to love her appropriately) that had been the main instigation of her later family romances. The various idealized, post-liberation sponsors who became solicitous of her welfare (as she first perceived the analyst in her transference, see Frosch, 1959), were on a deeper level, for Lilli, temporarily idealized adoptive mothers. As her analysis went on, I became convinced that the early trauma to her self-esteem and the sense of ordinariness felt in childhood had directly resulted from maternal deprivation, rather than from her father's inattentiveness and family abandonment. Even as a child she felt a yearning for a more exalted environment which might help her find a better future. Her family romances following liberation, however, all proved invariably unsuccessful, so quickly did she become disenchanted with her repetitive "adoptions."

Lilli recovered a seemingly innocuous childhood memory of seeing her father in the parental bedroom in his nightgown. This primal scene fragment, however, captured in caricature her lifelong sexual devaluation of her father. I mentioned that the maculacy of the primal scene had much to do with instigating as well as determining the quality of the family romance. Freud (1896) first introduced the primal scene as a real traumatic event experienced by children who had actually witnessed parental coitus. In his analysis of the Wolf Man (1918), he acknowledged its capacity to become blended with other realities, such as with images of copulating animals, and he noted its predilection to become embellished with themes of castration and debasement of the sexual partner. Freud was struck by the reactions of the witnessing child, including feelings of abandonment, excitation, or helplessness. He felt that the reproduction of these experiences in adolescence, as well as their re-creation in analysis, served as a powerful defense against recollection. In *Moses and Monotheism* (1939) he specifically discussed adolescent sadomasochistic masturbation fantasies that had been triggered by repeated observations of parental coitus.

Since Freud, analysts have come to acknowledge primal scene content as universal in the mental life of post-oedipal human beings, finding few specific pathological reactions in those who witnessed the primal scene. In Esman's (1973) study, certain elements of parental behavior, particularly their aggressions, were held accountable for actuating pathology in their children. Employing the term primal scene to mean the fantasies associated with the scene rather than the actual witnessing thereof, Greenacre (1973) suggested that actual exposure is particularly traumatic to the vulnerable child. She also admitted, however, that children acquire a certain feeling of the sexual nature of their parents via the primal scene, even though what they perceived might have been viewed largely as a physical struggle. She concluded that witnessing the actual event could be overwhelming in its strangeness, an experience that could arouse infantile feelings of loneliness and alienation or even promote altered states of consciousness.

Using the term primal scene as Freud originally defined it, as something actually witnessed, Peto (1975a) expressed the feeling that the primal scene played a decisive role in the etiology of certain cases of fetishism and perversion. According to Peto it offered an early fixation point to which patients could regress, although he saw fetishistic reactions as helping some patients escape a traumatic replay of the oral-depressive abandonment and annihilation originally experienced in the primal scene. In effect, he suggested that the re-creative repetition compulsion involved in fetishism was a way of resolving a passively experienced, traumatic primal scene. He observed that in its internalized poorly structured, bisexual representation of parents, the primal scene made it difficult for the child to establish a firm sense of self or object. The gradual internalization of dangerous parental images brought on precocious superego development of a cruel and threatening nature in the character

formation of the witness. Peto postulated that precocious
and frightening awareness of the anatomical difference
between the sexes, particularly in the case of the boy, could
lead to exaggerated identification with the mother (seen as
castrated), thereby setting the stage for further fixations,
fetishism, or perversions. Isay (1975) picks up the theme of
repetition, observing that in some couples there is a continued need to reproduce the primal scene in their sexual
practices, such as in the use of a mirror during coitus, or by
subtly encouraging offspring to invade the bedroom during
the parental act.

ROMANTIC LOVE

There is a psychoanalytic cliché to the effect that a
major aim of psychoanalytic treatment is to help the patient
achieve a genitality. With Lilli, I found this quite a chal-
lenging and ambitious ideal; to expect a girl to achieve a
normal love life and satisfying heterosexual fulfillment,
even with the help of psychoanalysis, when she had spent
the formative years of her adolescence in a Nazi concentration camp would be to expect an heroic accomplishment.
At the risk of appearing apologetic for my therapeutic
limitations, I suggest that Lilli's handicap definitely compromised the efficacy of analysis in clearing the path either
for the timelessness of love or for a consummation of what
psychoanalysts refer to as a genital sexual adaptation.

Psychologists and philosophers since Plato have tried to
explain the phenomenon of love. Bonaparte (1940) described its ecstasy as a flight from time, comparing it to the
addictions of drink and drugs. Reik (1944), in his days of
dissent with Freud, defined it as a mysterious psychic power
of undiscovered origins and of unknown character. His
particularly compelling thesis rejected Freud's libido theory
as a magnificent mistake, charging Freud with stretching

the concept by robbing the psyche (of love) to pay biology. Reik was all for establishing love as a power in its own right, rather than as an appendage of sex. The view of love as aim-inhibited sex was lambasted as fanciful nonsense, as Reik argued that love, unlike sex, required certain psychological and social conditions for fulfillment; its frequent conjunction with sex did not make the two identical, despite the confusion of love with infatuation. He compared the *release* of physical sex with the *relief* of the psychical tension of love, wherein the object is idealized rather than idolized, and where you cannot force love from the object any more than you can force it from yourself.

Reik contended that like the ebb and flow of hunger for food, sex was bound up with time, and time with sex. Love, by contrast, was timeless, the existence of time being acknowledged only on the parting of lovers, since one's beloved was irreplaceable. Just as sex could exist without love, so love could exist without sex; it could emerge before the desire for sex and last long after it was gone. And contrasted with the ecstasy of orgasm, the climax of love was beatitude. Branding the Freudian version of narcissism a misnomer and arguing that self-love originated in the earliest love of the parent for the child, Reik dismissed "love as an arrested sexual drive" as rubbish!

Clearly, this view of narcissism and libido, antedating Reik's return to the Freudian fold, was biased in favor of primary object love between mother and infant in the earliest months of life, a position to which Reik was surely entitled. It is surprising, however, that he confused Freud's views, ignoring the distinction Freud drew between genital sexual urges and the distributions of narcissistic libido that have a stake in determining all forms of love—romantic, sexual, or otherwise. Again, to postulate some mysterious and perhaps transcendental power beyond libido to account for nonsexual love is surely acceptable, but to condemn the Freudian concept of libido in a zealous search for self-mystification is throwing out the baby with the bath water. Contrast this with Balint's (1948) view, which also acknowledges a primary love between mother and infant antedating narcissism, but which identifies the tenderness of romantic love as deriving from the pregenital phases of child development.

Hitschmann (1953), too, saw romantic love as something of a higher order, recognizing its transcending mystical quality, which existentialists likened to an embeddedness in infinity and God. Yet Hitschmann conceded the validity of identifying a narcissistic component, as Freud (1921) did in *Group Psychology*, wherein the ego ideal of the lover was posited within the love object, promoting inhibition of reality testing and loss of the judgmental appraisal of the love object while under the spell of love. Focusing on the lover's mood of elevation, Hitschmann favored Freud's model of love as rooted in the child's ecstasy of feeding at the breast. Evans (1953), describing "troubadour love" (masochistic), felt it to be primarily based on illusion; the lover sought obstacles to prevent him from consummating his passion, an attempt at disguising the dread of regressing to a masochism once endured in relationship to the mother.

Kohut (1966) observed that for the average individual, idealization survives in the state of being in love, whereas in gifted individuals, it touches one's work as well, as work becomes invested with transitional narcissistic libido. In describing some transitional types of love, Modell (1968) portrays the lover who encapsulates himself in a magical cocoon or plastic bubble; the disdain for acknowledging a dependency on the outside environment affords this lover the illusion of choosing himself as his own object, a self-contained love between "him" and "himself." Gediman (1975) describes what she calls a twin narcissism, a type of

love in which the libidinal investment of the self is trans-
fered to an object sharing a common esteemed activity, so
that self and object are loved as one. According to Gediman, this twin narcissism is common to lovers and creative
artists. Bak (1973) places being in love between mourning
and melancholia, since in all three conditions there is an
identification with an object. In the case of mourning, there
is an identification with the deceased; for the lover, it is
with the beloved; and for the melancholic, it is with the self
as a representation of the lost object. Mourning is the
process of grieving over a lost object. Melancholia is the
expression of lowered self-esteem associated with a withdrawal of love from the object to the self. Being in love is
inspired by the wish to achieve a sense of self; the attempt is
to reach in actuality what cannot be reached intrapsy-
chically. While mourning and melancholia create an
impoverishment as a result of the emptying of narcissistic
cathexes, love leads temporarily to a sense of enrichment
and enhancement, to a sense of being alive and hopeful that
the object will offer replenishment. When followed by
sexual gratification, such an exalted state gives way to
loving. Kernberg (1974a, 1974b) offers two stages of
falling and remaining in love: the first includes the early
capacity for sensuous stimulation, coupled with a capacity
for object relations; the second involves a complementary
sexual identification with one's partner. Kernberg observes
that the fear of loss through abandonment or death is
greatest where love is deepest—an observation that deserves
emphasis, since we are accustomed to thinking that the
burden of fear falls to those less capable of profound object
relations.

Returning to Reik's mysterious psychical force, one
wonders if he had in mind a quality of love that one might
label *charismatic*. I suspect that Reik may well have been
struggling with that intrusive transitional process that

becomes enmeshed in charismatic love. Earlier it was mentioned that the self-replicating qualities that charac- terize the early transitional process can either become reactivated later on during stress or extended into one's adult cultural attitudes. This can also apply to love, where the object becomes distorted and moulded into the psychic image created by the beholder in a narcissistic replication of the original dyad that existed in infancy between the child and its first not-me possession. Like the soft cloth or the teddy, indeed sometimes like a fetish, the charismatic love object can become as irreplaceable as the transitional object of infancy. By further analogy, such a love object is neither internalized, nor mourned, nor lost, but eventually rele- gated to limbo, as in the rise and fall of a charismatic leader. During the period of worship, however, the object is a savior who is capable of inspiring poetry or other forms of transitional creativity in worshippers hungering for charis- matic illusion.

The physical and emotional state of the charisma-prone lover is in itself often pathognomonic—the distraught and disheveled look, the deportment showing the agonies of love—these are the stamp of the individual "in love with love"! In some instances, charismatic love approximates Romain Rolland's description of his oceanic feeling (see Freud, 1930), although the degree of regression to the primary narcissism that stamps the oceanic experience is usually more profound than in charismatic love, where some degree of separateness between self and object permits the development of a not-me effect. The main characteristic of charismatic love is a narcissistically inspired projection, by which the lover permits himself the illusion of having created his own possession in an effort to rescue himself from his own impoverishment (an immature and transi- tional attempt to validate his enfeebled efforts at object love). Among other functions, it serves to blur his protracted incapacities to individuate through the necessary internalizations of meaningful objects. The dwarfed state of the charismatic lover's superego is camouflaged, as with humor, by the legitimizing effect of a creativity tainted with impaired object relations. The lover plays with his love like the humorist with his "homemade transformer," concocting a love object that is neither in himself nor truly existent in the outside world. More often than not, such a choice of love is ultimately fated to the limbo of the teddy or the soft cloth (as is the puppy love of earlier years). The temporarily impassioned quality of such love, rooted in the original compulsion of the child to replicate himself in milk and excrement, is destined to evaporate like synthetic milk or to become flushed down the drain like stools.

Romantic love or love in general is relevant to my thesis since it is yet another intoxicant for the adolescent to employ in his effort to cheat time. Regardless of the kind of love—narcissistic or transitional, romantic or troubadour, degrading or idealizing, charismatic or object-oriented— one must logically conclude that all reflect the state of maturation of the particular individual in love. It is logical to classify two kinds of love, one largely illusory and emphasizing oneself (narcissistic), and the other more appreciative of someone real and separate from oneself. In these terms, it seems apparent that love heavily tainted with narcissism offers a respite from a confrontation with time, since a more object-differentiated love demands greater individuation between lover and object (and individuation demands postponement). As with intoxicants, or with mystical or religious states, idealization impairs the lover's judgmental faculties, as the ideal is given over to the image of the object, including the lover's burden of the sense of time. In a reactivation of the transitional process, the romantic lover is belatedly afforded a protective shield against the exigencies of erupting genitality. He is allowed a postponement of commitment to the care and compassion associated with more developed object love. More importantly, he enjoys a reprieve from trusting or being trustworthy, since these are rarely tested in romantic love as they inevitably are in later years, when romance fades and object fidelity is subjected to the test of time.

Lilli did not fall in love in the concentration camps. Not only did she lose her menarche for the entirety of her internment, but her sexual interest as well. She experienced little conscious awareness of either romantic feelings or sexual excitation during her imprisonment. One might think she would have been exposed to expressions of primal scene sexuality; she only recalled being witness to random acts of lesbianism. Several of the inmates and a guard on one occasion made sexual advances; they were spurned. Fellow inmates became suspicious of one guard who occasionally supplied Lilli with extra rations of food (which she shared with others); they were unaware that Lilli simply reminded her benefactor of his own little girl back in Berlin. Her youthful attractiveness particularly interested a young inmate, who arranged a tryst by the bridge after dark (the lover's lane of the concentration camp). Nothing happened. Lilli was to all intents oblivious of the sexual undercurrents of her suitors, although this same "innocence" was to continue long after liberation and, indeed, right up to her marriage. Her premarital admirers received the same treatment—first subtle seductiveness, then withdrawal when the relationship threatened to become sexualized.

Not that things improved much after marriage. Her husband became rapidly frustrated by her bouts of anxiety, and many times Lilli would fake passionate responses. Coincident with her analytic treatment, there was gradual development of real orgasmic experience, and always of a vaginal quality. Startlingly absent were the clitoridal elements, not only in sexual response, but in her fantasy life as well. This desexualization of foreplay, the lack of clitoridal excitations, went along with her passive role. Never did she take the initiative in sex; her anaclitic responses had to be either compulsively related to the act of biological procreation or expressed as an obvious acquiescence to her husband's needs, which created the impression that her vagina was a lower mouth rather than an erotized genital orifice. In sex, one might describe her as an old-fashioned young lady, or a young "old lady." Jacobson (1976), discussing certain women with strong fixations of vagina as lower mouth, observes that as long as such women feel secure with the man they love, they are capable of vaginal pleasure and orgasm; they became dependent on the partner's penis for their sexual excitement, experiencing his genital as belonging to their own body. Jacobson considers such genitality a sham, a narcissistic identification with the man. She observes that this may have been the usual for women of the last generation, but not for the liberated women of our times. I do not entirely agree with this generalization; it places a woman like Lilli in the category of a parasite paying homage to the penis, a concept that negates her hard-earned capacity to overcome her cynicism toward men, as well as her passion for creating new life. This is not to say that if Lilli were in analysis with me today, I would not heed Jacobson's admonition and be more explorative of the earlier phallic components of her psychosexual development.

THE PHALLIC PHASE

It is well recognized that although everyone has his own individual phallic symbols, some symbols have a universality, that is, they are shared by a relatively large proportion of a given population. Naturally, these symbols change from one era to another. Because of its copying function,

the xerox machine is offered by Boesky (1976) as a modern
day vehicle for the symbolization of the phallic-reproduc-
tive function. In the same vein, the car and the house
remain classic symbols, respectively, of man and woman
and their relationship. The changes in the configuration of
these objects from one decade to another, like wearing
apparel, serve as a kind of symbolic barometer of the sexual
attitudes of men and women. The house reflects the same
vicissitudes of architecture and decor as its female
occupant, just as the model and style of automobile
reveal aspects of the male's sense of self, including his
economics.

Consider the matter of trading in the car. The passion
invested in this transaction reflects in many instances its role
in the struggle with time. Granted that phallic pride is
involved in the waxings, the washings, and the massages,
and that size and shape are important issues for the young
particularly; but the addictive compulsion of exchanging
one's car is a ritual one cannot ignore in taking stock of
man's hunger for a *tabula rasa*. A new car always brings
excitement. For some it is rebirth, a completely fresh start—
and with a more youthful model. There is the novelty of the
brand new name, for example, the Grand Prix. Even for
those who have mellowed as prosperous members of the
establishment, there is the Oldsmobile or the Centurion,
which promises a majesty and longevity that belies the
limits of endurance of our modern transport vehicles.
Indeed, while some try to cheat time with suntans and
facelifts, with travel or diets, others count on a fast paint-
job to disguise their "mileage" come trade-in time.

As with the developmental phases of an airborne missile,
the phallic phase carries the imprints of its earlier pregenital
boosters, whose energies provide the fuel and the will to
loosen the phallus from its moorings and launch it into the
uncharted horizons of "outer space." Whether its voyage

will achieve timelessness ultimately depends on the firmness of one's resolve to abandon hope for pregenital re-entry into "paradise lost" in favor of taking a chance on a genital route to "paradise regained." Greenacre (1964) observes that at the onset of the phallic stage (age four), when in its immobility excrement has been acknowledged as dead, the child becomes fascinated with life, with moving objects, with running and jumping, and exults in the up and down dimension of motility. After cars and houses become separate from the self, and the cosmos becomes filled with all the unseen giants that make things go, there is the sensation of an erectile organ, the penis or clitoris, and a gravity-defying magic enters dream-life in disguise (as flying or tossing a ball). It's a new autonomy. Erection, the tumescence of pregnancy, and the extrusion of childbirth offer an awesome prototype for creative inspiration, as dreaming, oedipal conflict, and conscience keep pace with an unfolding world that engages the enigmatic generative force within.

The conflictual views, current and past, on phallic development not only reflect a considerable range of opinion, but offer their share of puzzlement. Freud (1923a) underlines an early phase of ignorance or innocence in boys, a phase of phallic monism in which the child perceives everyone as built like himself. A subsequent phase delineates two classes of people, those with a penis and those who are "castrated." According to Freud (1925a), a castration complex provoked in both sexes by the anatomical sex differences particularly weakens the male's oedipal strivings. This drives him from the mother into a narcissistic position, flavored with omnipotent self-centeredness, a weak impulse to penetrate, a conviction of possessing unsatisfactory genital equipment—and all this accompanied by a dread of the vagina and recoil from the female.

Whereas in the second phallic phase Freud relates the

male's terror of the female and her vagina to the fear of the
oedipal father and to fear of castration for incestuous
heterosexuality (a fear promoting partial surrender to the
father to safeguard his penis), Horney (1932) ascribes the
inhibited penetrative capacity to wounded self-esteem, a
fear of female ridicule directed at an organ not large
enough to satisfy "the cavernous vulva." Drawing on both
Horney and Freud, Jones (1933) perceives yet a deeper
reason for the shame, specifically the feminine attitude
toward the father, whose penis becomes incorporated inside
the mother's body in a maneuver that switches the surrender to a *woman with an in-dwelling penis.* In effect,
claims Jones, what such a boy (or man) is really ashamed of
is not that his penis is small, but the reason why it is small
(surrender). Furthermore, Jones sees the penis at the phallic
stage as mouthlike in its acquisitiveness, a sadistic and penetrating instrument whose aim is oral possession and destruction of the dreaded in-dwelling penis. Yet, in explaining the
reason for transposing the father's penis to the mother,
Jones offers the motive of reassurance to the male ego that
by so endowing the woman, she will no longer have cause
to sadistically castrate the male. Jones joins Freud, then, in
the sentiment that it is to avoid the imagined and self-
created dangers of the Oedipus complex that the boy in the
second phallic phase abandons the masculine attitude of
penetration by backtracking to phase one, to an assured
existence of his own (and his mother's) *external* penis. But
alas, the renunciation of the mother means but a later
retracing of steps to reclaim what was renounced—the
masculine drive to reach the vagina.

THE ILLUSORY PHALLUS

Somehow the thesis of a "floating penis," passing from
the father to inside mother and then to outside mother, has

never been a compelling idea to me, especially since I have found it difficult to corroborate with clinical material. Yet patients do present the theme of a woman's penis, both in-dwelling and external, and there is ample clinical evidence that the Oedipus complex is characterized in both sexes by fears surrounding incestuous heterosexual preoccupations. Perhaps an alternate explanation that accommodates the phases of sexual development telescoping each other would obviate the need for the aggressive version of the origins of the in-dwelling penis which Jones offers.

If we bear in mind the fragility of the ego during the phallic phase in both sexes, influenced as it is on the one hand by the fears of the oedipal rival and on the other, by the still active residues of pregenital life, then we should expect this ego to seek to reconcile both influences. I can acknowledge, with Freud and Jones, that the male surrenders his phallic penetrative power in deference to his rival, in an abdication that leaves him incapable of psychologically mounting an activity toward the female (the mother). After all, from the very beginning the child endows the mother with psychological power (primal knowledge), which becomes compounded by the child's gradual awareness of her physical procreative majesty (her immortality); now the boy is all the more vulnerable to the woman and her "secrets." I see little reason, however, for the male (or the female, for that matter), as he approaches the phallic level with its new challenges, to abruptly abandon all residues of earlier transitional elements of illusion which served him as defense and comfort. Just as he perceives the enigma of his mother's handbag as a bottomless pit, reminiscent of a magician's hat, from which she can extract sundry items, the phallic boy fantasizes the vagina as a magical replication of the pregenital cavities, as it is recessed in contrast to his genital. In his fantasy it produces a variety of spices—a set of teeth, a cutting shears, maybe a meatgrinder, perhaps a phallus, or even an unborn child. One should not leave out money (or excrement), in all likelihood stashed away in the family vault as well! I should point out that the male is by no means alone in such illusory ideas, although in the female these elements are more subdued and shrewdly displaced from overt associations with sex onto themes of family hygiene or health care such as the giving of enemas, and so forth.

Transitionally derived illusions help compound the aura of maternal omnipotence in the child's gradually elaborating imagery. Not only do they offer auxiliary strength and comfort, they offer an alibi for the boy's bailing out from further ideas of penetration. Even men utilize such illusions as aphrodisiacs for pregenital sexual play. And the abundant clinical evidence of fantasied castrative coitus is in my experience by no means peculiar to those males who perceived their mothers as barracudas or their fathers as monsters. As to the acquisitive aspect of the phallus, which in Jones's view is bent on destroying the in-dwelling maternal penis, in my clinical experience, phallic conflict in male adults with phallic fixations more often reflects a scouring function of the penis, which is seen as a rummaging vaginascope aimed at validating a "Pandora's box" that would justify continued caution against bolder penetration.

The telescoping of this scouring quality into phallic activity, stamped as it is with the replicating passions of transitional process, is exemplified in the case of a mechanical engineer who came to me for treatment of a sexual maladaptation. In his sexual activity this man perceived himself as a time-machine, a mechanized robot when it came to sex. A mortifying fear of surrender to the female underlay his defensive narcissistic position. He had two modes of sexual expression: in one he was a free spirit, penetrating women with abandon, then bailing out of the relationship like a vanishing stud; in his more stable relationships with women, sexual activity was characterized by the search for succor.

It was in his more constant relationships that his inventive preoccupation with time was most apparent. In action as in fantasy, he concocted an intricate scheme of transformatory devices dating back to an experimentation with rubber tubing employed during his pubertal masturbation, and clearly embodying both an identification with his paraplegic father (spinal cord injury) and his robust mother, who had nursed her sick husband. Coitus for this man was a "transfusion," that is, the fantasied use of the tubing (an idea derived from the father's in-dwelling urinary catheter) allowed him to envisage the act as a sexual injection of his partner with carefully calibrated doses of ejaculate, a "slow-drip" infusion regulated by a psychic pacemaker modelled after the stopcock on his paraplegic father's catheter. And there was a reverse infusion from the woman. In fantasy, his penis acted as a two-way catheter or as an extension pipe of a vacuum cleaner, which could successfully scour the woman's abdominal innards in a dredging for some primordial elixir that would provide the patient with the "immortal powers" of a woman.

His penis also served as an umbilical cord, suggesting yet a deeper explanation for the small-penis complex which reflects the feelings of some men of having an inadequate organ for fulfilling the task of "docking" with the woman's womb (thereby bridging the gap back to timelessness). The fetishistic undercurrent of aggression linked with this patient's wish to maraud the woman of her powers related to the extension of a self-replicative passion which began with his childhood conviction that women lived longer than men because of their child-bearing capacity. They had an immortal "juice" inside them. Once he decided that only the female had this formula, he demanded this replicating elixir (of milk and excrement) for himself. From adolescence he began fetishistically scouring various females for this magic—between their toes, in their armpits, or in any other crevice of their body that could conceivably produce the odorous secretions of timeless self-replication. Obviously the dawning trauma of his own biological limits regarding procreation had become buffered in the alchemy of his fetishism.

Most psychoanalysts agree that fetishism derives from the illusion of the existence of a female phallus. Freud (1927) viewed the fetish as a substitute for this maternal phallus which the little boy believes in and cannot relinquish, as a token triumph over the fear of castration as well as a protection against such a happening. He felt the mechanism allowed the fetishist to maintain two opposing images of the female genitals in a splitting of the ego (Freud, 1940a). Hermann (1949) questions Freud's assumption that the male child takes the maternal phallus for granted, maintaining that the little boy fabricates or confabulates the mother's penis, simply out of the gigantic image that he holds of his mother's cavernous vulva. Weissman (1957), again doubting Freud's view of fetishism as a development in the child for surmounting his castration anxiety, sees it as the use of a nongenital object for resolving a specific pregenital disturbance that often appears in the form of a castration threat. He argues that the sexual activity that accompanies fetishism is by no means under the impetus of a heightened genital wish; even in sexual intercourse where gratification is achieved, fetishism in no way aids the genital sexual activity. Rather it is quite the reverse, claims Weissman; sexual activity in fact augments the role of the fetish, safeguarding against the ego disequilibrium of pregenital anxieties by temporarily creating a transient state of ego balance. I support Weissman's thesis, since rage against separation seems to me the motivation of all fetishism.

To Sperling (1963) the fetish serves as a substitute for the preoedipal mother. Sperling believes that to view it as a benign transitional extension (as she feels Winnicott does) is not only fallacious, but dangerous, because the potential for the development of future perversions might be overlooked. Sperling compares the pervert, who seeks gratification in reality, to the neurotic, who accepts gratification in fantasy or in symptom. She suggests that the fetish makes it impossible for the child to individuate psychologically by magically undoing the physical separation. In this way, only the façade of normality is established. Gratifications not obtainable from the mother are gained from the fetish. Its formation interferes with the process of internalization and with ego and superego development, supporting the persistence of part-object relations and deflections of unmodified instinct onto the fetish. Sperling unfavorably compares the use of a fetish to the use of the imaginary companion; at least, in the latter instance, the object is given qualities of a live being and is thus more object-oriented than the lifeless fetish. Sperling observes that in some instances the fetish may be abandoned without resolving the fetishistic fixation, with the result that the person treats another person's body as if it were a fetish. The compelling feature in such object relations is not the person, but only a part of the body or a certain quality of that part. Sperling's view of the fetish also stresses the importance of separation anxiety over the castration complex, since Sperling believes that Freud's concept of the illusory maternal penis does not properly apply to childhood fetishism.

Greenacre (1968) lists qualities the fetish must possess, all representing body parts or body attributes in slightly concealed form: the fetish must be visible, tangible, inanimate, invested with body odors, and not easily destructible. Greenacre's stages of fetish development include a genital body identity that is not firmly established, an unusually severe castration complex, a conception of the female genitals as mutilated and cloacal, failure in separation-individuation with strong primary identifications particularly activated in crowds, and most significantly, a feeling of being castrated when confronted with the female genital. Like Freud, Greenacre sees the fetish as serving to concretize the female phallus and thereby salvage the potency of the male. She points out that since Freud's time, there is clinical evidence that the castration fear of the anal period is not merely related to giving up stool, but to losing the phallus as well, since repeated enemas provoke fear not only of castration, but of disintegration and death as well.

According to Greenacre, unique guilt due to the castration complex of the oedipal period differentiates fetishists and perverts from neurotics. She feels there is a special intensity to the oedipal hostility, wherein the role of injuries, particularly those accompanied by bleeding or mutilation, are likely to embellish the fetishistic syndrome, lending credence to the child's fantasied anticipation that amputation of the penis is indeed a realistic danger (the female is perceived as castrated). As to why the female phallus must be depicted by something concrete in order to serve the purpose of the fetishist, Greenacre's explanation is that an early-witnessed accident involving mutilation of some sort supposedly shocked the child sufficiently to dissuade him from taking a second or third look—something that might have prevented the child from developing the conviction of having witnessed an actual castration (loss of a penis). Instead, the reality is denied and the castration stands uncorrected. In Greenacre's reasoning, it is to offset such fantasied castration that an indestructible fetish is necessary, an object that is also tangible, visible, and smellable.

I am not entirely in agreement with Greenacre. My

outlook on the repetition compulsion suggests that, in childhood trauma, a second or third look neither establishes nor corrects the first fleeting impression; it alters it. If an actually witnessed mutilation were to be the source of fetishistic development, it seems more likely to me that such a mutilation would register on the potential fetishist as a confirmation of the natural frailty of the human body. The male child particularly would in all likelihood attribute this frailty to the penis; the idea of an accident to explain the mother's lack of a penis would perhaps follow. His identification with his mother (as a woman with a penis) would lead to a transitional creative endowment of the woman with an indestructible, even removable, penis—a logical protection against the idea that anyone might easily become "an amputee."

Greenacre also cites the game of pin the tail on the donkey played by children during latency. The blindfolded child is whirled about until dizzy, then directed to pin the tail. Does not such play, Greenacre asks, reflect the child's bewilderment over where the appendage belongs?

Her compelling illustration touches on a theme that I find frequently permeates the clinical material of those tainted with fetishism. So many childhood games seem to lend themselves to this theme, such as "horsey" and "piggyback," in which one child "rides" the other while gesticulating like a jockey whipping his horse. More than one of my patients with strong predilections for anal intercourse have brought memories and fantasies incorporating the flavor of such anal play. A case in point is the male offspring of a hardened old crone, a man who entered treatment predominantly because of a problem in self-esteem. Gifted in economics and seeking fame and fortune in his chosen field, he struggled with a profound sense of inferiority largely derived from his illegitimate birth. His lack of paternal roots led to problems in identity, which were only temporarily assuaged by a guardian uncle who proved to have feet of clay. In his adult years, following the marriage of his only sister, my patient developed a compulsive interest in anal intercourse. There was an eruption of masturbatory activity associated with altered states of consciousness and involving fantasies of sexual play with the girl. A common fantasy cast the girl as companion animal—piggy, horsey or doggy. His fantasied raid from the rear, climbing into her skin like a surgeon into his operating gown, included inserting a fetish into his rectum that was meant to stand for the animal's tail. By transforming himself into the girl, the patient achieved the body image of woman with phallus, his unconscious childhood imagery of his mother. The feelings permeating these bouts of fetishistic masturbation involved what Greenacre would describe as congealed aggression, rage at being abandoned by a sister as well as by an exalted father for whom he still searched with the undying passions of his family romance.

McDougall (1972) emphasizes the element of play in sexual perversions, where the game of role reversal is permitted, including the castration of the partner. In such play, McDougall sees the fantasied symbolic recovery of lost objects. Most importantly, there is a capturing of the eye of the anonymous spectator, a significant third dimension. What has been denied or disavowed, says McDougall, is retrieved through a form of illusion contained in the perverse act.

Stoller (1974) suggests that the term perversion be used to denote a preferred habitual sexual fantasy or act at the root of which lies hostility. He feels that something was done to the pervert by his parents, although the victim cannot specify just what was done, when it was done, or why it was done. Stoller identifies this element of mystery as vital not only to the perversions, but to sexual excitement in general, and related to the convoluted way in which society

obscures the discovery of the anatomical differences between the sexes. To me, the sense of mystery springs from
far deeper than preoccupation with anatomical sex differences; it emanates from man's passion for preserving his
"immortality"—his passion for surmounting the riddle of
time. I go along with Stoller's (1974) metaphorical descrip-
tions of the female genital as something possessing danger
that comes from silence, or as a secret that stems from its
growth in the darkness. I think such imagery is attributable
to the largely unconscious awe the male harbors for the
"immortal" capacity of the female to create new life. I
agree with Stoller that perversions are more common in the
male. He attributes this to the separation the boy must
undergo from his mother's female body in order to become
masculine, a task that in itself promotes perversion—out of
rage, fear, and revenge.

The matter of identification is, of course, crucial to
phallic development. In this phase, the identifications demanded by the instincts of both sexes commonly draw on
the images of live animals as embodiments of those aggressively phallic, sexuality-defining impulses that are incompatible with the child's developing conscience and with the
outside world. Not just at the infantile phallic phase, but
again at puberty and at the climacteric, do such instinctual
strivings pose a risky burden to an unequivocating ego. It is
not surprising that animals in each instance are selected to
embody these base cravings—leashed or harnessed pets
that are chosen to portray this raging struggle between the
ego and the instincts. At the same time, the telescoping of
transitional solutions (an indwelling maternal magic)
continues to offer its element of balm, particularly against
the penetrative-sadistic components of the phallic thrust.

The dog is particularly suitable as a self-image for
connoting the wanderings of the exploring child who, on
release from his fetters in the yard, is permitted to roam the

streets, first like a puppy on a leash, then on his own, in an enactment and resolution of his protracted rapprochement; in his scamperings back and forth between harness and mischief, he busies himself with a new sexualized universe. Clinically, the reactivation or extension of such an instinctual struggle with rapprochement into adult life, couched, as it often is, in animal imagery, produces symptoms and characterological features in adult neurotics that further attest to the equation human beings make between phallic sexuality and the animal nature of man. Patients of both sexes, sorely tempted toward partially censored acts of promiscuous sexual wanderings, commonly present fantasies and associated muscular conversions that they correlate with childhood imagery of harnessed household pets. The very demeanor of these individuals often reflects their struggle—the roving eye, the look of the dog with tongue hanging out, sometimes a compulsive "bark" which comes on at the most inappropriate times (part of the Tourette syndrome).

As with most psychological symptoms, a compromise solution to a conflict can be identified behind these phenomena. Not only does such animal imagery embody instinctual cravings, as well as the policing efforts of the ego against these craving, but like the child's protective parent or the household police dog, the imagery serves as an identificatory defense against the anticipated punitive response of the community. Some adults are ridden with indiscriminate impulses toward promiscuity and fearful of losing the love of a parent or spouse because of the strong sexual wish to rum amuck in the streets (agoraphobics). Symptomatic relief for these people often is only gained through the regressive reliance on the outside agency of a chaperone. Indeed, sometimes a huge dog is selected for that role, an instance of an animal with a human on the leash. Conversely, some people have a dog phobia, in which there is a defensive displacement of oedipal castration anxiety from parent to animal.

Just as the repression of early oral and anal-sadistic trends can lead to depression and obsessional neuroses respectively, so the repression of pubertal phallic strivings can predispose in adulthood to phobias or other hysterical neuroses, especially in those who are reluctant to assume responsibility for their phallic impulses. To mind comes a patient who was squeamish about providing his wife with the sexual fulfillment to which she was entitled. He would recurrently lapse into hypochondriacal fears for his own health or for hers. Such brooding illusions of illness not only yielded some secondary gain, but provided a way out from resolving the anxieties surrounding his phallic strivings— through rescue by some stronger agent (the broad shoulders of the physician). Another vehicle for extricating himself from resolving his instinctual phallic conflict took the form of proxies, by which his forbidden impulses were altruistically relinquished for others to fulfill. Aided by the mechanism of denial, he would permit his wife to engage in sexual intimacies with his best friend, the man who lived next door. In compensation, he would indulge in the pastime of leisurely walking the dog, a model that offered vicarious fulfillment with minimal risk. After all, in a world that lauds the animal lover, who could fault him for walking his dog—even if it "unloaded" on his neighbor's lawn, or mounted the man's wife in the heat of frolic?

The diffidence surrounding the act of coitus, especially during the conflict-ridden phallic period of adolescence, cannot be explained by castration anxiety alone, whether it is directly related to the oedipal father or to some projection of his menacing organ into or onto the body of the female (as Jones seemed to feel). Involved as well is a stalling for time, which is significantly assisted by the telescoped residues of pregenital and transitional development; the adolescent's need for continued narcissistic supplies and his dependency on the strengths (real or imagined) of parental figures allow him to indulge the illusion of obstacles standing in the path of full sexual consummation. These hindrances can take the form of exaggerated oedipal anxieties, fear of the woman with the dangerous vulva, or other more hypochondriacal alibis. Underlying such excuses in many cases may be the narcissistic struggle with time, either the fear of relinquishing the inchoate hope of a timeless reunion with the sustaining breast, or a more contrived stalling to consolidate security and power while allaying the fear of depletion.

Fear of the oedipal father can be properly put into perspective only when it is seen to straddle the shoulders of the earlier pregenital fear of encroachment of time (Father Time). The intrusion of the father into the maternal program of pregenital sustenance of both the male and female child should logically remain as an underpinning of the later oedipal rivalry. This would explain why the scouring phallus of narcissistic males so often disguises an underlying vein of transitional illusion, yearnings of childhood lurking in the penetrative act to "strike oil (milk) when the drill goes in." Naturally a "dry run" adds to their disappointment and justifies a breaking from further exercises in futility. With some relief, the phallic explorer might turn to compensatory diversions (like searching elsewhere for timelessness) or join the father in commiseration, perhaps to enlist his help in building up Superman for another day. A struggle with the pregenital father over time can be clinically confused with the oedipal struggle with the same figure over sex; one tends to disguise the other. Even historically, in ancient Greek art Time was depicted as old man Cronus with a sickle (with which he castrated his father Uranus, according to Greek mythology). Cronus became confused with Chronos, the mythological personification of Time, the symbol of eternal youth and agedness. A similar confusion can often occur clinically when the psychology of the female is examined, again a consequence of telescoping.

FEMALE SEXUALITY

Jones (1933) and Klein (1928) agreed with Freud that girls originally envy a "bird in the hand" in contrast with "childbirth in the bush," but with genitality, this becomes ultimately transformed into the preoccupation with having a child. Jacobson (1968) outlines three developmental phases in a girl's wish for a child. The first is colored by a narcissistic object relation to the mother, with ambivalence and oral envy of that parent's procreative capacities. The second phase is characterized by envy of the father's organ, the girl perceiving her vagina as a lower mouth with which to rob the father of his penis. The third phase of "castration" allows her an oedipal conflict with her mother and genital wishes for a child. Her clitoris brings not only compensatory excitation and pleasure, but shame as well, especially in the unenlightened child, who thereby suffers greater damage to her genital self-confidence.

Other psychologists had early on taken issue with Freud's castration theory of female sexual development. Horney (1932), for example, felt that the masculinity complex in girls, along with its penis envy, stemmed from the repression of a femininity attained in much the same natural way as the boy's masculinity. Others (Marmor, 1954) observed that it was the clitoris rather than the vagina that was the original organ for female orgastic experience, as it is innervated from centers in the sacral segment of the spinal cord. Still others (Barnett, 1966) explained the sexual emphasis that females placed on the clitoris as resulting from an inability to maintain vaginal

awareness without anxiety, cathexis of the vagina thereby
becoming reduced in favor of clitoridal excitations.

It has long been fashionable for psychologists from
various points of view to pillory Freud for many of his
psychological concepts. A primary rationale for these
attacks has been what they consider his chauvinistic view of
female sexual development. The concept of the little girl
suffering penis envy and arriving at her femininity via
castration is for many neo-Freudians quite unacceptable;
and rightfully so. But the quality and tone of the dissent
against Freud's views in more recent times have a most
suspicious ring. In the early postwar period, it was a mark
of sophistication to take exception to Freud's views, but
with a degree of subtlety, with a diplomacy, if you will.
Deferential phrases such as "Freud may have been over-
zealous" or "I think Freud was presumptuous" keynoted the
discretion that marked the salad days of the Freudian critic.
But we've come a long way since then—in our critical
bluntness, if not in our constructive thinking. In these times
our eyes are being opened to the real facts! Reading Schafer
(1974), for example, one gets the feeling that poor Freud
really had a "problem"—when it came to women, Freud
could see no further than the end of his cigar!

At the risk of sounding anti-intellectual, I must say that
listening to some modern day psychologists harangue over
the issue of female sexuality, one cannot help but become
more profoundly taken with the emotional undercurrent
than with the actual issues of the debate. A kind of tempest
in a teapot seems to invade these discussions, even when
delivered in sober academic terms. Particularly noteworthy
is the supreme confidence of the champions of the "new
sexuality" with their "Aha, I told you so" manner. Many of
the female members of this "enlightened society" behave as
if Freud had once hit them in the crotch with an axe. And
their all-too-gallant male counterparts seem to condescend

to the rest of us male chauvinists, as if only they truly love women and know how to give the fair sex their due (which I still suspect is a penis).

I consider myself neither old-fashioned nor a traditionalist when it comes to psychology. I require little convincing that times have changed and that perspectives on human nature are bound to alter. I even agree that Freud erred in some of his judgments and in some of his formulations. But I am also aware that the insistence of some, such as Schafer, on ascribing Freud's views on female psychology to massive blind spots, when in other regards he was so lucid, indeed carries a missionary urgency. Schafer is in too much of a hurry to convince us that Freud missed the boat when it came to female sexuality. Surely whatever new developments unfold in the future, no one will ever be able to make a strong case for washing out *the* basic psychological difference between man and woman. Freud understood and emphasized that difference. In his attempts to formulate a female psychology, he may well have been wrong in his undue emphasis on the anatomy of the genital apparatus; and yes, Schafer is correct in drawing our attention to the psychic portion of psychosexuality. But it is Schafer and not Freud who is trying to get around a basic and fundamental fact of sexuality, namely the biological fecundity of the woman and her reproductive apparatus. It is this creative endowment—her organic endowment—that has to stand at the center of her sexual development. The male does not share in this fecund process except through his role as inseminator. No wonder males develop such a compulsive creative mental activity! In fact, when something aborts or obstructs the female's biological reproductive capacity, a compensatory shift toward mental creativity often follows in the female as well.

When Schafer says that we should not emphasize or assume a self-fulfilling instinctual drive in women toward

the propagation of the species, let him speak for himself!
That is exactly what we should and must assume. It is
toward this very point that this thesis is directed—toward
the repetition compulsion of a woman whose neurosis
stemmed from a direct threat to her biological procreativity, and not from some cultural threat to her clitoris
or from the expectations of some bumbling old patriarch
who was baffled beyond coherent thought on the topic of
female sexuality. In fact, despite women's liberation, new
views on female sexuality, refreshing as they are, do not
seem all that revolutionary. The consensus of a recent panel
on the psychology of women (as reported by Galenson,
1976) was that although female sexual development includes a disappointment at not being male, nonetheless
women enjoy a primary femaleness. Horney told us this 45
years ago. True, Kleeman pointed out in the same panel
that such primary femininity was seen to arise in the first
year of life, rather than after the phallic phase, and was not
initiated by penis envy. Galenson and Roiphe, though
substantiating Freud's position on penis envy and the
castration complex, nonetheless felt that they developed
earlier than Freud thought and were complexes that only
continued to shape an already developing sense of feminine
identity. Buxbaum even proposed a pregenital form
of penis envy, in my opinion quite a logical premise, since
envy of the sexual apparatus can have its roots in other than
sexual performance. For Bernstein the onset of the
girl's latency was the signal for relinquishing oedipal wishes
—out of fear of loss of the mother's love, out of fear of
penetration by the father's penis, or out of disappointment
in the wish for a child. It was left to Elizabeth Kaplan to
support tomboy behavior during latency as a culturally
acceptable vehicle for facilitating the girl's outlet for
aggressive drives.

All these current views on female sexual development

only point up how remarkably few are the major changes from Freud's time. Despite all the clamor and dissension, the new outlook on female sexual development is not as new as some would contend, and what does appear novel seems to have theoretical rather than practical significance. Regarding Freud's views on masochism as a female charac-teristic, Blum (1976) offers a timely and gentle refutation by observing that the so-called compliance of the female may well be a feminine value, rather than a masochistic dcfi-ciency. When Blum states that motherhood, as inspired by the maternal ego ideal, is a basic feminine wish rather than a "sour grapes" secondary compensation, I seriously doubt that he believes Freud would have differed with this sentiment.

Perhaps the most compelling and current case for an updated outlook on female sexual development is the one offered by Chasseguet-Smirgel (1976), who first observes that Freud's theory of sexual phallic monism more logically relates either to a splitting of the ego or to the repression of an earlier piece of knowledge, rather than to a lack of knowledge of the vagina. Her thesis is much like Horney's and in a nutshell proposes that the mother, rather than being seen by the child as castrated, is held in awe for possessing a vagina which the child is unable to fill; since only the father possesses the faculties for doing so, the child is forced to recognize the difference between the gener-ations. A narcissistic wound results, which the idea of phallic monism aims to erase. Underlying the natural scorn of males for women is this powerful maternal image, both envied and terrifying. The need to detach oneself from the omnipotent primal mother by denying her faculties, her organs, and her feminine features is a need shared by both sexes. The girl's penis envy rests neither on her ignorance of the vagina nor on feelings of castration, but on her desire to triumph over this omnipotent primal mother by hoping to possess the penis that the mother lacks. The intensity of the envy is proportionate to the power of the maternal image. Chasseguet-Smirgel concludes that when we underestimate the importance of the maternal image, we allow paternal law to dominate; and conversely, when we neglect the organizing effects of the Oedipus complex, we thereby restore a maternal omnipotence.

I have already supported in part this alternative to Freud's phallic monism through my concept of the infiltration of the transitional process into phallic development, which I have described as lending a mysterious majesty to the maternal body. I questioned the concept of a primary ignorance of the vagina by suggesting that such ignorance was but an illusion concocted to perpetuate the riddle surrounding sexual reproduction (Schiffer, 1973). Stoller (1974), too, feels that one aim of fetishism is to extend this mystery and excitement. Indeed, a large part of sexual pleasure comes from the element of ignorance, without which, who knows, we might lose all interest in sex. In relation to man's struggle with time, I have long been impressed with the evidence offered by so many patients that their ignorance of the anatomy of the human reproductive organs was in fact feigned. The last thing that even the psychoanalyst gets around to understanding appears to be the psychology of phallic development—not at all surprising considering the respite and the transitional joy in analyzing all the illusory sequelae to sexual ignorance. In truth, when we finally discover just where to "pin the tail," it's then that we feel like donkeys for spoiling all the fun that stems from the repression of our deeper knowledge.

As in the case of the male, an element of bluff does, in fact, pervade certain aspects of phallic development in girls—and for the identical reason as in the male, to stall for time. Particularly in the phase when the vagina is for all practical purposes but a lower mouth for snatching the envied penis, an underlying residual quest for the breast (disguised as penis) can be clinically discerned. Left unresolved into adulthood, this lends a bluffing quality to the manifest heterosexual activity of the woman still searching for timeless maternal union. Phallic narcissism (or phallic bluff) is but a compromise then, one that transpires in both sexes, a covert procrastination often disguised in a cloak of precocity. The façade of oedipal resolution in both the male and the female may hide the understructure of dependency or submission to the father and the mother respectively. Just as the adolescent or adult male may continue to disguise or repress the object of his submission (father) by transitional surrender to the in-dwelling maternal magic, so the adolescent or adult female with her lower mouth may unconsciously hope (as Lilli did) to retrieve the maternal breast in the guise of the oedipal penis.

Reich (1949) has described characteristics of adults of both sexes in whom fixated development produced phallic narcissism. He profiled a confident and arrogantly vigorous male of cold reserve, unwanting in self-regard, whose strong attachment to people and things was motivated by infantile and neurotic factors. He cited the courage of certain aviators and athletes and their reactionary boldness in the face of underlying feelings of phallic intimidation and orgastic depletion, which nonetheless buffered the residue of sadistic rage. For Reich, the narcissistic male's degrading attitude toward his partner during the act of penetration is often matched by the disdain of a female counterpart willingly colluding in the confirmation of his impotence (thereby disguising her envy as well as her deeper cathexis of the mother). Reich offers early disappointment in love to account for such fixations, where an identification with a disappointing object can lead to homosexual compensation. This contrasts with Jacobson's view (1976) that whereas oedipal castration anxiety causes male narcissism to take precedence over object love, phallic narcissism in the female merges into object love. In keeping with the animal complex mentioned earlier, I would add another trait to this profile of phallic narcissism, a coat of arms that aggrandizes narcissistic sexual instabilities. As the flip side of the phobic so to speak, promiscuity and object inconstancy are the hallmarks of liberation for some of today's adults. In this sophistry, object constancy becomes equated with timidity, as robust actualization lends an aspect to phallic narcissism that particularly in our times looms as the new standard of human sexual adaptation.

With all the complexity of the struggles of phallic development, one might logically conclude that its early stages, occurring in childhood, are of the order of bluff that reappears not only in puberty but sometimes in adult life. When we are small and young, we wish to be bigger and older; when we are bigger and older, we wish to be even bigger and younger. The protracted, pregenital flavor of bluff that permeates phallic development is especially pronounced in those who need more time (for securing timelessness), in those who find it difficult to acknowledge limits. When either the castration or the separation anxieties of puberty and adolescence are especially intense, we can expect excessive phallic narcissism to become a reconciliatory solution. Such narcissism gains its earlier impetus in the natural course of latency, when disgust with sexuality and shame for harboring a potential for genital object love reinforce the child's cathexis of the self. It is not surprising to find adults driven to repetitive yet abortive efforts at genitality (genitality is defined here as sexual relations with mutual regard between partners), without the necessary sacrifice of some of their narcissism. This is often reflected in bisexual escapades or in theatrical and hysterical attachments to props in postponement of the forward step.

To Reich's explanation that early disappointment

triggers phallic narcissism, one might add simple failure or neglect in reciprocating genital feelings, to which the overly indulged as well as the unduly frustrated or intimidated are prone. Of course, failure of early influences to offer a sense of protection and trust, or to make demands of appropriate return of genital feelings, will take their toll in subsequent phallic fixations which promote an aura of protracted adolescence. As Erikson (1956) has observed, prolonged adolescence involves an urgency about time; yet paradoxically, there is a loss of its consideration as a dimension of living, wherein youth feels babylike, yet aged beyond rejuvenation, unwilling to believe that time may bring change, while terribly fearful that it might. Erikson describes the feeling as a moving in molasses, a mistrust of time where every delay is a deception, every hope a danger, and every plan a catastrophe. For youth, Erikson concludes, time must stand still—either through magic immobility or death.

Orgasm and Timelessness

Reik (1945) explains the criminal's predilection for returning to the scene of his crime as the transgressor's wish for re-experiencing his ghoulish pleasure, as well as his need for self-betrayal, punishment, and expiation. By returning, the criminal challenges the fates either to apprehend him or to allow him a total escape. This thesis suggests an alternate conclusion, that a deeper narcissistic dynamism is operative, namely the compulsive wish to reanimate the dead victim through a magical reincarnation. This would not only offer proof of the criminal's, as well as the victim's, invincibility (the timeless immortality of all mankind), but would also offer an opportunity to engage in the re-enactment of the repetition compulsion (by committing the same crime over again).

In a successful killing of time, if such an achievement were possible, both time and timelessness would need recapturing, for without the resurrection of the victim (time), there could be no target for repeating the liquidation. In his thesis on "the great man," Freud failed to satisfactorily explain why the father was more powerful in provoking group bondage when dead than when he was alive. I suggest that the father was never perceived as dead, but rather as immortalized, a dynamism that lies at the core of the active re-creative repetition compulsion. Reik raises the issue as to why unsolved murders or assassinations provoke an uncanny aura, as if some supernatural force were standing in the way of a solution to the crime. I suggest that rather than anticipating a solution that would bring the true culprit to justice, the general public has an unconscious preference for a magical reincarnation of the victim (a confirmation of man's immortality). I offered a similar view on man's perpetuation of the enigma of the primal scene (Schiffer, 1973), contending that despite diligent research into the facts, man still prefers to compound, rather than to clarify, the riddle of human sexuality—to keep it suspended in its enigmatic mist. This human revulsion for intrusion into the sanctuary of his "original sin" reflects an extended compulsion to maintain safeguards on perpetuating the aim of sex, namely to abolish time toward reinstatement of an original timelessness. In the re-creative compulsion of coitus, I see man drawn to "the scene of the crime" in perpetuity, prepared for both progressive and regressive paths toward securing his goal. Like the adolescent, he is often far from equipped to do the job successfully; in his nostalgia he is not disposed to abandon his more familiar infantile modes in favor of a thrust toward the more tangible solutions of biological pro-creativity.

Our need to maintain the mystery of sexuality may

explain why the novelist and the playwright intuitively portray our favorite detective, whether Sherlock Holmes or his modern-day counterpart, as a man with a questionable sexual life! Cast as maladjusted or as a celibate, he is out of his depth when it comes to sex. His image assures us that one mystery he will never solve is the secret of human sexuality. Sitting in a cafe over a bowl of chili, our modern shamus makes minimal reference to "the little woman" at home. As with our political heroes, a flagrant link between sexual activity and sleuth would only inject a discordant note; the public are as loath to entrust their protection from crime to an investigator who engages in licit sexual intercourse as they are to place the national safety in the hands of a politician who is a homebody. On the surface, we may claim that we look for a figurehead who is the epitome of the mature, sexually knowledgeable leader, one who offers a model for national emulation; but I suggest that more often than not, we choose a leader (not by coincidence) whose sexual life is far from resolved—indeed often illicit and heavily tainted with intrigue (we feign surprise and indignation when the facts come out after the leader has long gone).

In the same vein, those who consult a psychiatrist, ostensibly to shed light on the deeper conflicts of their sex lives, are often unconsciously hopeful that their carefully selected investigator, like the detective, will help preserve the mystique of both the patient's and the therapist's sexual adaptation (or maladaptation). Not that this study can claim to offer a solution to the mystery of the sex act, though I have proposed that it has to do with the recapturing of a timelessness in a re-enactment of the primal scene. There are some who prefer to emphasize its physical and anatomical aspects—workers in the sexology clinics who observe coitus "under glass," under supposedly scientific conditions which only reflect the exhibitionistic theatricality of all those involved. The limits in an academic exercise in sexuality are clearly drawn; sex meant for an audience, whether for the general reading public, for filmgoers, or for scientific voyeurs in the laboratory, will fail to capture the flavor of the primal scene. The squeaking bedsprings under enraptured young lovers which send messages to landlords through paper-thin walls probably come closer to creating a replication of that happening. Fliess (1961) observed that aside from the influence of toxic agents, the only condition that met the requirements of total blockage of self-observation beyond infancy was the experience of orgasm. I would hasten to add that orgasm itself will not entirely do that job. For an orgastic timelessness to be achieved, a *genital* coital act in the psychological sense is required—a sexuality in which both partners, the male and the female, have acknowledged a mutual caring beyond phallic narcissistic exploitation. Such an emotional engagement can only occur between those committed to a psychological perpetuity of parental identifications, as well as the biological perpetuity of themselves (coital conception). Only this provides the incentive for man to undergo the struggle toward individuation and to renounce some of his narcissism in favor of a nonincestuous partner.

There is considerable controversy over the position Freud took in relation to his perception of Eros as a drive remaining outside the domain of the repetition compulsion. The core of his views on the death instinct drew on the phylogenetic development of the lower animal kingdom to support his theory that man is dedicated to a return to the inorganic. Although he toyed with the idea of including Eros in his death instinct theory, allowing himself to briefly entertain the possibility that the repetition compulsion might be energized by Eros (Freud, 1923b), he concluded that because Eros had to do with union, creation, and progress, rather than movement to a previous state, it should be abandoned as an instigator of the repetition compulsion. He equivocated briefly thereafter (Freud, 1933) but ultimately reaffirmed his conclusion (Freud, 1940). He reasoned that including Eros in the service of a death instinct would imply that living substance was once a unity, that it had been torn apart and had come under a subsequent compulsion to reunite the torn particles.

Freud's (1939) speculations concerning the delayed sexual development of human beings (insofar as is known, the only one of the animal species to have a latency period) involves his theory of the slaying of the primal father, as well as its re-enactments, with Moses and Christ as the victims on these occasions. Freud's theory of an incubation period between the disapproval by the Jews of the Mosaic doctrine and its later acceptance after a period of repression became the model for Freud's understanding of the role of time in mental life: "it takes time for the reasoning activity of the ego to overcome the objections that are maintained by strong affective cathexes" (p. 67). His formula for traumatic neuroses and the repetition compulsion (early trauma —defense—latency—neurotic illness) offers a phylogenetic view of the dilatory nature of man's sexual development, in contrast to my ontogenetic concept of the trauma of time. Freud identifies the trauma as the actual killing of a patriarch, resulting in a psychology passed down to individuals within the group as a repetition compulsion in response to that traumatic event.

Though supporting Freud's version of the death instinct as well as drawing on his earlier view that sexuality was in some way included, Ferenczi (1923), in his parallel between the individual experience of birth and its psychological repetition in the act of coitus, decided that genitality was a belated abreaction of the individual aimed at mastering the trauma of his rupturing emergence into the world. In sex, Ferenczi saw separate, repetitious acts releasing fractional amounts of unpleasurable tension toward undoing the trauma. His thalassal theory deserves elaboration insofar as it has a specific bearing on the theme of orgasm as a quest toward the restoration of timelessness.

In Ferenczi's view, the human organism returns to the womb in three ways, through psychologically hallucinated return, in the form of the penetrating penis, and through the secretion of germ cells. Reality for Ferenczi (1913) involved a renunciation of the regression that normally appears in sleep, in dream, in sex, and in fantasy, and only a fully developed genital function could achieve what Ferenczi called an erotic reality sense. Yet he was convinced that the genital act would have undercut latency in man's ontogenetic development (and at an incestuous level) had it not been for the social taboos against incest. I have already expressed my reasons for disagreeing with this view in my psychology of phallic development.

According to Ferenczi, self-induced castration anxiety in the male was prompted by the unconscious wish to get rid of his organ, to drop all or part of it into the receptacle of the woman, since it produced such unpleasurable tension. He perceived the emotions mobilized in the coital act as stemming from the re-experiencing of painful birth merged with happiness at the re-establishment of intra-uterine life. This produced a reduction or cessation of consciousness during orgasm—a cataleptic hallmark of hallucinatory fulfillment. He compared sex to wit, where there is playful pleasure in the negation of an original trauma and where one can play with danger in attenuating the fear of living in an overpowering external world. Ferenczi agreed with Darwin that the intrauterine existence of higher mammals replicates an original piscine period. He hypothesized that birth may be but a recapitulation of a recession of the oceans that forced our ancestors to adapt to land existence by substituting the human uterus for the ocean's waves. Reminding us that the genital secretion of the human female has a distinct fishy odor, Ferenczi compared the amniotic fluid to an introjected sea.

Contemporary theorists and clinicians harbor serious reservations not only about Ferenczi's theory, but about Freud's death instinct as well. Szasz (1952), for example, accepts but one primary instinct, the life instinct, the aim of which is to keep the life processes in continuous operation by drawing a negative entropy from the environment. Basing his dissension with Freud's theory (and implicitly with Ferenczi's) on its derivation from Fechner's principle and the Second Law of Thermodynamics, he suggests that, in general, it is the frustration of instinct that leads to either progressive or regressive adaptation, and that while primitive systems adapt progressively, complex ones adapt regressively toward earlier archaic patterns of behavior. Binstock (1973) perceives Ferenczi's theory as naive, concrete, and literal—indeed, as male chauvinistic. He sees a paradox in the idea of instinctually regressive triumph being placed alongside the renunciation of aggressions toward the establishment of the sense of reality. The failure to distinguish between psychological development before and after the establishment of individual autonomy is the fault he finds with Ferenczi's thesis. Binstock is skeptical, as am I, that man is dominated from birth by a regressive trend toward re-establishing intrauterine life, and he disdains the description of the sex act as but a clumsy effort at returning to the womb.

Needles (1953) goes beyond Ferenczi, taking particular issue with Freud's (1909a) nihilistic concept of the adult sexual act as habitually terminating in orgastic loss of consciousness, again a Freudian view backed by Ferenczi (1923) and others, such as Keiser (1952), who also ascribe to normal individuals a momentary state of unconsciousness in orgasm resulting from the massive withdrawal of cathexis from body ego. Indeed, Keiser views the failure to achieve unconsciousness during climax as a sign of unhealthy repression and a reflection of undue fear of death during the act. Needles, by contrast, allows for an alteration of consciousness at climax, but like Abraham (1917), perceives total loss of consciousness as symptomatic of pathology, such as that which occurs in cases of premature ejaculation, where orgasm is often an effortless "dying."

Regarding repetition compulsion, Needles (1962) reminds us of the hermaphroditic tendencies in man as well as in nature, where human autoeroticism, fetishism, and transvestitism suggest that Eros is motivated by life instinct in the service of the repetition compulsion. According to Needles, man, rather than seeking minimal excitation beyond the pleasure principle, seeks maximal stimulation in the service of pleasure. He further counters (Needles, 1973) that lack of clinical data supporting a loss of consciousness at orgasm forces one to suspect that Freud's idiosyncratic personality may have well been responsible for his view on orgasm—in Needles's opinion, as nihilistic an outlook as Freud's theory of the death instinct. What may hold true for instinct may not be true for ego, Needles argues, and man's adventuresome ego allows him an act with forepleasure that reflects a far less enigmatic passion than Freud (and Ferenczi) would have us believe. Unpleasure to the point of unconsciousness, claims Needles, is a reflection of castration anxiety, which is Needles's diagnosis of Freud's idiosyncrasy.

Dizziness or unconsciousness associated with sex may well have implications beyond those that can be accounted for by the physiological phenomena associated with the coital act. Giovacchini (1958), for example, links the symptom of dizziness to precocious sexual stimulation in childhood, which leaves the victim vulnerable to later experiences that re-create the past sexual trauma. He describes patients who are prepared for every contingency, in anticipation of and defense against being caught unawares in sexual relationships. I, too, have encountered patients with "sexual dizziness." For one individual, the sex act involved a fantasied insertion of his entire head (or brain) into the vaginal canal of his partner. Another man invariably experienced giddiness as his genital became turgid in the prelude to the act; the abrupt release of fluid and tension at orgasm was experienced as a sudden emptying of the contents of his brain, associated with a momentary sense of loss of consciousness. His symptom was ameliorated when his erotic strivings were separated from the phallic erotization of his head and transferred to a more localized genital sensation.

Ferenczi's thalassic theory and Freud's death instinct theory, although probably academic, are nonetheless fascinating subjects for controversy. It is my own impression that Ferenczi's theory is itself a reflection of a re-creative repetition compulsion, wherein the author engaged in an exercise in controlled illusion that reflected his struggle to divert the symbolism of the incestuous mother into a vast cosmic force, perhaps in an effort to deobjectify incest and minimize the regressive implications. Ferenczi's further perception of a close relation between the sexual act and hypnosis upholds his view of hypnosis as love in its true sense. Yet such a view makes one suspect that Ferenczi either denied or ignored the transitional element of controlled illusion and the theatrical make-believe that is implicit in hypnotic suggestion, re-creating as it does the mutually manipulative aspects of play where one partner feigns surrender to the other in the hope of borrowing the imagined powers of that partner (Schilder, 1923). Indeed, the macabre vignette of the ejaculatory death throes of the criminal about to be hanged, which Ferenczi puts forth as an example of sexual excitement, is to my mind an over-zealous pitch for including Eros in the service of the death instinct. To me, a more likely explanation of this grisly ejaculatory response is castration terror at facing such a dire fate.

Rather than finding Ferenczi too naive and literal, as does Binstock, I see an expansive and robust egoism which presents the act of coitus as larger than life. Even Ferenczi would agree that something more modest and personal than a "cosmic orgasm" occurs in the conscious and preconscious life of most people during coitus, even in those reacting to fading hopes of self-procreation in the face of the aging process. The phallic grandeur of Ferenczi's thalassal theory hints at an underlying uterine envy. I think it is fair to observe that as an instrument for achieving timelessness, the male organ pales alongside the nine-month stretch that the uterus undergoes as cradle for the creation of life. Such envy in men has long been documented and has been recently reviewed by Jaffe (1968).

As for the psychoanalyst's fascination with the idiosyncratic sex life of Freud, one need only point out that Needles, like many other analysts, seems to be substituting Freud for the father in demonstrating his passion for returning to the primal scene. What more classic illustration is there of this psychological process than our academic interest in what the father of psychoanalysis was doing under the sheets? Even our lofty scholarly pursuits fail to disguise the theme. Like the criminal and the investigating detective who are both compelled to return to the scene of a crime, so humanity seems drawn to the primal scene, to both replace and restore the oedipal parents in a bid to transform self and primal objects toward the illusory achievement of timelessness (immortality).

Freud (1936) himself never claimed to be above this narcissistic venture, as evidenced by a personal vignette—his experience while standing on the Acropolis. He acknowledged the process of transformation and the feelings of derealization I offered earlier as features of the repetition compulsion—a derealization which Freud likened to hallucination. Freud refers to the transitional element of illusion enmeshed in his symptom, a reflection of his endeavor to surmount dissatisfaction with home and family, particularly his undervaluation of his father that took the place of earlier idealization. Freud concluded that it was his filial piety in reaction to the forbidden desire to excel over his father that had persisted right up to his experience on the Acropolis. Psychoanalysts have long enjoyed offering their own analyses of Freud's experience at "the top," and I am loath to add mine to the ever-growing list. Nonetheless, there is a strong tone of blended complexes in this Freudian pastel, an activation of old repressions, including sibling rivalries, oedipal residues, and primal scene ingredients— all flavored with Freud's family romance and, more significantly, with the sense of his immortality in the face of transience.

The temporary sense of derealization Freud experienced while standing on the Acropolis, and the altered states of consciousness he experienced during coitus, are phenomena we all experience to a degree when something triggers our harking back to the past. Some have emphasized developmental crises, such as castration anxiety in the face of oedipal triumph, as the key element in such "acropolisian" phenomena, while acknowledging as well the overpowering grandeur of antiquities (see Harrison, 1966). I prefer to offer the trauma of time as the bonding factor, a trauma that comes from the awareness of being an insignificant speck, sharing a common space and sense of transience with others.

In coitus, it is the trauma of time we aim to overcome when we return to the primal scene as participants. Perhaps for some of us such a scene has an aggressive and traumatic quality, but it is a crucial psychological event nonetheless. Our return is the very quintessence of the active re-creative repetition compulsion, a uniquely human transformation of the coital act, a compulsion that offers testimony to our undying hopes for continuity and for achieving the ecstasy of timelessness.

VIII

An Exile from Eden

Mystery stories customarily conclude with the so-called wrap-up in which the triumphant supersleuth unravels the intricate skein of clues and motives at a last gathering of the harassed suspects. This traditional ritual culminates in the climactic unmasking of the criminal. I would deviate in one respect from this classic format by ending my narrative on a note of self-effacement, for as the author of this study, I am as patently guilty as any of the killing of time. To some, man's emotional and sexual development may appear motivated by an aversion to birth or death, while to others, the wish to escape oedipal castration seems to be the consideration. To me, such procrastinations are the passionate reflections of man's heroic efforts to alter the trauma of time through an undoing of the separation from those who gave him life. Although the clues to this process may be found in the illusions of the transitional process and in the family romance, nevertheless such transformatory expressions must inexorably reach their climax in the coital act, where each of us stands exposed as a participant in this universal "crime."

241

The clinical narrative presented herein portrayed a girl in a world at war, where the traumata of everyday life contrasted sharply with the routine living of today. Fortuitous mishap, disease, man's everyday aggressions toward man, all these we have become accustomed to taking in our stride: but not Nazi death camps. Although I have acknowledged the basic force that drove one girl toward a precocious adulthood in a compulsion to replicate her genes, I made only tentative efforts to relate this to the more ordinary conflicts that most of us encounter in our odyssey toward biological fulfillment. This final chapter inventories the role of time in our here and now, where, in search of our rightful share of longevity, we all draw on a reservoir of transitional devices to uphold our personal dignity in the face of our transience.

I have proposed that beyond the cognitive process of assimilation, the human compulsion to repeat is a universal, psychological mechanism prompted by our instinctual need to both merge with and individuate from the mother in order to fulfil our procreative capacities, a heritage passed down by our ancestors in repetition of some primordial cosmic force. As a fate forced on us from birth, this compulsion becomes transformed from passivity to creative activity, wherein our imaginative symbolizing capacities in reaction to threatened loss help us rediscover our communion with parents in the form of controlled illusion. I have compared the process to the modern electronic device that faithfully and objectively records human or elemental happenings and then allows instant replay; yet in no way does it completely eradicate the subjectivity of the observer, whose task is to alter the actuality through his creative and imaginative psychology. This playback allows us the freedom of subjectively manipulating our time experience, wherein images can be shrunken or enlarged, telescoped or stretched, and, most significantly, relived in an endless repetition.

Freud (1927a) pronounced that the most important item in the inventory of a civilization was its illusions. He perceived their task as a defense against nature, but he expressed grave misgivings as to the efficacy of some of our illusions to achieve that goal without considerable harm to mankind. Recognizing that the fountain of human illusion was derived from the wellspring of man's wishes and acknowledging that without neurosis man could be left helpless and insignificant in the face of an overpowering environment, Freud still charged society with the task of preserving man's cathexis of earthly matters, which he felt held greater promise for the welfare of civilization than did the spiritual anticipation of a life after death. He was particularly taken with the benefits that humanity derived from the illusions of the creative arts, and he (Freud, 1930) also offered emphatic acknowledgments of other auxiliary constructions, such as deflections, substitutions, intoxicants, and displacements, which were available for lifting libido to the higher planes of imagination, humor, and love. Perhaps he foresaw the holocaust when he warned that it was aggression that posed the greatest impediment to civilization. Freud perceived aggression as a death instinct unobtrusively operating within the living organism, at all times standing in opposition to Eros. Although he was optimistic about crucial benefits accruing to civilization from controlled illusion, he was concerned generally about obstacles to a victory for Eros and especially about the power of the destructive instincts, which he perceived as ominous to our civilization. According to Freud, survival for mankind rested on neurosis-free men and women unflinchingly turning the tide by facing up to the truth toward building a more civilized world.

In this particular regard, I have a less courageous outlook than Freud's. In the absence of hard statistics, I have speculated that the frailties of man, especially the tenacity of his narcissism in the face of the trauma of time, are indeed more profound and universal than Freud was inclined to believe. Man's ignorance of the primal facts surrounding life and death has shown little sign of amelioration despite scientific progress; and though this may be an observation from impotence, a human posture that Freud both deplored and countenanced (1927a), it is my contention that to be convinced of man's knowledgeability of the whole truth is but another controlled illusion. I have offered man's ignorance as a truth that matches the fact of his knowledge, an understructure defended by an illusion of omniscience. Many illusions are embedded in validated "facts" and thus may appear less offensive to the intellect than those based on belief. Nonetheless, they are natural protrusions of the transitional process into our reality, and apparently necessary for the psychological survival of those who require a lifetime to come to terms with the passage of time. The illusory elements of the transitional process invade the lives of all of us, even our adult sexual lives. They play a major role in first postponing and then embellishing the act of coitus. Without such illusions, man would be hopelessly locked in a barren repetition compulsion without the re-creative features that permit him a return to the primal scene to achieve the sense of continuity and timelessness that is embedded in this nuclear imprint.

The reader might conclude from this that I support homage to transcendence as the salvation for mankind, the kind of undoing of the denial of death that Becker (1973) suggests, or the repair of impaired death imagery that Lifton (1976) prescribes. Becker chided Freud for his lack of spirituality and for aggrandizing sexuality instead of acknowledging its limitations in the face of man's more impassioned struggle with death. Becker's hero was Rank, a man who understood the need for illusion and afforded it the stature of an ultimate salvation, a transitional balm for the human agony. For me, Rank's trauma of birth as the cause of neurosis is no more acceptable than Freud's death instinct as the explanation for man's repetition compulsion. On the contrary, genital sexuality in all its corporeal flesh-iness has always been the main thrust of mankind, enlisted as it is, with the aid of transitional illusion, in the service of the timelessness of procreation. Although Rank's views on creativity are to be lauded and the beauty of Becker's prose applauded, their indignant reactions to Freud's atheism, weighted by an argument for spirituality that belabors the mortification of the psychobiological aspects of sexuality, to me show disdain for the creative power of the body. Eros is seen as too puny a weakling, and Death is left with too heavy a clout.

As to the impaired death imagery which Lifton offers as the predisposing and premorbid factor in the traumatic neuroses, his concretization of death allows a kind of existential deal with death *qua* death; the specter can be confronted rather than avoided—allegedly the habit of the Freudian analyst in his countertransference to his patient's fear of death. Jousting with one's impending annihilation by arming oneself with "death imagery" rests on the un-proven and unprovable conviction that the unconscious, like the conscious mind, not only knows of life but of death, a burdensome concept indeed. Examining the posture of those who espouse it, one invariably discovers the intro-duction of the theme of the hereafter, and one suspects that transcending one's denial of death through bold encounters with the human nemesis is in itself a mechanism of denial, a wrestling match with a pale but comforting messenger from the realm of the hereafter. It is yet another example of controlled illusion with which there is no cause to quibble—provided one is not upbraided for identifying it for what it is.

THE LIMITS OF NARCISSISM

It appears to me that Freud's philosophic exercise in foreseeing the future of an illusion is even more relevant to society today than it was in Freud's day. A new narcissism that conceptualizes a limitless reservoir of self-invested libido following its own developmental path implies not only progressive directions for such investments, but an infinite variety of regressive ones as well. One might compare this new concept to the Prigoginian view of a decreasing or negative entropy which holds promise of an infinite timelessness for mankind.

If we were to accept out of hand a theory of independent narcissism, it would raise certain obvious questions germane not only to the future of an illusion, but to the future of object responsibilities. For example, what kind of mental illnesses might one expect to find in societies that continue to encourage an ever-broadening spectrum of narcissistic options? As for the quality of culture, what kind of appreciative posture toward the creative arts would be spawned under conditions where the sluices of self-indulgence were opened even wider? More importantly, what sense of responsibility should one expect man to shoulder in a world that offered rewards for ever more liberated narcissistic expressions? Some of these questions have been tentatively answered by the inroads that narcissism has already made into our present culture.

Today's acceptance of narcissism as a necessary investment for the maintenance of a sense of balanced self may have precipitated a tendency in some to negate the traditional psychoanalytic view of object love, which involves a certain necessary renunciation of narcissism. Few will deny, however, that previous tendencies to condemn self-investments categorically as undesirable overlooked some of their more healing benefits. And despite the barrage of criticism from traditionalists who continue to attack today's cultural revolution, people's psychological outlook on issues of identity is considerably healthier than it was half a century ago. For example, through our increased understanding of narcissism, we have a more humane and empathic view of the so-called sexual perversions, expressions of delayed development typical among those who equate growth with death. Psychopathic personality as a blanket diagnosis for certain character trends is no longer as acceptable as it conveniently was in the past, and a new enthusiasm on the part of clinicians treating narcissistic disorders has replaced the previously gloomy outlook for their cure. There is little doubt that the cultural liberations of today have allowed long overdue relief from certain artificial burdens, shams, and pretenses, such as blind displays of muscle-flexing male chauvinism and penis worship "femininity," that marked yesterday's version of sexual respectability.

Notwithstanding these progressive features, and despite the psychoanalysts' enthusiasm for detailed analyses of narcissistic problems, there are good reasons to be concerned that the cultural deviation toward narcissistic license poses a setback to some of the earlier contributions that Freud agonizingly made in his sober appraisal of the future of an illusion in the mental life of mankind. As a practitioner treating ever-increasing numbers of individuals with narcissistic disorders, not a day goes by that I am not acutely aware of my collusion in the therapeutic exercise of killing time. The homage that our present culture seems so willing to pay to those who uncover, or expose narcissistic fantasies in the name of artistic expression is likewise amazing. Even our theater and other forms of entertainment seem bent on a relentless repudiation of a value system that used to respect the privacy of the self. Today's exaggerated emphasis on unveiling the whole truth in the name of honesty seems to have led to a wholesale dispensing with the notion that there may be some value in leaving certain aspects of humanity in the protective obscurity to which they have been accustomed.

It seems to me that man's responsibility to his fellowman particularly suffers when exaggerated narcissistic traits become exalted, since it is a fact of human nature that self-indulgence fosters its own form of aggression, *the aggression of negligence.* Throughout this study I have stressed this type of aggression, which is often subtly intermeshed with the illusory elements of the transitional process. Perhaps this is the strongest argument of all against exaggerated narcissism. A necessary way station it is, for creativity it may be mandatory, it may indeed have its own developmental autonomy. But when it comes to human relationships, it carries the potential for negligence, for dereliction of one's consideration toward others—sometimes the cruelest form of aggression. For neurotics, finding an oasis in narcissism may mean a new opportunity for elevating self-esteem and acquiring a zest for living. As with tranquilizer pills, however, there is the possibility of overdose, even from "higher narcissistic expressions." As often as not, self-investments bring rewards that are hollow; they bring boredom rather than vitality, and sometimes tension and guilt instead of respite and serenity. Well-being calls for qualitative limits on narcissism, since too random a license promotes sickness rather than health. Illusion that helps people perpetuate mystery, that adds zest to sexuality by its veil of ignorance or by helping to disguise certain abysmal facts—such harmless illusion is one thing; but a fetishistic and necrophilic narcissism that destroys in the name of a transcending ethic, that would service aggression masked as a cultural purge, this is a frightening narcissism. In support of the conviction that there is a more intricate balance between narcissism and object love

than some have postulated, I propose a maxim for appraising the desirable limits of narcissism: narcissistic investments can be considered healthy when they are in the direct
service of either an immediate or an eventual reinforcement
of maturing, *object-oriented responsibilities.*

TIME AND PREJUDICE

If anyone was entitled to look for answers regarding
man's predilection toward genocidal prejudice, my patient
Lilli had that right. And although my profession calls for
delving into the deepest aspects of human psychology, on
this subject psychoanalysts have been remarkably unforth-
coming. My exposure to the details of Lilli's experiences
only heightened my own sense of conviction about the link
that I believe exists between the hatreds of prejudice and
the passions surrounding time. Over the years, I have been
exposed to many theories, and some I have developed on
my own. There is the theory that prejudice stems from envy,
and there is the theory of stranger anxiety (xenophobia).
There is the concept of projective scapegoatism based on
unresolved oedipal conflict that leads to pathologically
displaced aggressions. There is the view that prejudice is
strictly a racist philosophy which calls for peoples with
undesirable traits to be exterminated. Several of my
analytic patients, some of them non-Jewish, have gratui-
tously offered the suggestion that anti-Semitism is nourished
by the perception of the victim as weakling or coward,
unwilling to defend himself. Others have suggested that the
capacity of a people to survive in the face of genocide makes
them uncanny, and all the more to be feared and hated.
Freud (1939) speculated that the burden of carrying the
yoke of a monotheistic religion might have been the earliest
precipitating factor for anti-Semitism. Perhaps a more
updated insight into the phenomenon comes from one

artless patient whose childhood exposure to anti-Semitism was epitomized in the guardedness of his parents against the "wandering Jew" in the family garden—a plant that was threatening the seedling grass. However one views the reality of prejudice, in Lilli's case I felt her particular qualms about bringing new life into a postwar world whose virulent predisposition to prejudice and racism has yet to be tempered were by no means neurotic. Prejudice is often intimately linked with the transitional demands of those who will settle for nothing less than a reified physical immortality, a passion whose lifeline depends on total global reinforcement. To individuals and groups demanding such absolute confirmation, any dissension casts unacceptable doubt. All skeptics are perceived as agents of the uncanny, dangerous in their threat to the concept of a body everlasting; they are seen as vermin or weeds, eating away at man's hope for immortality. Ironically, the accused are often more "religious" than the accusers, who in all their piety begrudge those who don't share their version of transcendence equal rights to life.

Eissler (1955) drew attention to the resistance man mobilizes against the investigation of both time and death. One wonders if this resistance might not stem from an inner awareness of the futility of such an investigation. Examination of the physical aspects of death at postmortem is a concrete procedure; there is a body to examine. But we have yet to bottle the corpse of a dead psyche or soul, and it is not clinically valid to claim that by examining the psyche of man as he lies dying, one is examining his psychic death. A phenomenon described by many who have been close to physical death—the separating out of the soul from the body—is in full keeping with my earlier accounting of depersonalization. As long as the individual lives, his dreams, hallucinations, and self-replicative reveries—live psychic images—cannot be represented as products of a dying

psyche simply because death did in fact ensue. As retro-
spectively reported (after the fact of death), they still are
phenomena that belong to the living. In presuicidal people
there is no way of knowing in advance whether the victim
will commit suicide or move in the direction of recovery.
The psychic productions of such people cannot therefore be
offered as products of a dying psyche, any more than can
any other regressive psychological processes. I believe it to
be wishful thinking to expect the study of the minds of those
close to death to free mankind from its obsession with life,
death, and time—or for that matter, from the illusion
mankind creates in quest of the truth.

Those who would meet death head-on in a reified
struggle with thanatos are the ones, I contend, who evade
confronting their countertransference to the patient's preoccupations with death. There are some who perceive the
unconscious as a devil with whom to joust or as a labyrinth
in which man has inchoately locked away his true knowledge
of death. The premise that Freud was guilty of reducing an
unconsciously imprinted archaic fact to symbolic castration
or separation anxiety, or that he shrewdly deflected our
attentions onto the overburdened shoulders of Eros, is to my
mind a misguided critique which translucently aims to
elevate the human psyche to some deified level where man
"knows" his fate. Paradoxically, it reduces and infantilizes
humanity to a horde of stream-of-consciousness creatures in
need of lessons in death. It fails to acknowledge that unlike
dying, death is not a phenomenon clinically accessible to
psychological investigation. In truth, as disease and aging
take hold, regressive processes within the human psyche
may demonstrate efforts at rejuvenation, with a return to
primary process thinking aimed at recapturing the life-
giving and life-sustaining forces associated earlier with the
fusion with primal love objects. Often the dying person
exudes an aura of liberated spirit as he transfers his vitality

to progeny, to friends, or to students. Perhaps man's flinching from investigating death is due to the realistic awareness that his efforts at communication with the dying can only reaffirm the limitations of his capacity to solve the riddle of death.

Whereas Freud perceived the passive repetition compulsion as a sign of man's death instinct at work (something not yet clinically confirmable), I have chosen to emphasize the restorative aspect of the process, as seen, for example, in soldiers in battle. Many shell-shocked survivors place themselves psychologically in the role of their dead comrades. This fascination of mankind for simulating death in dress rehearsal is found even in childhood play. The living have always had an awe for the dead; the soldier with the medal of honor is more revered if he achieves it posthumously. In fact humanity reserves its charisma primarily for the deceased. Artists, for example, are more commonly acknowledged by society after their demise. In *Totem and Taboo* and his theory of the primal father, Freud (1913) observed that the dead father was psychologically a more powerful force than he was in life. In *Civilization and Its Discontents* (1930), he attributes this to a remorse resulting from the primordial ambivalence of sons, in which their love came to the fore over their hate; for Freud, such ambivalence stemmed from the eternal struggle between Eros and the death instinct. I have submitted the counterproposal that when replaced by the living through narcissistic identification, the dead are thereby immortalized; we afford them (and us) omnipotence in order to fulfill our own demands for eternity. To the dead we offer that extra endowment of charisma, as well as the secret key to the riddle of death. Out of envy as well as out of remorse, we glamorize the dead, provided they have not died by their own hand. The frenzy to achieve a closeness with death has frequently led to suicide, perceived by many as a cheating, as an act outside the bounds of fair play. Although it may be a despairing admission of defeat, it may in some instances express a futile bid for acknowledgment. Humanity, however, pays little homage to suicides, whether they be merely attempts or actualized. Like the process of aging, suicide draws the posthumous impeachment of humanity; both are relegated to a footnote in the archives of human indiscretion. I compare our strenuous efforts to revivify the memory of our dead to our repetitive and compulsive return to the scene of the crime. Not only do we mourn the dead, we identify with their psychic resurrection. In some instances we incorporate and plagiarize their spirit and their work; we take their place—in fact sometimes to the point of fearing that they might come back to reclaim the entitlements that they held in life.

Returning to the treatment of the traumatic neuroses and to Lilli, Loewald (1971) observes that re-creative transformation allows an opening up of the ego. Borne to fruition by the destruction and dissolution of the Oedipus complex, a maturing conscience leads to new psychic structure and to the development of object relations of a higher order. Through the mourning of childhood cathexes and the abandonment of incestuous objects, freed instinctual life can be mobilized elsewhere, and out of the ruined love affair with parents, libido can become reinvested in the self (secondary narcissism). What was originally repressed and split off from the ego becomes internalized and integrated within it. Even the way station of identification with parents is ultimately abandoned and mourned, as one's individuated self becomes more sharply differentiated from one's objects. This fuller internalization implies emancipation, and the individual becomes enriched rather than burdened by relationships with parental objects. Lilli's therapy exemplified a psychoanalytic attempt to clear the obstacles blocking the natural evolution of an active re-creative repetition compulsion, which would allow the traumatized girl to abandon her cathexes of primary objects in favor of newer investments. Only in this way could she properly validate herself, her husband, and her children as individuals deserving something more than the genocide that the Nazis had prescribed. The task was to help her acknowledge not only her entitlement to sex and procreation, but her obligation to surmount an identification with the dereliction of parents, so that she might be able to actively offer her own offspring the protection she herself had not enjoyed (the transformational aspect of the recreative repetition compulsion). To achieve this, the treatment had to contend with both the concentration camp experiences and with the early familial traumata that had provoked her original flight from time.

Lilli did extricate herself from the illusory intangibles that had invaded her psychological life. Through the interaction with her analyst, which reactivated attitudes toward certain figures from her past (the transference neurosis), she managed to abandon and then to mourn her primal objects, including the preoedipal mother. She came to cathect her husband and her children. To suggest that she completely resolved her narcissistic problems through the pacemaking mediations of her therapy would be wishful thinking. Since her treatment years ago, however, she has maintained the patience and the anticipation involved in being a mother and a housewife. Follow-up on her present reveals that she is approaching the menopause. By reviving an old love of music, she is sustaining a creative outlook. As for her past, through her marriage and her children—the girl and the two boys she has brought into the world—she has resurrected her mother, her father, and herself, as well as an early familial constellation that included two little cousins. And as for her *future*, when someday she becomes blessed with grandchildren, it will be a day of affirmation for Lilli, a day of fulfillment of her grandparent's prayer.

In summary, the biological function of coitus is man's logical hope for ameliorating the agony of his transience. The man and woman who inspire each other with their constancy and trust, especially when reinforced by the offspring they produce, may therein find timelessness, for constancy and trust are the anchors of civilization. Freud (1930) acknowledged this, too, despite his paradoxical concern about woman's capacity to undermine society's foundations by her interest in family and her claims on man's love. Whether one shares this Freudian cynicism or not, one must respect the ability of genital love to defend mankind against the indictment of time killer. Rather than viewing man's postponement of coitus as an escape from oedipal castration, I favor Róheim's (1940) interpretation of the biblical myth that "in the eating of the Fruit of the Tree," man acknowledges his physical transience. To this I would add the rider that in relinquishing his ensconcement in Eden, man acts in the service of a biological continuity, a means of surmounting the trauma of time.

References

Abraham, G. (1976), The sense and concept of time in psychoanalysis. *Internat. Rev. of Psycho-Anal.*, 3:461-472.

Abraham, K. (1917), Ejaculatio praecox. In: *Selected Papers on Psychoanalysis.* New York: Basic Books, 1953.

―――― (1921), Contributions to the theory of the anal character. In: *Selected Papers on Psychoanalysis.* New York: Basic Books, 1953.

―――― (1924), The influence of oral erotism on character formation. In: *Selected Papers on Psychoanalysis.* New York: Basic Books, 1953, pp. 393-406.

Allen, D. W. (1974), *The Fear of Looking.* Charlottesville: University Press of Virginia.

Apostel, L., with Mandelbrot, V. & Piaget, J. (1957), Logique et equilibre. In: *Etudes d'épistemologie genetique*, 2:1-26a. Paris: Presses Universitaires de France.

Ardrey, R. (1961), *African Genesis.* London: Collins (New York: Atheneum).

―――― (1966), *The Territorial Imperative: A Personal Inquiry Into the Animal Origins of Property and Nations.* New York: Atheneum.

Arlow, J. (1959), The structure of the déjà vu experience. *J. Amer. Psychoanal. Assn.*, 7:611-632.

―――― (1960), Fantasy systems in twins. *Psychoanal. Quart.*, 29: 175-199.

―――― (1966), Depersonalization and derealization. In: *Psychoanalysis—A General Psychology. Essays in Honor of Heinz Hartmann*, eds. R. Loewenstein, L. Newman, M. Schur, and A. Solnit. New York: International Universities Press, pp. 456-478.

Bak, R. (1973), Being in love and object loss. *Internat. J. Psycho-Anal.*, 54:1-8.

Balint, M. (1948), On genital love. In: *Primary Love and Psychoanalytic Technique.* New York: Tavistock, 1959, pp. 109-120.

257

Barnett, M. (1966), Vaginal awareness in the infancy and childhood of girls. *J. Amer. Psychoanal. Assn.*, 14:140.

Becker, E. (1973), *The Denial of Death.* New York: The Free Press.

Benedek, T. (1938), Adaptation to reality in early infancy. *Psychoanal. Quart.*, 7:200-215.

Benson, R. M. & Pryor, D. B. (1973), "When friends fall out: Developmental interference with the function of some imaginary companions. *J. Amer. Psychoanal. Assn.*, 21:457-473.

Beres, D. (1960), Perception, imagination and reality. *Internat. J. Psycho-Anal.*, 41:327-334.

Bergler, E. (1950), Further studies on depersonalization. *Psychiat. Quart.*, 24:268-277.

Bergman, P. & Escalona, S. K. (1949), Unusual sensitivities in very young children. In: *The Psychoanalytic Study of the Child*, 3/4: 333-352.

Bergson, H. (1889), *Time and Freewill: An Essay on the Immediate Data of Consciousness.* New York: Torchbooks, 1960.

Bibring, E. (1943), Repetition compulsion. *Psychoanal. Quart.*, 12: 486-519.

———— (1953), The mechanism of depression. In: *Affective Disorders: Psychoanalytic Contributions to their Study*, ed. P. Greenacre. New York: International Universities Press, pp. 13-48.

Bion, W. R. (1961), *Experiences in Groups.* London: Tavistock Publications, Ltd.

Binstock, W. (1973), On the two forms of intimacy. *J. Amer. Psychoanal. Assn.*, 21:93-107.

Blank, H. R. (1954), Repression, hypomania and depersonalization. *Psychoanal. Quart.*, 23:20-37.

Blum, H. (1976), Masochism, the ego ideal, and the psychology of women. *J. Amer. Psychoanal. Assn.*, 24:157-191.

Boesky, D. (1973), Déjà raconté as a screen defense. *Psychoanal. Quart.*, 42:491-524.

———— (1976), Xerox: A new symbol. *Psychoanal. Quart.*, 45:290-295.

Bonaparte, M. (1940), Time and the unconscious. *Internat. J. Psycho-Anal.*, 21:427-468.

Brandon, S. G. F. (1964), Time as god and devil. *Bulletin of the John Rylands Library*, 47:12-31.

Brenner, C. (1974), On the nature and development of affects—A unified theory. *Psychoanal. Quart.*, 43:532-556.

Breuer, J. & Freud, S. (1893), Studies on hysteria. *Standard Edition*, 2. London: Hogarth Press, 1955.

Brodsky, B. (1959), Self-representation, anality and dying. *J. Amer. Psychoanal. Assn.*, 7:95-108.

Burlingham, D. (1952), *Twins: A Study of Three Pairs of Identical Twins.* New York: International Universities Press.

Calhoun, C. J. (1976), Continuity and change: The significance of time in the organization of experience. *Internat. Rev. Psycho-Anal.*, 3:291-304.

Chasseguet-Smirgel, J. (1976), Freud and female sexuality: The consideration of some blind spots in the exploration of the "Dark Continent." *Internat. J. Psycho-Anal.*, 57:275-286.

—— (1976a), Some thoughts on the ego ideal. A contribution to the study of the "Illness of Ideality." *Psychoanal. Quart.*, 45:345-373.

Cohn, F. (1957), Time and the ego. *Psychoanal. Quart.*, 26:168-189.

Coltrera, J. (1965), On creation of beauty and thought. *J. Amer. Psychoanal. Assn.*, 13:634-703.

Coppolillo, H. P. (1967), Maturational aspects of the transitional phenomena. *Internat. J. Psycho-Anal.*, 48:237-246.

Deutsch, F. (1959), On the creative passion of the artist and its synesthetic aspects. *Internat. J. Psycho-Anal.*, 40:38-51.

—— (1959a), *On the Mysterious Leap from the Mind to the Body.* New York: International Universities Press.

Deutsch, H. (1926), Occult processes occurring during psychoanalysis. In: *Psychoanalysis and the Occult*, ed. G. Devereux. New York: International Universities Press, 1953, pp. 133-146.

—— (1930), Melancholic and depressive states. In: *Neuroses and Character Types.* New York: International Universities Press, 1965, pp. 145-156.

—— (1933), Motherhood and sexuality. In: *Neuroses and Character Types.* New York: International Universities Press, 1965, pp. 190-202.

—— (1937), Folie à deux. In: *Neuroses and Character Types.* New York: International Universities Press, 1965, pp. 237-247.

—— (1942), Some forms of emotional disturbance and their relationship to schizophrenia. In: *Neuroses and Character Types.* New York: International Universities Press, 1965, pp. 262-281.

—— (1955), The impostor. *Psychoanal. Quart.*, 24:483-505.

Doyle, A. Conan (1901), *A Treasury of Sherlock Holmes.* New York: Hanover House.

Einstein, A. (1905), *Sidelines on Relativity.* London: Methuen, 1922.

Eisenbud, J. (1956), Time and the oedipus. *Psychoanal. Quart.*, 25:363-384.

Eisnitz, A. (1974), Reply to Muller and Weinberger on boredom. *Internat. J. Psycho-Anal.*, 55:587-590.

Eissler, K. (1955), *The Psychoanalyst and the Dying Patient.* New York: International Universities Press.

—— (1966), A note on trauma, dream, anxiety, and schizophrenia. In: *The Psychoanalytic Study of the Child*, 21:17-50.

Eister, A. (1974), Culture crises and new religious movements. In: *Religious Movements in Contemporary America*, ed. Zaretsky and Leone. Princeton, New Jersey: Princeton University Press, pp. 612-627.

Engel, C. L. (1962), *Psychological Development in Health and Disease*. Philadelphia: Saunders.

Erikson, E. (1950), *Childhood and Society: Basic Trust and Basic Mistrust*. New York: W. W. Norton & Co., pp. 247-251.

_____ (1956), The problem of ego identity. *J. Amer. Psychoanal. Assn.*, 4:56-121.

_____ (1962), Reality and actuality. *J. Amer. Psychoanal. Assn.*, 10:451-474.

Esman, A. H. (1973), The primal scene: A review and a reconstruction. In: *The Psychoanalytic Study of the Child*, 28:49-81.

Evans, W. (1953), Two kinds of romantic love. *Psychoanal. Quart.*, 22:75-85.

Fairbairn, W. R. D. (1952), *Psychoanalytic Studies of the Personality*. London: Tavistock Publications.

Fenichel, O. (1939), Trophy and triumph. In: *Collected Papers*, second series. New York: W. W. Norton & Co., 1954.

_____ (1945), *The Psychoanalytic Theory of Neurosis*. New York: W. W. Norton & Co.

Ferenczi, S. (1913), Stages in the development of the sense of reality. In: *First Contributions to Psychoanalysis*. London: Hogarth Press, 1952.

_____ (1923), Thalassa—A theory of genitality, Part I. *Psychoanal. Quart.*, 2:361-403; Part II, *Psychoanal. Quart.*, 3:1-29; Part III, *Psychoanal. Quart.*, 3:200-222.

_____ (1934), Gedanken über das Trauma. *Internat. J. Psycho-Anal.*, 20:5-12.

Finkelstein, L. (1974), The impostor: Aspects of his development. *Psychoanal. Quart.*, 33:85-114.

Fintzy, R. T. (1971), Vicissitudes of the transitional object in a border-line child. *Internat. J. Psycho-Anal.*, 52:107-114.

Fliess, R. (1956), The déjà raconté: A transference-delusion concerning the castration complex. *Psychoanal. Quart.*, 25:215-227.

_____ (1961), *Ego and Body Ego: Contributions to their Psychoanalytic Psychology*. New York: Schulte, pp. 179-205.

Fodor, N. (1949), *The Search for the Beloved*. New York: Hermitage Press.

Fraser, J. T. (1975), *On Time, Passion and Knowledge*. New York: George Braziller, Inc.

Freud, A. (1936), *The Ego and the Mechanisms of Defense*. New York: International Universities Press, 1946.

_____ (1952), Bodily illness in the mental life of children. In: *The Psychoanalytic Study of the Child*, 7:68-81.

_____ (1967), Comments on trauma. In: *Psychic Trauma*, ed. S. S. Furst. New York: Basic Books.

_____ (1972), Comments on aggression. *Internat. J. Psycho-Anal.*, 53:163-171.

Freud, S. (1893), On the psychical mechanism of hysterical phenomena. *Standard Edition*, 3:27-39. London: Hogarth Press, 1962.

_____ (1895), Project for a scientific psychology. *Standard Edition*, 1:289-317. London: Hogarth Press, 1966.

_____ (1896-97), Extracts from the Fliess papers. *Standard Edition*, 1:175-280. London: Hogarth Press, 1966.

_____ (1899), Screen memories. *Standard Edition*, 3:301-322. London: Hogarth Press, 1962.

_____ (1900), The interpretation of dreams. *Standard Edition*, 4:79. London: Hogarth Press, 1953.

_____ (1900a), The interpretation of dreams. *Standard Edition*, 5:399. London: Hogarth Press, 1953.

_____ (1905), Three essays on the theory of sexuality. *Standard Edition*, 7:173-206. London: Hogarth Press, 1953.

_____ (1905a), Jokes and their relation to the unconscious. *Standard Edition*, 8. London: Hogarth Press, 1960.

_____ (1908), Creative writers and day-dreaming. *Standard Edition*, 9:142-153. London: Hogarth Press, 1959.

_____ (1909), Family romances. *Standard Edition*, 9:237-241. London: Hogarth Press, 1959.

_____ (1909a), Some general remarks on hysterical attacks. *Standard Edition*, 9:227-234. London: Hogarth Press, 1959.

_____ (1912), On the universal tendency to the debasement in the sphere of love. *Standard Edition*, 11:178-190. London: Hogarth Press, 1957.

_____ (1913), Totem and taboo. *Standard Edition*, 13:140-161. London: Hogarth Press, 1955

_____ (1914), Fausse reconnaissance (déjà raconté) in psychoanalytic treatment. *Standard Edition*, 13:201-207. London: Hogarth Press, 1955.

_____ (1915), The unconscious. *Standard Edition*, 14:166-215. London: Hogarth Press, 1957.

_____ (1915a), Instincts and their vicissitudes. *Standard Edition*, 14:119. London: Hogarth Press, 1957.

_____ (1917), General theory of neurosis. *Standard Edition*, 16:358-377. London: Hogarth Press, 1963.

_____ (1917a), Mourning and melancholia. *Standard Edition*, 14:243-258. London: Hogarth Press, 1957.

_____ (1918), From the history of an infantile neurosis. *Standard Edition*, 17:29-81. London: Hogarth Press, 1955.

_____ (1919), The uncanny. *Standard Edition*, 17:219-256. London: Hogarth Press, 1955.

_____ (1920), Beyond the pleasure principle. *Standard Edition*, 18:7-64. London: Hogarth Press, 1955.

_____ (1921), Group psychology and the analysis of the ego. *Standard Edition*, 18:67-143. London: Hogarth Press, 1955.

_____ (1923), The ego and the id. *Standard Edition*, 19:57-59. London: Hogarth Press, 1961.

_____ (1923a), The infantile genital organization. *Standard Edition*, 19:141-145. London: Hogarth Press, 1961.

_____ (1923b), The two classes of instincts. *Standard Edition*, 19:40-47. London: Hogarth Press, 1961.

_____ (1924), A note upon the mystic writing pad. *Standard Edition*, 19:225-232. London: Hogarth Press, 1961.

_____ (1925), Negation. *Standard Edition*, 19:233-239. London: Hogarth Press, 1961.

_____ (1925a), Some psychical consequences of the anatomical distinction between the sexes. *Standard Edition*, 19:243-258. London: Hogarth Press, 1961.

_____ (1926), Inhibitions, symptoms and anxiety. *Standard Edition*, 20:91-142. London: Hogarth Press, 1959.

_____ (1927), Fetishism. *Standard Edition*, 21:149-157. London: Hogarth Press, 1961.

_____ (1927a), The future of an illusion. *Standard Edition*, 21:3-56. London: Hogarth Press, 1961.

_____ (1927b), Humour. *Standard Edition*, 21:160-166. London: Hogarth Press, 1961.

_____ (1928), Dostoevsky and parricide. *Standard Edition*, 21:175-196. London: Hogarth Press, 1961.

_____ (1930), Civilization and its discontents. *Standard Edition*, 21:64-132. London: Hogarth Press, 1961.

_____ (1933), New introductory lectures on psychoanalysis. *Standard Edition*, 22:81-111. London: Hogarth Press, 1964.

_____ (1936), A disturbance of memory on the Acropolis. *Standard Edition*, 22:238-248. London: Hogarth Press, 1964.

_____ (1939), Moses and monotheism. *Standard Edition*, 23:3-137. London: Hogarth Press, 1964.

_____ (1940), An outline of psychoanalysis. *Standard Edition*, 23:145-207. London: Hogarth Press, 1964.

_____ (1940a), Splitting of the ego in the process of defense. *Standard Edition*, 23:271-278. London: Hogarth Press, 1964.

Fromm, E. (1973), *The Anatomy of Human Destructiveness*. New York: Holt, Rhinehart & Winston, pp. 1-32.

Frosch, J. (1959), Transference derivatives of the family romance. *J. Amer. Psychoanal. Assn.*, 7:503-522.

Galenson, H. (1976), Reporter on panel on psychology of women: (1) Infancy and early childhood, (2) Latency and early adolescence. *J. Amer. Psychoanal. Assn.*, 24:141-160.

Gediman, H. (1971), The concept of stimulus barrier: Its review and reformulation as an adaptive ego function. *Internat. J. Psycho-Anal.*, 52:243-257.

———— (1975), Reflections on romanticism, narcissism, and creativity. *J. Amer. Psychoanal. Assn.*, 23:407-423.

Gifford, S. (1960), Sleep, time and the early ego. *J. Amer. Psychoanal. Assn.*, 8:5-42.

———— (1964), Panel report: Repetition compulsion. *J. Amer. Psychoanal. Assn.*, 12:632-649.

Giovacchini, P. (1958), Some affective meanings of dizziness. *Psychoanal. Quart.*, 27:217-225.

Glenn, J. (1974), Twins in disguise: A psychoanalytic essay on sleuth and the royal hunt of the sun. *Psychoanal. Quart.*, 43:288-302.

Greenacre, P. (1947), Vision, headache, and the halo. *Psychoanal. Quart.*, 16:177-198.

———— (1952), Respiratory incorporation and the phallic phase. In: *Trauma, Growth and Personality.* New York: W. W. Norton, pp. 259-293.

———— (1955), Mutual adventures of Jonathan Swift and Lemuel Gulliver. *Psychoanal. Quart.*, 14:20-62.

———— (1957), The childhood of the artist. In: *The Psychoanalytic Study of the Child,* 12:47-72.

———— (1958), The impostor. *Psychoanal. Quart.*, 27:359-382.

———— (1960), Woman as artist. *Psychoanal. Quart.*, 29:208-227.

———— (1964), A study on the nature of inspiration. *J. Amer. Psychoanal. Assn.*, 12:6-31.

———— (1968), Perversions: General considerations regarding their genetic and dynamic background. In: *The Psychoanalytic Study of the Child,* 23:47-62.

———— (1969), The fetish and the transitional object. In: *The Psychoanalytic Study of the Child,* 24:144-164.

———— (1972), Crowds and crisis. In: *The Psychoanalytic Study of the Child,* 27:136-155.

———— (1973), The primal scene and the sense of reality. *Psychoanal. Quart.*, 42:10-41.

Greenson, R. (1953), On boredom. *J. Amer. Psychoanal. Assn.*, 1:7-21.

Grotjahn, M. (1942), The process of awakening. *Psychoanal. Rev.*, 29:1-19.

Hacker, F. J. (1964), The reality of myth. *Internat. J. Psycho-Anal.*, 45:438-451.

Haining, P. (1974), *The Sherlock Holmes Scrapbook.* New York: Clarkson N. Potter, pp. 30-31.

Hamburg, D. A. (1968), Evolution of emotional responses: Evidence from recent research on non-human primates. In: *Animal and Human,* ed. J. Masserman. New York: Grune & Stratton, pp. 39-52.

———— (1972), An evolutionary perspective on human aggressiveness. In: *Modern Psychiatry and Clinical Research. Essays in Honor of*

Roy R. Grinker, Sr., eds. D. Offer and D. Freedman. New York: Basic Books, pp. 30-43.

—— (1973), An evolutionary and developmental approach to human aggressiveness. *Psychoanal. Quart.*, 42:185-196.

Hanly, C. & Masson, J. (1976), A critical examination of the new narcissism. *Internat. J. Psycho-Anal.*, 57:49-66.

Hardwick, M. & Hardwick, M. (1962), *The Sherlock Holmes Companion*. London: John Murray, pp. 39-40, 130-178.

Harrison, I. (1966), A reconsideration of Freud's "A Disturbance of Memory on the Acropolis" in relation to identity disturbance. *J. Amer. Psychoanal. Assn.*, 14:518-527.

Hartmann, H. (1937), *Ego Psychology and the Problem of Adaptation*. New York: International Universities Press, 1958.

—— (1950), Psychoanalysis and developmental psychology. In: *Essays on Ego Psychology*. New York: International Universities Press, 1964, pp. 99-141.

Hartmann, D. (1969), A study of drug-taking adolescents. In: *The Psychoanalytic Study of the Child*, 24:384-398.

Hartocollis, P. (1972), Time as a dimension of affects. *J. Amer. Psychoanal. Assn.*, 20:19-108.

—— (1974), Origins of time: A reconstruction of the ontogenetic development of the sense of time based on object-relations theory. *Psychoanal. Quart.*, 43:243-261.

—— (1976), On the experience of time and its dynamics, with special reference to affects. *J. Amer. Psychoanal. Assn.*, 24:363-375.

Heiman, M. (1976), Psychoanalytic observations on the last painting and suicide of Vincent van Gogh. *Internat. J. Psycho-Anal.*, 57:71-79.

Heimann, P. (1962), Notes on the anal stage. *Internat. J. Psycho-Anal.*, 43:406-424.

Hermann, I. (1949), The giant mother, the phallic mother, obscenity. *Psychoanal. Rev.*, 36:302-307.

Hitschmann, E. (1953), Freud's conception of love. *The Yearbook of Psychoanalysis*, 9:23-36.

Horney, K. (1932), The dread of woman. *Internat. J. Psycho-Anal.*, 13:348-360.

Hunter, R. C. A. (1966), The analysis of episodes of depersonalization in a borderline patient. *Internat. J. Psycho-Anal.*, 47:32-41.

Isaacs, K., (with Alexander, M. & Haggard, E.) (1963), Faith, trust and gullibility. *Internat. J. Psycho-Anal.*, 44:461-469.

Isakower, O. (1938), A contribution to the patho-psychology associated with falling asleep. *Internat. J. Psycho-Anal.*, 19:331-345.

—— (1939), On the exceptional position of the auditory sphere. *Internat. J. Psycho-Anal.*, 20:340-348.

Isay, R. (1975), The influence of the primal scene on the sexual behavior of an early adolescent. *J. Amer. Psychoanal. Assn.*, 23:535-554.

Jacobson, E. (1953), Contributions to the metapsychology of cyclothymic depression. In: *Affective Disorders*, ed. P. Greenacre. New York: International Universities Press, pp. 49-83.

———— (1957), On normal and pathological moods. In: *The Psychoanalytic Study of the Child*, 12:73-113.

———— (1959), Depersonalization. *J. Amer. Psychoanal. Assn.*, 7:581-610.

———— (1964), *The Self and the Object World*. New York: International Universities Press.

———— (1968), On the development of the girl's wish for a child. *J. Amer. Psychoanal. Assn.*, 37:523-538.

———— (1976), Ways of female superego formation and the female castration conflict. *Psychoanal. Quart.*, 45:525-538.

Jaffe, D. (1968), The masculine envy of women's procreative function. *J. Amer. Psychoanal. Assn.*, 16:521-548.

Janet, P. (1928), *L'Evolution de la Memoire et de la notion du Temps*. Paris: Maloine.

Jones, E. (1918), Anal-erotic character traits. In: *Papers on Psychoanalysis*. Baltimore: William & Wilkins, 1949, pp. 413-437.

———— (1932), The phallic phase. In: *Papers on Psychoanalysis*. Baltimore: Williams & Wilkins, 1949, pp. 452-484.

Joseph, B. (1959), An aspect of the repetition compulsion. *Internat. J. Psycho-Anal.*, 40:213-222.

Kafka, J. S. (1972), Panel reporter on the experience of time. *J. Amer. Psychoanal. Assn.*, 20:650-667.

Kahne, M. J. (1967), On the persistence of transitional phenomena into adult life. *Internat. J. Psycho-Anal.*, 48:247-258.

Kant, I. (1781), *Critique of Pure Reason*. New York: Humanities Press, 1950.

Keiser, S. (1952), Body ego during orgasm. *Psychoanal. Quart.*, 21:153-166.

———— (1967), Freud's concept of trauma and a specific ego function. *J. Amer. Psychoanal. Assn.*, 15:781-794.

Kernberg, O. F. (1974), Contrasting viewpoints regarding the nature and psychoanalytic treatment of narcissistic personalities: A preliminary communication. *J. Amer. Psychoanal. Assn.*, 22:255-267.

———— (1974a), Barriers to falling and remaining in love. *J. Amer. Psychoanal. Assn.*, 22:486-511.

———— (1974b), Mature love: Prerequisites and characteristics. *J. Amer. Psychoanal. Assn.*, 22:743-768.

———— (1975), *Borderline Conditions and Pathological Narcissism*. New York: Jason Aronson.

Kierkegaard, S. (1849), *Sickness unto Death*. New York: Doubleday, 1954.

Klauber, J. (1974), Notes on the psychical roots of religion with particular reference to the development of Western Christianity. *Internat. J. Psycho-Anal.*, 55:249-258.

Klein, M. (1923), Infant analysis. In: *Contributions to Psychoanalysis.* London: Hogarth Press, 1948.

―――― (1928), Early stages of the Oedipus conflict. In: *Contributions to Psychoanalysis.* London: Hogarth Press, 1948.

Knapp, P. (1953), The ear, listening and hearing. *J. Amer. Psychoanal. Assn.*, 1:672-689.

Kohut, H. (1966), Forms and transformations of narcissism. *J. Amer. Psychoanal. Assn.*, 14:243-272.

―――― (1971), *The Analysis of the Self.* New York: International Universities Press.

Kris, E. (1938), *Psychoanalytic Explorations in Art.* New York: International Universities Press, 1952.

―――― (1940), Laughter as an expressive process. *Internat. J. Psycho-Anal.*, 21:314-341.

Kubie, L. (1953), Some implications for psychoanalysis of modern concepts of the organization of the brain. *J. Amer. Psychoanal. Assn.*, 22:21-52.

Kucera, O. (1959), On teething. *J. Amer. Psychoanal. Assn.*, 7:284-291.

Kupper, H. & Rollman-Branch, H. (1959), Freud und Schnitzler (Doppelgänger). *J. Amer. Psychoanal. Assn.*, 7:109-127.

LeBon, G. (1895), *Psychologie des Foules.* Paris: T. Fisher Unwin, 1920.

Lewin, B. (1946), Sleep, the mouth and the dream screen. *Psychoanal. Quart.*, 15:419-434.

―――― (1950), *The Psychoanalysis of Elation.* New York: Norton.

Lifton, R. J. (1976), *The Life of the Self: Toward a New Psychology.* New York: Simon and Schuster.

Lipin, T. (1963), The repetition compulsion and "maturational" drive-representatives. *Internat. J. Psycho-Anal.*, 44:389-406.

―――― (1964), Panel report: Repetition compulsion (reporter, S. Gifford). *J. Amer. Psychoanal. Assn.*, 12:630-649.

Lipps, T. (1898), *Komik und Humor.* Hamburg and Leipzig: L. Voss.

Loewald, H. (1971), Some considerations on repetition and repetition-compulsion. *Internat. J. Psycho-Anal.*, 52:59-67.

―――― (1973), On internalization. *Internat. J. Psycho-Anal.*, 54:9-19.

―――― (1975), Psychoanalysis as an art and the fantasy character of the psychoanalytic situation. *J. Amer. Psychoanal. Assn.*, 23: 277-299.

Lorenz, K. (1932), *Studies in Animal and Human Behavior.* Cambridge: Harvard University Press, 1970, 1:57-258.

―――― (1950), *Studies in Animal and Human Behavior.* Cambridge: Harvard University Press, 1971, 2:115-195.

Maclean, P. (1949), Psychosomatic disease and the "visceral brain." *Psychosomatic Medicine,* 11:338-353.

Mahler, M., Pine, F. & Bergman, A. (1975), *The Psychological Birth of the Human Infant.* New York: Basic Books.

―――― (1975a), Discussion of "Early ego development and the déjà-vu" by B. Pacella. *J. Amer. Psychoanal. Assn.*, 23:322-333.

Malev, M. (1974), Discussion of "Notes on the psychical roots of religion, with particular reference to the development of Western Christianity" by John Klauber. *Internat. J. Psycho-Anal.*, 55:257-259.

Mann, J. (1964), Reporter on panel on Clinical and theoretical aspects of religious belief. *J. Amer. Psychoanal. Assn.*, 12:160-170.

Marcovitz, E. (1952), The meaning of déjà vu. *Psychoanal. Quart.*, 21:481-489.

Marmor, J. (1954), Some considerations concerning orgasm in the female. *Psychosomatic Medicine*, 16:240-245.

Masler, E. (1973), The subjective perception of two aspects of time: Duration and timelessness. *Internat. J. Psycho-Anal.*, 54:425-429.

McDougall, J. (1972), Primal scene and sexual perversion. *Internat. J. Psycho-Anal.*, 53:371-384.

McDougall, W. (1920), *The Group Mind.* Cambridge: Harvard University Press.

McLaughlin, J. (1961), The analyst and the hippocratic oath. *J. Amer. Psychoanal. Assn.*, 9:106-123.

―――― (1975), The sleepy analyst: Some observations on the states of consciousness in the analyst at work. *J. Amer. Psychoanal. Assn.*, 23:363-382.

Milner, M. (1952), Aspects of symbolism in comprehension of the not-self. *Internat. J. Psycho-Anal.*, 33:181-195.

Mittelmann, B. (1954), Motility in infants, children and adults: Patterning and psychodynamics. In: *The Psychoanalytic Study of the Child*, 9:142-177.

Modell, A. (1968), *Object Love and Reality.* New York: International Universities Press.

Montagu, A. (1952), *Darwin, Competition and Cooperation.* New York: H. Schuman.

―――― , ed. (1968), *Introduction to Man and Aggression.* London and New York: Oxford University Press.

Mooney, W. (1968), Gustav Mahler—A Note on life and death in music. *Psychoanal. Quart.*, 37:80-102.

Myerhoff, B. (1974), *Peyote Hunt.* Ithaca: Cornell University Press.

Nagera, H. (1969), The imaginary companion: Its significance for ego development and conflict solution. In: *The Psychoanalytic Study of the Child*, 24:165-196.

Needles, W. (1953), A note on orgastic loss of consciousness. *Psychoanal. Quart.*, 22:512-518.

―――― (1962), Eros and the repetition compulsion. *Psychoanal. Quart.*, 31:505-513.

_____ (1973), Orgastic loss of consciousness: Its possible relation to Freud's nihilism. *Internat. J. Psycho-Anal.*, 54:315-322.

Neu, J. (1973), Fantasy and memory: The aetiological role of thoughts according to Freud. *Internat. J. Psycho-Anal.*, 54:383-398.

Niederland, W. G. (1975), Scarred: A contribution to the study of facial disfigurement. *Psychoanal. Quart.*, 44:450-459.

_____ (1976), Psychoanalytic approaches to artistic creativity. *Psychoanal. Quart.*, 45:185-212.

Nunberg, H. (1932), *Principles of Psychoanalysis.* New York: International Universities Press, 1955.

Oberndorf, C. P. (1950), The role of anxiety in depersonalization. *Internat. J. Psycho-Anal.*, 31:1-5.

Orgel, S. (1965), On time and timelessness. *J. Amer. Psychoanal. Assn.*, 13:102-121.

Ostow, M. (1958), The illusory reduplication of body parts in cerebral disease. *Psychoanal. Quart.*, 27:98-100.

_____ (1960), The metapsychology of autoscopic phenomena. *Internat. J. Psycho-Anal.*, 41:619-625.

Pacella, B. (1975), Early ego development and the déjà-vu. *J. Amer. Psychoanal. Assn.*, 23:300-318.

Pederson-Krag, G. (1949), Detective stories and the primal scene. *Psychoanal. Quart.*, 18:207-214.

Penfield, W. (1952), Memory mechanisms. *Archives of Neurology and Psychiatry*, 37:178-198.

Peto, A. (1973), The olfactory forerunner of the superego: Its role in normalcy, neurosis and fetishism. *Internat. J. Psycho-Anal.*, 54:323-329.

_____ (1975), On crowd violence: The role of archaic superego and body image. *Internat. Rev. Psychoanal.*, 2:449-466.

_____ (1975a), The etiological significance of the primal scene in perversions. *Psychoanal. Quart.*, 44:177-189.

Piaget, J. (1927), *The Child's Conception of Time.* London: Routledge & Kegan, 1964.

_____ (1937), *The Construction of Reality in the Child.* New York: Basic Books, 1954.

Prigogine, I. (1955), *Introduction to the Thermodynamics of Irreversible Processes.* New York: Interscience, 1967, p. 91.

Prince, R. (1974), Cocoon work: An interpretation of the concern of contemporary youth with the mystical. In: *Religious Movements in Contemporary America*, ed. Zaretsky and Leone. Princeton: Princeton University Press, pp. 255-271.

Rado, S. (1926), The psychic effect of intoxicants: An attempt to evolve a psychoanalytical theory of morbid cravings. *Internat. J. Psycho-Anal.*, 7:396-412.

_____ (1928), The problem of melancholia. *Internat. J. Psycho-Anal.*, 9:420-438.

—————— (1933), The psychoanalysis of pharmacothymia (drug addiction). *Psychoanal. Quart.*, 2:1-23.

Rangell, L. (1952), The analysis of a doll phobia. *Internat. J. Psycho-Anal.*, 33:43-53.

—————— (1953), The analysis of a doll phobia. *The Yearbook of Psychoanalysis*, 9:178-198, postscript 196-198.

—————— (1976), Lessons from Watergate: A derivative for psychoanalysis. *Psychoanal. Quart.*, 45:39-40.

Rank, O. (1909), *Myth of the Birth of a Hero—A Psychological Interpretation of Mythology*. New York: Robert Brunner, 1952, pp. 65-91.

—————— (1936), *Will Therapy and Truth and Reality*. New York: Alfred Knopf, 1945.

Rapaport, D. (1953), Some metapsychological considerations concerning activity and passivity. In: *Collected Papers*, ed. Merton Gill. New York: Basic Books, 1967, pp. 539-541.

Rappaport, E. (1968), Beyond traumatic neurosis. *Internat. J. Psycho-Anal.*, 49:719-731.

Reich, W. (1949), *Character Analysis; The Phallic-Narcissistic Character*. New York: Orgone Institute Press, pp. 200-207.

Reik, T. (1944), *A Psychologist Looks at Love*. New York: Farrar and Rinehart.

—————— (1945), *The Unknown Murderer*. New York: Prentice-Hall, pp. 76-91.

Róheim, G. (1940), The Garden of Eden. *Psychoanal. Rev.*, 27:1-26.

Roiphe, H. & Galenson, E. (1975), Some observations on transitional object and infantile fetish. *Psychoanal. Quart.*, 44:206-231.

Rycroft, C. (1957), The detective story. *Psychoanal. Quart.*, 26:229-245.

—————— (1962), Beyond the reality principle. *Internat. J. Psycho-Anal.*, 43:388-394.

Sadger, I. (1910), *Anal Erotism and Anal Character*. Vienna and Leipzig: Die Heilkunde.

Saravay, S. (1975), Group psychology and the structural theory: A revised psychoanalytic model of group psychology. *J. Amer. Psychoanal. Assn.*, 23:69-89.

Sarlin, C. (1962), Depersonalization and derealization. *J. Amer. Psychoanal. Assn.*, 10:784-804.

Savitt, R. (1963), Psychoanalytic studies on addiction: Ego structure and narcotic addiction. *Psychoanal. Quart.*, 32:43-57.

Schafer, R. (1968), On the theoretical and technical conceptualization of activity and passivity. *Psychoanal. Quart.*, 37:173-198.

—————— (1974), Problems in Freud's psychology of women. *J. Amer. Psychoanal. Assn.*, 22:459-485.

Schiffer, I. (1962), The psychoanalytic study of the development of a conversion symptom. *Internat. J. Psycho-Anal.*, 43:169-174.

_____ (1973), *Charisma: A Psychoanalytic Look at Mass Society*. Toronto: University of Toronto Press.

Schilder, P. (1923), *Medical Psychology*. New York: International Universities Press, 1953, pp. 256-265.

_____ (1935), *The Image and the Appearance of the Human Body*. New York: International Universities Press, 1950.

_____ (1936), Psychopathology of time. *J. Nerv. Ment. Dis.*, 83:530-546.

Schimek, J. G. (1975), The interpretations of the past: Childhood trauma, psychical reality, and historical truth. *J. Amer. Psychoanal. Assn.*, 23:845-865.

Schur, M. (1960), Phylogenesis and ontogenesis of affect and structure formation and the phenomenon of repetition compulsion. *Internat. J. Psycho-Anal.*, 41:275-287.

Scott, C. (1975), Time, sleep and dreams. In: Remembering Sleep and Dreams. *Internat. Rev. Psychoanal.*, 2:299.

Siegman, A. J. (1956), The psychological economy of déjà raconté. *Psychoanal. Quart.*, 25:83-86.

_____ (1964), Exhibitionism and fascination. *J. Amer. Psychoanal. Assn.*, 12:315-335.

Silbermann, I. (1963), The jamais phenomenon with reference to fragmentation. *Psychoanal. Quart.*, 32:181-191.

Simon, N. (1977), Primal scene, primary objects and nature morte: A psychoanalytic study of Mark Gertler. *Internat. Rev. Psychoanal.*, 4:61-70.

Sontag, L. W. (1948), Determinance of predisposition to psychoanalytic dysfunction and disease: Problem of proneness to psychosomatic disease. In: *Synopsis of Psychosomatic Diagnosis and Treatment*, ed. F. Dunbar. St. Louis: C. V. Mosby.

Sperling, M. (1963), Fetishism in children. *Psychoanal. Quart.*, 32:374-392.

Spitz, R. & Wolf, K. (1949), Autoerotism: Some empirical findings and hypotheses on three of its manifestations in the first year of life. In: *The Psychoanalytic Study of the Child*, 3/4:85-120. New York: International Universities Press.

_____ (1957), *No and Yes: On the Genesis of Human Communication*. New York: International Universities Press.

_____ (1965), *The First Year of Life*. New York: International Universities Press.

_____ (1972), On anticipation, duration and meaning. *J. Amer. Psychoanal. Assn.*, 20:721-735.

Sterba, R. (1940), Aggression in rescue phantasy. *Psychiat. Quart.*, 9:505-508.

Stern, E. M. (1977), Narcissism and the defiance of time. In: *The Narcissistic Condition*, ed. M. C. Nelson. New York: Human Sciences Press.

Stern, M. (1972), Bio-trauma, fear of death and aggression. *Internat. J. Psycho-Anal.*, 53:291-299.

Stoller, R. J. (1974), Hostility and mystery in perversion. *Internat. J. Psycho-Anal.*, 55:425-434.

Swift, J. (1726), *Gulliver's Travels*, ed. P. Pincas. Toronto: Macmillan, 1968, pp. 1-286.

Szasz, T. (1952), On the psychoanalytic theory of instincts. *Psychoanal. Quart.*, 21:25-48.

———— (1958), The role of the counterphobic mechanism on addiction. *J. Amer. Psychoanal. Assn.*, 6:309-325.

Tarachow, S. (1966), Coprophagia and allied phenomena. *J. Amer. Psychoanal. Assn.*, 14:685-699.

Tinbergen, N. (1968), Of war and peace in animals and men. *Science.* 160:1411-1418.

Trotter, W. (1916), *Instincts of the Herd in Peace and War.* London: Unwin.

Truzzi, M. (1974), Towards a sociology of the occult. In: *Religious Movements in Contemporary Americs*, eds. Zaretsky and Leone. Princeton: Princeton University Press, pp. 628-645.

Weinberger, J. & Muller, J. (1974), The American Icarus revisited. Phallic narcissism and boredom. *Internat. J. Psycho-Anal.*, 55:581-586.

Weissman, P. (1957), Some aspects of sexual activity in a fetishist. *Psychoanal. Quart.*, 26:494-507.

———— (1971), The artist and his objects. *Internat. J. Psycho-Anal.*, 52:401-406.

Wieder, H. & Kaplan, E. (1969), Drug use in adolescents. In: *The Psychoanalytic Study of the Child*, 24:399-431.

Winnicott, D. W. (1953), Transitional objects and transitional phenomena. *Internat. J. Psycho-Anal.*, 34:89-97.

———— (1960), The theory of the parent-infant relationship. *Internat. J. Psycho-Anal.*, 41:585-595.

———— (1963), Dependence in infant and child care and in the psychoanalytic setting. *Internat. J. Psycho-Anal.*, 44:86.

———— (1965), Ego distortion in terms of true and false self. In: *The Maturational Processes and the Facilitating Environment.* London: Hogarth Press, pp. 140-152.

Winterstein, A. (1934), Contributions to the problem of humor (first offered in 1932, *Psychoanalytische Bewegung*, IV.). *Psychoanal. Quart.*, 3:303-316.

Wulff, M. (1946), Fetishism and object choice in early childhood. *Psychoanal. Quart.*, 15:450-471.

Zaretsky, I. & Leone, M. (1974), The common foundation of religious diversity. In: *Religious Movements in Contemporary America*, eds. Zaretsky and Leone. Princeton: Princeton University Press, Introduction, pp. xvii-xxxvi.

Index

273